The Meaning of Sociology

EIGHTH EDITION

The Meaning of Sociology

Joel M. Charon
Professor Emeritus
Minnesota State University Moorhead

Lee Garth Vigilant
Associate Professor
Minnesota State University Moorhead

PEARSON

Prentice
Hall

Upper Saddle River, New Jersey 07458

Library of Congress Cataloging-in-Publication Data

Charon, Joel M.

The meaning of sociology / Joel M. Charon, Lee Garth Vigilant. — 8th ed.

    p. cm.

 Includes bibliographical references and index.

 ISBN-13: 978-0-13-813328-3 (alk. paper)

 ISBN-10: 0-13-813328-X (alk. paper)

 1. Sociology. I. Charon, Joel M. Vigilant, Lee Garth. II. Title.

HM585.C4475 2009

301–dc22

2008010840

Editor-in-Chief: Dickson Musslewhite
Full Service Production Liaison:
 Joanne Hakim
Editorial Assistant: Nart Varoqua
Marketing Manager: Lindsey Prudhomme
Marketing Assistant: Craig Deming
Operations Specialist: Christina Amato
Cover Art Director: Jayne Conte
Cover Design: Bruce Kenselaar
Cover Photo: Avenue of the Arts © Doree
 Loschiavo
Manager, Cover Visual Research &
 Permissions: Karen Sanatar

Director, Image Resource Center:
 Melinda Patelli
Manager, Rights and Permissions:
 Zina Arabia
Manager, Visual Research: Beth Brenzel
Photo Coordinator: Ang'john Ferreri
Photo Researcher: Francelle Carapetyan
Full-Service Project Management:
 Shiny Rajesh/Integra Software Services
Composition: Integra Software Services

Credits and acknowledgments borrowed from other sources and reproduced, with permission, in this textbook appear on appropriate page within text.

Pearson Education LTD., London
Pearson Education Singapore, Pte. Ltd
Pearson Education, Canada, Inc.
Pearson Education–Japan
Pearson Education Australia PTY, Limited

Pearson Education North Asia Ltd., Hong Kong
Pearson Educación de Mexico, S.A. de C.V.
Pearson Education Malaysia, Pte. Ltd.
Pearson Education, Upper Saddle River,
 New Jersey

ISBN 13: 978-0-13-813328-3
ISBN 10:   0-13-813328-X

Contents

PART V: CONCLUSION

15   The Meaning and Uses of Sociology   215

Index   221

Preface

It is difficult to know what "the meaning of sociology" actually is. Like everything else, it changes. A simple definition does not capture the subtle aspects of the discipline, nor the complex disagreements and divisions within it. Sociology really became a recognized academic discipline in the nineteenth century, and throughout the twentieth century, it was altered by the major social events, as well as by the individuals who have contributed questions, issues, and ideas to it.

The twenty-first century is here. If living in the twentieth century has taught me anything, it has taught me that everything changes. The twenty-first century reaffirms to me the prediction that change is everywhere. I was born in 1939, at the very beginning of World War II. Perhaps all periods are characterized by change, but it seems that there was an acceleration of change that I witnessed in the second half of the twentieth century. Change is so complex and dramatic that it is difficult to understand and appreciate. Nothing seems to stay the same; the future is difficult to predict, except that we know it will bring events and qualities we cannot even imagine today.

It is difficult to accept change. Each of us has attempted to believe that our world will not change; once we are challenged by change and recognize that our world is no longer the same, it seems "crazy" to us, "terrible," "not like it used to be."

The 1980s and 1990s saw the world increasingly becoming a truly global economy. The Soviet Union is no more. Western Europe is moving toward unity, and Eastern Europe is becoming more and more part of a larger European community. Immigration from North Africa and the Middle East has had a great impact, not only changing societies, but also bringing fear and sometimes violence. In the United States, the economic and social problems that have been hidden to most of us for so long are increasingly coming to the surface—for example, excessive concentration of wealth, increasing violence, limited job opportunities for much of the population, great inequalities in educational achievements, and a decline in feeling for community. The issues related to globalization, terrorism, and environment divide us and make compromise very difficult. We even wonder if our institutions have become obsolete. The societal issues of this first decade of the twenty-first century divide us considerably. The opening of Dickens's *Tale of Two Cities* continues to haunt me: "It was the best of times; it was the worst of times." While many of us proclaim the triumph of capitalism, it seems as though fewer and fewer people in our society are benefiting very much even though salaries may increase. Our population is older, our society is more bureaucratic and secularized, and our role in the world is not yet clear in the post–Cold War period. All over the world, societies are changing at rates unequaled in the history of this planet, and most of them are learning from us—in a very ambiguous and, some would say, negative way—about what is and is not worth-while in this life. In social science and humanities, scholars are proclaiming the arrival of postmodern society—new possibilities and new challenges. Tremendous opportunities and serious social problems exist for societies in this world.

Sociology is one important way we can begin to understand all of this: the nature of society, social change, and social problems. It is an attempt to take something that most of us regard to be sacred—society—and examine it carefully and objectively. It is an attempt to cause all of us to look back on ourselves and our lives, to understand what we are in the context of society's past and present: that we are located; that social location matters to all of us; that social location is one of the most important ways we can understand our lives.

Sociology is not simply a bunch of facts or a list of definitions. It is a way of look-ing at the world. That is why this book was written: to introduce the sociological perspective and show its relevance to understanding. That is why there is a logic to the organization of this book.

Part I, The Nature of Sociology, describes sociology as an academic discipline that takes a certain approach to understanding the world of the human being. This discipline emphasizes why we are social, how social patterns affect us, and how we are socialized into our social world.

Part II, The Nature of Social Organization, starts with the idea that we are social. We are social actors, we interact socially, and we form social organization. Social organization is made up of three patterns: social structure, culture, and institutions. We should understand humans in the context of these patterns because in every organization we are shaped and controlled to a great extent by such patterns.

Part III, Order and Power in Social Organization, focuses on the question that many thinking people ask about the modern world: How is order established in social organization, and what role does social power play in society? And in looking at order and power, we encounter deviance. Why do we have deviance in society? Who, after all, do we declare to be a threat to the order we seek?

Part IV, The Dynamic Nature of Human Social Life, describes social change. Individuals change; society changes. Why? Four chapters look at change. The first looks more closely at the nature of the human being and describes how humans are able to make free choices in spite of the tremendous power of society. We are in control of our own lives and, to some extent, are able to change the society in which we live. The second chapter examines how and why society changes. Individuals make a difference, but other forces must also be considered. The third chapter in this part is an examination of one part of the society: the family. The theme of the family is change. This chapter shows what forces in society cause that change, how the family has changed, and how the changing family plays a major role in every aspect of society.

The fourth chapter on change is a new chapter in this eighth edition of this book. It is entitled "Religion, Society, and the Individual." More and more religion is play-ing a major role in our thinking, our politics, and our view of the past, present, and future. The theme of the chapter is change: What are the important ideas, our con-flicts, our theories, and our research related to religion? Is our society becoming increasingly secular? Is modern life in conflict with traditional religion? What will be the important trends in the future?

Part V, the *Conclusion*, summarizes the ideas emphasized throughout the book, and it tries to answer the serious question that many students rightfully ask: Why study sociology?

This eighth edition is an attempt to continue my search for the "Meaning of Sociology." I have asked Professor Lee Vigilant, a dedicated and intelligent sociologist, to become a second author of this book. Many of the changes from the eighth edition are his. Much of the discussion of globalization is his. The chapter on religion was a joint venture.

I am especially indebted to Nancy Roberts, editor at Prentice-Hall, who has supported me for many revisions of this book. She has inspired me and guided me. Thanks also to Shiny Rajesh for all her help in producing the book, and to Professor David Olday who advised me on the family chapter. I am also heavily indebted to Lee Viglant, who read and improved the manuscript.

I would like to dedicate this book to Susan, my wife, best friend, and partner for 40 years.

The Meaning
of Sociology

Isabel Bishop, American (1902–1988). Men and Girls Walking, 1970.
Mount Holyoke college Art Museum.

1

The Discipline
of Sociology

I like understanding human beings. As a teenager, philosophy fascinated me. In college, history did. I majored in history simply because I was totally absorbed by questions about people and how we have developed the kind of world we have. I taught high school for a while, and there I dabbled in psychology, which, at the time, held great promise for unlocking mysteries concerning the human being.

I love music, too, yet when I go to concerts, I am sometimes more interested in the people there than in the music. What kind of person is the conductor? What is his or her relationship with the orchestra? How much conflict is there? Do they really enjoy practicing? Do they see each other as competitors for the top or as part of a team? Do they enjoy making music or is it just a job for them?

I came to sociology late in my career. My first sociology class in college was not very interesting. I took the minimum amount required and never thought I would return. I barely understood what sociology was all about (something concerning social problems such as crime, alcoholism, and divorce), but I really did not take it very seriously. All I knew was that it was something like psychology, so I was mildly attracted to it. Psychology studied the individual, I thought; sociology studied groups. I wasn't very sure we had to understand groups if we understood individuals.

Taking a class in social organization changed my whole view. As I listened to the instructor and as I read the material, a whole new world began to open up for me. I realized that sociology was a way of looking at the human being that I really never considered. We are, I was told, part of social organization—not sometimes, but all the time. This is our very central human quality. Everything is linked to this. I remember a student asking the instructor about freedom and social organization: If we are embedded in organization, then do we have free choice? That question has stayed with me. I also remember the instructor's answer (which I did not want to hear): Sociology is a highly deterministic perspective, one that sees much of what we do resulting *from* organization. From the sociological perspective, we are much less free than we think.

What happened to me was that I was drawn progressively more into sociology. It became a passion for me. It offered explanations I had never encountered before.

1

It never gave me final answers, but kept pointing out aspects of the human condition that I should consider if I was going to understand.

I have found that my early experience with sociology is not unique. Most people do not understand what it is. News commentators, psychologists, economists, high school teachers, and college administrators—many of whom have taken courses in sociology—generally do not have any idea of what sociology is. There are many stereotypes of sociologists. Supposedly, we are social reformers, scientists in love with statistics, social workers, cold observers of human beings, testers of ideas that everyone knows. Most people seem to think of us as another version of psychology. I am even embarrassed to say that many sociology majors graduate with courses, with facts, with some ideas, but somehow without the ability to "think sociologically" about situations they encounter.

The purpose of this book is to give an introduction to the central ideas that make up the sociological perspective. I hope you will come to understand it and see its usefulness. If this book is any good, you will see the world differently, and you will see yourself differently. Sociology has many facts and many specialized fields one can study; here the purpose is not to describe these facts and fields, but to introduce the core ideas.

WHAT IS SOCIOLOGY?

Sociology Is an Academic Discipline

The university normally does not offer us certainty. If a university education works, we are left instead with a thirst for understanding more and the humility to admit that we are not yet wise and all knowing, and that if we are going to understand anything well, we must use care and control our tendency to be sloppy in the search.

The university introduces us to a number of *academic disciplines*. They are "academic" because they exist primarily in universities, and scholars there research and debate the knowledge gathered. They are "disciplines" because each has a long history, each has an accumulated body of knowledge, and each is a systematic and careful (hence "disciplined") approach to developing ideas. Philosophy, psychology, sociology, history, physics, mathematics, and art, for example, are usually considered academic disciplines.

Each discipline has its own focus. Each is a different *perspective*. Each examines a different aspect of reality. Each, by its very nature, tends to emphasize certain points and ignore others. Psychology examines the development of the individual, chemistry treats reality as a mixture of chemicals, and biology understands life as genes and environment. No single academic perspective can capture every aspect of reality or give us certainty, but each perspective can be a useful guide.

Sociology is one academic discipline; it is one perspective found in the university. Its history goes back to at least the nineteenth century (some would date it earlier than that). It has an accumulated body of knowledge, and over the years, it has developed a systematic approach to understanding. For many, sociology is a very useful perspective. For some, it becomes a passion because it constantly drives them to apply it to their world and to their own lives, truly altering their understanding in a very profound way.

Sociology Focuses on Our Social World

Sociology is one attempt to understand the human being. It centers on our social life. Typically, it does not focus on the individual's personality as the cause of behavior, but examines *social interaction, social patterns* (for example, roles, class, culture, power, conflict), and ongoing *socialization.* For example, sociologists examine the rules that develop as people interact, the expectations that arise among them, and the truths they come to share. Sociologists see the significance of the "student role," being "middle class," and being a "man" or a "woman" in modern American society, and how these have developed historically. We notice how actors change as they shift groups or organizations, influenced by the inevitable socialization (attempts by people in the organization to form them) that comes with joining. Sociology begins with the idea, then, *that humans are to be understood in the context of their social life, that we are social animals influenced by interaction, social patterns, and socialization.*

Most people are used to seeing the world psychologically, where action is thought to spring from the characteristics of the individual rather than from interaction and social patterns. From this psychological perspective, people may explain the mass suicide of a religious cult, say, as the result of religious fanaticism or a magnetic leader or irrational and sick persons. Although this may indeed be a partial explanation, sociologists believe that any religious group must be understood as a kind of society, as an organized group sharing a culture, as individuals influencing one another in social interaction, and as a structure with people filling positions and acting in roles, conforming to one another's expectations, influenced by a power structure, as in any other group or society. As another example, instead of examining the characteristics of individuals who end up in prison, sociologists are generally more interested in factors relating to the positions these people occupy in society: how the poverty "position" might influence criminal action, arrest, and imprisonment; or how power in society might play a part in how crime is defined in the first place. Sociologists will study crime *rates,* the role of law and crime in society, the history and philosophy of punishment and corrections in society, and the working of the criminal justice system, as well as its role in keeping order and/or protecting the wealthy and powerful in society.

Sociology, then, is a perspective and an academic discipline that studies the human being in a social context.

Sociology Asks Three Questions

One way of understanding sociology is to recognize what holds the discipline together. In my view, it is held together, first of all, by its continuous attempt to answer three basic questions concerning the human being: What is the human being? What holds society—or all social organization—together? What are the causes and consequences of social inequality?

From the beginning of sociology, sociologists have sought to understand the nature of the human being. *What are we, anyway?* Emile Durkheim, an important early French sociologist, described it well: Human beings are socialized into society. Society gets inside our very being. We take on society's rules, its morals, its truths, its values. In a sense, the individual becomes society. Charles Cooley and George Herbert Mead, two important American social scientists, emphasized that human beings are born unfinished: Human nature is learned; our very being results as we interact with others.

That interaction continues throughout our lives, so we constantly change as we meet new people and take on new rules and ideas. Throughout the history of the discipline, sociologists have uncovered a host of ways that human beings are, by their very nature, *social, socialized, and forever changing in social interaction.*

What holds society together? What is the nature of order? Why are humans able to cooperate? This is the second concern of the discipline of sociology. Many call it "the problem of order." We are born into the world prepared to do very little. As we become socialized, we learn the ways of our society. Its ways become our ways, and that, in part, is how we begin to see how order is possible. However, it is far more complex than this. Order is developed through the social patterns we establish, through the rules, truths, and structure we create. It is maintained through families, media, schools, political leaders, and religion. Ritual, rules, punishment, and continuous interaction aid order. Karl Marx, another important early sociologist, showed the contribution of force and manipulation to order; Max Weber examined the role of legitimate power, which ultimately means that order in society exists, at least in part, because people are willing to obey those who are perceived to represent that society. Much of sociology is an examination of the nature of order in society.

The third big question is also one that unites the discipline: *Why is there inequality in society and what are its consequences?* Is it inherent in the nature of organization? How does it arise? How is it perpetuated? What are the problems it brings, and how does it affect the individual? Marx saw inequality inherent in all class societies; Weber saw it inherent in the nature of lasting organization. Some sociologists see it as contributing to order; all see it as one source of social change. Sociologists are fascinated by the way inequality persists and by the way it weaves itself through our lives. Many see it as the source of many of the injustices in our world; all see it as part of almost all social organization.

There are, of course, other questions that unite the discipline, but these three are the most basic. Examining these questions carefully should give you a good start at understanding what the discipline of sociology is all about.

Sociology, then, is a perspective and academic discipline that focuses on humans as social beings, believing that humans are social to the core of their being, that society is an order that develops and continues over time, and that inequality is a key to understanding both society and social problems.

Sociology Focuses on Five Topics

Although sociologists are united in the importance they give to society, and although they generally agree that both social order and social inequality are central to understanding society, they differ on their focus of investigation. There are five topic areas that sociologists tend to choose from:

1. Some sociologists focus on society. Sociology to them is the "science of society." Society is that very large and abstract entity in which humans exist. Those who focus on society are sometimes called "macrosociologists."
2. A second focus or topic area is *social organization.* Sociology is the study of all social organization, from the largest unit — society — to the smallest — a pair of interacting individuals (a dyad). Human beings live in organization; studying the nature of all organization is a desirable goal.

3. American sociology has typically become more specialized, tending to look at *institutions* or *institutional systems*. Some sociologists specialize in the family, some in schools, and others in government. There are, for example, sociologies of law, criminal justice, health, religion, and military. Specialization has created experts who understand a certain part of society as well as its relationship to the whole of society.
4. Many sociologists are interested in the *micro* world of *face-to-face interaction*, how individuals act in relation to one another in everyday life. There is interest here in how individuals in social interaction shape organization, share a view of the world, influence one another, and are socialized.
5. Finally, there is an emphasis among some sociologists on *social problems*, a concern about understanding poverty, family disorganization, child abuse, sexism, and racism, and careless misuses of the environment among other things.

These five focuses, like the three questions, both divide sociology and unite it. On one hand, sociologists differ in which question they are driven to answer, and also on which of the five general topic areas they concentrate. On the other hand, most of us recognize that sociology is a combination of all of these elements, that together these constitute the outline of the discipline. Sociology might therefore be defined as *(1) a perspective and (2) an academic discipline that (3) examines the human being as a social being, (4) who is a product of social interaction, socialization, and social patterns. (5) Sociology tries to concern itself with the nature of the human being, the meaning and basis of social order, and the causes and consequences of social inequality. (6) It focuses on society, social organization, social institutions, social interaction, and social problems.*

Sociology Is a Scientific Discipline

Some academic disciplines are sciences; some are not. From the beginning of sociology, sociologists have regarded it as a science. However, what exactly does it mean to be a "science"? My goal here is to describe science by highlighting five principles.

First, *the purpose of science is to understand the universe in a careful, disciplined manner.* Although science is often used to change the world and solve problems, its first goal remains to understand. Science developed because it was recognized long ago that casual observation of the universe is often misleading and sometimes incorrect. Science tries to control personal bias and go beyond casual observation. To argue that sociology is a science is to claim, first of all, that sociology is an attempt to understand the human being in a careful, disciplined manner.

Second, *proof is the requirement for accepting ideas in science, and proof must be empirical.* The fact that someone who is intelligent tells you something is not good enough; the fact that experience confirms your opinion is not good enough; the fact that you feel something intuitively may be good enough for you, but not for science. The ideas that characterize the field of sociology, and most of the ideas contained in this book, are ideas that have been slowly and carefully developed through accumulating evidence. That evidence must be *empirical* evidence. This simply means that evidence must be gathered through human senses. Normally, we mean by this that evidence is observed. Science is different from religion, which usually bases its ideas on faith, authority, and sometimes logical debate. It is also different from many nonscientific disciplines, such as philosophy and mathematics, which tend to base their ideas on good logic. Logic is certainly part of the scientific approach, but scientists want more: *empirical observation as the basis for proof.* In sociology, therefore, as in all sciences, carefully developed tests are created—experiments, surveys, interviews, case studies, and analysis of government data, for example—where results can be counted, observed, and shared with others who are also able to count and observe.

Third, science should be thought of as *a community of scholars, checking each other's work, criticizing, debating, and together slowly building a body of knowledge.* In sociology, as in all sciences, this community gets together at meetings to discuss research studies and publishes those studies in professional journals and books for all to see and for all to learn, check, and criticize.

Fourth, *science is an attempt to generalize.* Scientists seek to go beyond the concrete situation and to establish ideas that relate to many situations. Scientists generalize about disease, gravity, animals, plants, stars, and people. In sociology, we generalize about roles, minorities, revolutions, social change, class, social power, families, religion, and so on. People are part of nature. Although all things in nature are to some extent unique, if we are careful, we can generalize intelligently. Sociology is a careful attempt to make generalizations about the social aspects of human beings.

Fifth, *science is an attempt to explain events.* Good science can tell us *why things happen,* what the causes or influences on a certain class of events in nature are. For example, Weber showed how Protestantism was an influence on the development of capitalism, and Durkheim showed how very low levels of social integration are an important cause of high suicide rates. Sociologists have explanations for (that is, describe the influences on) crime, school success, change, and social conflict. They also are able to show the effects of racism, sexism, poverty, socialization, and role on other matters. *Science is an attempt to develop ideas about cause–effect relationships.*

From its beginnings, sociology has claimed to be a science and to be guided by these five principles. There has been great diversity in how sociologists "do" science. It is rare, for example, to find laboratory experiments in sociology (or astronomy, for that matter). Sociology has instead relied on experiments done by the government or other organizations (affirmative action, busing, segregated education, and Head Start, for example), on surveys, on real-life observation, and on data carefully collected by various agencies and organizations. Sociologists try to generalize from historical documents. Sociology is a science of *diversity and creativity,* attempting to break away from simply accepting the traditional techniques borrowed from other sciences.

To many, Max Weber's work represents the best approach to science in sociology. A German sociologist, Weber was faced with a personal dilemma that he tried to resolve: Can he simultaneously be both a scientist and an involved member in the world of politics? Will involvement in politics sacrifice objectivity in science? Will devotion to objectivity become an excuse to avoid acting on social issues important to him? How, in the end, can one be a sociologist and also work for a better society? Weber resolved this conflict by emphasizing the fact that sociology as a science must be *value free*—that is, every sociologist must self-consciously try to control his or her values in doing scientific work. We must try to see *what is,* rather than *what we would like to see.* Weber knew that values can never be perfectly controlled, but that still must be our goal. He also taught that, as citizens of society, sociologists should take political stands: We should, for example, work for justice, equality, freedom, or whatever else we might favor, but this effort must be separated from our work as scientists as much as possible because, as scientists, we must dedicate ourselves to describing and explaining human beings. Why believe us if we do not try to control our personal bias, however noble or attractive our ideas might be?

Weber also believed that science is an organized and systematic approach to investigating nature and that, although it seeks to find truth, science can never really attain truth in any final sense. It is an excellent way of understanding, but it is never perfect. Although as scientists we must always try to control our personal bias, everything we do in scientific investigation—the questions we ask, the concepts we use, the techniques we set up—influences what we find. Our truths, therefore, cannot be pure or final. Although this applies to all science, it especially applies to social science. Recognizing this as a sociologist, Weber called for a science that is open—where many methods are employed, many approaches to understanding are taken, and different concepts are used. He respected diversity in science as a way of limiting our biases. He pointed out that scientists must be prepared in their own lifetimes to see their ideas replaced by others because new evidence will almost always be found to question, alter, refine, or replace what we believe at any one time in our history. To Weber, science is not truth; it is an imperfect method but often the best one for finding out something. It will be frustrating to those of us who seek certainty!

Science is therefore a process of investigation that attempts to understand reality as it is. It is an attempt to be "objective": to capture and understand the "object" as it exists rather than to impose our subjective views on it. It is imperfect, as are all approaches to understanding the world. Unlike many other approaches, because objectivity is so important to science, scientists will study their own discipline and try to understand its own assumptions and imperfections. For example, science focuses on what cause events to occur in nature (it assumes that all natural events are caused by other natural events), and it is willing to accept only empirical evidence in its search for understanding (assuming that intuition and subjectivity, for example, are not good enough). Such core ideas have been very useful in uncovering some understanding of the universe, but increasingly many scientists are discovering that science is able to uncover only part of reality, not all of it.

Science is an open search for understanding, where ideas are debated; the ideas that ultimately win usually have been researched and supported by evidence and the scrutiny of the scientific community. Yet science also has its own problems. For example, scientists sometimes get stuck trying to understand trivial things, which can be easily studied, rather than the more complex and important things, which are difficult. It is, for example, much easier to study rats than people—why not understand people by studying rats? Sometimes, good creative ideas are discouraged because "everyone knows" what the experts have found. Other times, scientific communities are controlled by a few powerful scholars, and often whoever pays for research controls what questions are investigated. Ethical questions also arise—for example, the rights of people and other animals studied, or the use of research by government or interest groups for purposes of distorting reality and defending policies.

The limits of science, however, must not cause us to ignore its importance for understanding reality. And the creative and diverse ways sociologists use science should not hide from us the fact that *sociology is a scientific approach to understanding the social life of the human being.*

The Meaning of Sociology: A Summary

Let us summarize here what sociology is. This chapter has described it as an academic discipline. It is one perspective. Its focus is on our social world, and it emphasizes that humans are social animals influenced by interaction, social patterns, and socialization. Sociologists are driven by questions about the nature of the human being, the problem of social order, and the causes and effects of social inequality. Sociologists study society, organization, social institutions, interaction, and social problems. Finally, sociology is a scientific discipline. It is one of those academic disciplines that takes a certain approach to understanding reality, an approach that emphasizes objectivity, proof, observation, a self-critical competitive community of scholars, generalization, and explanation.

THE BEGINNINGS OF SOCIOLOGY

People have not always asked the questions sociologists ask, nor have they gathered data about society as sociologists presently do. Sociology is really a late arrival to the academic community and is one of the youngest sciences. Most sociologists find it convenient to place sociology's origins in the early nineteenth century with the work of French philosopher Auguste Comte (1798–1857), the first to use the term "sociology" and who defined sociology as the "science of society."

Like all perspectives, the development of sociology was linked to social conditions. After all, perspectives are ways of defining what is "out there," and not all societies encourage their members to examine society objectively and carefully. Nineteenth-century Europe, however, was ripe for self-analysis. Several developments came together to bring about the right climate for the questioning spirit to grow and flourish. Let us briefly examine them.

Science Was an Inspiration . . .

Sociology was defined by Comte as the science of society, and it was indeed the development of science that was an important inspiration for early sociologists. Sociology grew out of a desire by some intellectuals to apply the techniques of science to the study of society. Before sociologists, there were social philosophers, historians, political scientists, economists, and religious thinkers who looked at society or aspects of it. Most of these intellectuals examined the political world primarily, and the majority of their efforts were a mixture of understanding human society and searching for what human society should be. Often, objective investigation was not the goal.

Sociologists, however, took the advice of the Enlightenment thinkers of the eighteenth century: We can understand the laws of human society through applying the tools of science. From its start, sociology borrowed from the natural sciences the tools that were being used to fashion new discoveries about the stars, the earth, and the human body. The universe is comprised of natural laws; so, too, society must be governed by such laws, and sociology would discover these laws by applying scientific procedures. Its purpose would be to describe what society *is* and *how it works*, instead of necessarily advocating what it *should be*.

Sociology, then, was born in a time of intellectual excitement about the possibilities of discovery; indeed, Comte was so excited about the future of the science of society that he naively predicted sociology (what he believed was the "queen" of all sciences) would be the focus of a new religion, and sociologists, as the bearers of knowledge, would be the "priests of the new order," moral leaders, solvers of the ills of humankind.

And So Were the Problems of Industrialization . . .

Sociology was born not only in a time of science, but also in a time when industrialization and urbanization were transforming the very basis of society. Some of the early sociologists saw industrialization as they saw science: a means by which the problems that plagued humanity would be banished. Poverty, disease, famine, and even war would be ended. Other sociologists, such as Karl Marx, reacted to the extremes of inequality and poverty that the Industrial Revolution telescoped; still others, such as Durkheim and Weber, saw basic changes occurring in the old ways of society—changes such as the declining importance of traditional religion and the growing bureaucratic organization of society.

In a real sense, sociology in the nineteenth and early twentieth centuries was an attempt by a number of thoughtful people to understand and clarify these profound changes.

And the Need to Understand Revolution . . .

The French Revolution exerted a powerful force on the development of sociology. The French Revolution was an unequaled social upheaval that began in 1789 and continued through the Napoleonic Wars ending in 1815, transforming the society of France and influencing all Europe and North America as well.

The intellectual community inherited that revolution—its ideals, its excesses, and the questions it posed. The debate of nineteenth-century Europe is still with us and has influenced the beginning of sociology: Why do revolutions occur? What do they accomplish? How is order maintained in society and problems solved? How can a society deal with the excesses of inequality of power and privilege?

Sociology grew out of the twin concerns of inequality and order that the French Revolution inspired. Some early sociologists feared change; some welcomed it. Some wondered about the effects of declining tradition; some were amazed at how well the old held on. Some feared disorder; some hated inequality. All, however, were influenced by the memory of the French Revolution.

As Well as Experiences with Other Peoples and Societies . . .

The new interest in society was also encouraged by "the march of empire"—the colonization of non-Western societies that followed centuries of discovery and exploration. As people learn about other societies, they may "be thankful we don't live like that," or they may come to see new alternatives of living never imagined; they may see opportunities to save those who are "less fortunate," or they may decide that other peoples are inferior and incapable of profiting from the benefits of civilization.

In any case, thinking people are encouraged to examine their own societies from a new angle, are forced to compare, contrast, and seek answers to new questions about the nature of society in general. European intellectuals began this kind of examination when other lands were first discovered, but it began in earnest as other societies became laboratories, places to explore rather than just to conquer. Out of this development, too, sociology was born—out of an interest in society spurred by the realization that "things don't have to be this way; after all, look at the way others live."

And a Climate for New Ideas Arose

Along with the Industrial Revolution, the French Revolution, science, and the exploration of new lands, something else happened to encourage the development of sociology. European society was increasingly open to new ideas. This was a trend that went back a long time, but in a way, the nineteenth century was ready for sociology, ready for a more critical, objective approach to society. Not all societies encourage scholars to investigate social issues objectively. The preference is too often praising society not studying it listing its virtues rather than trying to discover its problems. The freedom that accompanied the great revolutions of the late eighteenth and nineteenth centuries encouraged the development of all the social sciences. Sociology's time had come.

THE DEVELOPMENT OF SOCIOLOGY

Montesquieu, Saint-Simon, Comte, and many others were the real "beginners" of sociology. However, in the nineteenth and early twentieth centuries, four European thinkers were especially important to the discipline; together, they might be called "the classical sociologists." They are Karl Marx, Max Weber, Emile Durkheim, and Georg Simmel. They exert a powerful influence to the present day: They are models for us, they inspire our ideas and studies, and their definitions of concepts are the places at which we still begin. By 1920, all four men had died, but together they left a strong sociological tradition in European universities.

The discipline of sociology came to the United States at the turn of the twentieth century. It quickly took on a distinctively American coloration, being imbued with a spirit of reform, and was at first not distinguishable from social work. This spirit of reform has always been important to many American sociologists: an incentive for research for some, a subject of debate for others. American sociology has been strongly influenced by pragmatism ("If it is to be worthwhile, show me how I can use it"), and right from the beginning it has had to deal with the problem of how to understand society both critically and objectively, yet also attempt to reform it. Although American sociology, as a practical reforming discipline, continues to be a variation, the dominant theme since these early years has been scientific understanding and explanation.

Between 1900 and 1920, sociologists increasingly put reform aside to gain respectability in the university and scientific communities. They worked to have sociology become a legitimate social science in major universities, especially in the midwestern and eastern United States.

After 1920, American sociology entered a period of major work in both scientific theory and scientific research. Here was an attempt to build a discipline of specialization, accumulated scientific studies, ideas that had good evidence to back them up. Also at this time, an important school (or perspective) in sociology known as *functionalism* developed in the United States. Until the 1960s, functionalism was very influential, but since then its influence has declined. People in this school have concerned themselves with the same issues as Durkheim—issues that focus on the problem of social order. Functionalists want to know how society works, how order is established, how the various parts of society—family, education, religion, law, and so on—function in society. There is an emphasis here on institutions, society's patterns, social organization, and social order. It is *macrosociology*. Functionalism contributed much to the study of social organization in the United States but has become progressively less important in the past 40 years.

Since the early 1960s, sociology has veered in several directions. First, in the United States, the scientific community has become increasingly specialized, building on the research studies of previous decades. New ideas and empirical studies have divided the discipline into distinct fields: family sociology, sex roles, religion, health, bureaucracy, deviance, the military, government, social mobility, and so on. This is a predictable direction for any science, and there is every reason to believe that it will continue.

Second, in the 1960s to the present, a conflict sociology has emerged, concerned less with science and more with social issues, especially those related to inequality: class, poverty, sexism, racism, corporate power, white-collar crime, and social conflict. Karl Marx, a nineteenth-century German thinker, and C. Wright Mills, a mid-twentieth-century American sociologist, are most influential in the development of this school. At first, this school was called radical sociology, but by the 1980s, it had clearly become a leading perspective in the discipline, had become broader in scope, and was associated with many who are less radical.

The study of social class has always been part of the conflict perspective, but race and gender have become increasingly an important part of this perspective. Like the functionalist, the conflict sociologist tends to be a *macrosociologist*. Conflict sociology is sometimes called critical sociology: It asks serious questions about society and the direction of sociology—our loyalty to science, for example, our claim to objectivity, and our refusal to work for change. This conflict sociology has put forward a number of exciting ideas and studies and has become a vital alternative to the scientific specialists and functionalists.

Conflict sociology tends to be macrosociology, and focuses on the nature of society. The scientific specialists focus on societal institutions, often at the macro level, sometimes at the micro level. The late 1970s and early 1980s have seen the emergence of yet a third trend: an increasing interest in *microsociology*—face-to-face interaction, socialization, communication, the creation and maintenance of social patterns in small groups, presentation of self to others in situations, language, identity, roles, and so on. A number of schools have taken a microsociological approach. Historically, the most important of these approaches is called "symbolic interactionism," but increasingly important are the "ethnomethodologists," "dramaturgical sociologists," social constructionists, and "phenomenologists." Grouping these together, we might call this a school—*interactionism*.

Specialization, conflict sociology, interactionism, and increasing focus on globalization are our important trends in the discipline of sociology in the United States. Other directions also seem to be driving the discipline, for example, more emphasis on understanding gender inequality, more concern about the future of modern—and "postmodern"—life, more attempts to understand human beings by relying less on "quantitative" science and using more techniques such as interviewing, observing in real-life situations, analyzing and comparing various societies, and using written content from historical and contemporary societies. Throughout its history, sociology has been filled with people who honestly and seriously disagree with one another about many basic issues and about the direction that we should go. We still disagree about the nature of good science and the meaning of society. We still disagree about what sociology should focus on and what concepts are the most useful for studying society. We disagree about the meaning and extent of inequality in society, the reasons for social change, the degree to which human beings are free within society, and which social problems are the most serious. Some are champions of Marx, others consider Max Weber to be the model sociologist. Others regard Emile Durkheim, George Herbert Mead, or Erving Goffman to be the most useful today, and still others are excited about some contemporary European thinkers, such as Anthony Giddens, Michel Foucault, and Jurgen Hamermas. There are also many sociologists who are not interested in any "big ideas," but are simply focused on testing concrete ideas in carefully done empirical studies.

The excitement of sociology is that it is so alive with controversy and self-criticism. Ideas and studies are not taken for granted because there are so many of us lying in wait to criticize. As in all science, disagreement and criticism are necessary to ensure that accumulated knowledge is accurate.

CONCLUSION AND SUMMARY

Of course, to those of us who work in the field, sociology is a very useful discipline. To many, it is a passion, driving us to apply its ideas to every aspect of human existence.

To many outside the discipline, sociology is often misunderstood. Most people really do not understand the meaning of society and its importance to all that we do, are, and think. It is easier and more concrete to understand human beings from a biological or psychological perspective. Many people are not willing to accept a scientific study of social life, often because they do not understand science, and sometimes because they do not think we can generalize about human life.

To sociologists, however, it is very important to understand the human being carefully and objectively, using scientific principles wherever possible. Nothing is as fascinating as understanding why human beings act as they do—and nothing is as important.

Sociology, then, is an academic discipline that began in the nineteenth century. It is one perspective on the human being, and its focus is on our social life, interaction, social patterns, and socialization. Sociologists are interested in the nature of the human being, social order, and social inequality. They examine society, social organization, institutions, interaction, and social problems. Sociology is a scientific discipline. Like other sciences, it tries to be objective in how it studies the universe, it seeks to understand cause, it requires empirical evidence, it is an attempt to generalize, and it consists of a community of scholars who criticize and build on one another's work. Sociology began with the work of Auguste Comte, and it was inspired by the development of science, industrialization, the French Revolution, exposure to other societies, and a climate favorable to new ideas. The most important founders were probably Marx, Weber, Durkheim, and Simmel. In the United States, sociology has gone in four different directions: functionalism, scientific specialization, conflict sociology, and interactionism or microsociology. Sociology is filled with disagreement and debate, but this is what makes it alive and exciting.

QUESTIONS TO CONSIDER

1. Based on your understanding of this chapter, how would you describe the discipline of sociology to someone who does not know what it is? What are the key points to understand?
2. According to this chapter, what are some of the ideas about human beings that sociologists believe?
3. Sociology claims to be a scientific discipline. What does this mean? Is it possible to study the human being scientifically? What are the strengths of studying the human being scientifically? What are some problems?
4. Do you think there is a need for sociology?

RECOMMENDED READING

The following works are good introductions to the perspective of sociology.

Babbie, Earl. 1998. *The Sociological Spirit.* 3rd edn. Belmont, CA: Wadsworth.
Berger, Peter L. 1963. *Invitation to Sociology.* New York: Doubleday.
Charon, Joel M. 2008. *Ten Questions: A Sociological Perspective.* 6th edn. Belmont, CA: Wadsworth.
Gordon, Milton M. 1988. *The Scope of Sociology.* New York: Oxford University Press.
Johnson, Allan G. 1997. *The Forest and the Trees: Sociology as Life, Practice, and Promise.* Philadelphia: Temple University Press.
Lemert, Charles. 2007. *Thinking the Unthinkable: The Riddles of Classical Social Theories.* Boulder, CO: Paradigm Press.
Mazlish, Bruce. 1989. *A New Science: The Breakdown of Connections and the Birth of Sociology.* University Park, PA: Pennsylvania State University Press.
Mills, C. Wright. 1959. *The Sociological Imagination.* New York: Oxford University Press.
Shibutani, Tamotsu. 1986. *Social Processes: An Introduction to Sociology.* Berkeley: University of California Press.

The following works are some examples of important scientific work done in sociology.

Ammerman, Nancy T. 2005. *Pillars of Faith American Congregations and Their Partners.* Berkeley, CA: University of California Press.
Baltzell, E. Digby. 1964. *The Protestant Establishment: Aristocracy and Caste in America.* New York: Vintage.
Becker, Howard S. 1953. "Becoming a Marihuana User." In *American Journal of Sociology,* 59:235–247.
Becker, Howard S. 1976. *Boys in White: Student Culture in Medical School.* Rev. edn. Chicago: University of Chicago Press.
Chambliss, William J. 1973. "The Saints and the Roughnecks." In *Society,* 11:24–31.
Currie, Elliot. 2004. *The Road to Whatever: Middle-Class Culture and the Crisis of Adolescence.* New York, NY: Owl Books.
Dudley, Kathryn Marie. 1994. *The End of the Line: Lost Jobs, New Lives in Postindustrial America.* Chicago: University of Chicago Press.
Durkheim, Emile. 1897. *Suicide.* 1951 edn. Trans. and ed. John A. Spaulding and George Simpson. New York: Free Press.
Durkheim, Emile. 1915. *The Elementary Forms of Religious Life.* 1954 edn. Trans. Joseph Swain. New York: Free Press.

Edin, Kathryn, and Maria Kefalas. 2005. *Promises I Can Keep: Why Poor Women Put Motherhood Before Marriage*. Berkeley, CA: University of California Press.

Erikson, Kai T. 1966. *Wayward Puritans: A Study in the Sociology of Deviance*. New York: John Wiley.

Erikson, Kai T. 1976. *Everything in Its Path*. New York: Simon & Schuster.

Fine, Gary Alan. 1987. *With the Boys: Little League Baseball and Preadolescent Culture*. Chicago: University of Chicago Press.

Goffman, Erving. 1961. *Asylums: Essays on the Social Situation of Mental Patients and Other Inmates*. New York: Doubleday (Anchor).

Gouldner, Alvin. 1954. *Patterns of Industrial Bureaucracy*. New York: Free Press.

Horowitz, Ruth. 1983. *Honor and the American Dream: Culture and Identity in a Chicano Community*. New Brunswick, NJ: Rutgers University Press.

Kanter, Rosabeth. 1977. *Men and Women of the Corporation*. New York: Basic Books.

Keister, Lisa A. *America's New Rich and How They Got That Way*. New York: Cambridge University Press.

Liebow, Elliot. 1967. *Tally's Corner*. Boston: Little, Brown.

Lipset, Seymour Martin, Martin Trow, and James Coleman. 1956. *Union Democracy: The Inside Politics of the International Typographical Union*. New York: Free Press.

Lofland, John. 1966. *Doomsday Cult*. Upper Saddle River, NJ: Prentice Hall.

Michels, Robert. 1915. *Political Parties*. 1962 edn. Trans. Eden Paul and Cedar Paul. New York: Free Press.

Mills, C. Wright. 1956. *The Power Elite*. New York: Oxford University Press.

Myrdal, Gunnar. 1944. *An American Dilemma*. New York: Harper & Row.

Newman, Katherine S. 1993. *Declining Fortunes: The Withering of the American Dream*. New York: Basic Books.

Piven, Frances Fox, and Richard A. Cloward. 1979. *Poor People's Movements: Why They Succeed, How They Fail*. New York: Vintage.

Sennett, Richard, and Jonathan Cobb. 1972. *The Hidden Injuries of Class*. New York: Random House.

Sewell, W. H., R. M. Hauser, and D. L. Featherman. 1976. *Schooling and Achievement in American Society*. New York: Academic Press.

Shils, Edward S., and Morris Janowitz. 1948. "Cohesion and Disintegration in the Wehrmacht in World War II." In *Public Opinion Quarterly*, 12:280–294.

Stouffer, Samuel A. 1949. *The American Soldier*. Princeton, NJ: Princeton University Press.

Straus, Murray A., Richard J. Gelles, and Suzanne K. Steinmetz. 1988. *Behind Closed Doors: Violence in the American Family*. New York: Doubleday.

Thomas, William I., and Florian Znaniecki. 1918. *The Polish Peasant in Europe and America*. 1958 edn. New York: Dover.

Thrasher, Frederic. 1927. *The Gang*. Chicago: University of Chicago Press.

Tocqueville, Alexis de. 1840. *Democracy in America*. 1969 edn. New York: Doubleday.

Wallerstein, Immanuel. 1974. *The Modern World-System*. New York: Academic Press.

Weber, Max. 1905. *The Protestant Ethic and the Spirit of Capitalism*. 1958 edn. Trans. and ed. Talcott Parsons. New York: Scribner's.

Whyte, William Foote. 1955. *Street Corner Society*. Chicago: University of Chicago Press.

Wilson, William J. 1987. *The Truly Disadvantaged: The Inner City, the Underclass, and Public Policy*. Chicago: University of Chicago Press.

Zimbardo, Philip. 1972. "Pathology of Imprisonment." In *Society*, 9:4–8.

The following works are good discussions of social research in sociology—how it is done, and some of the issues involved.

Alford, Robert R. 1998. *The Craft of Inquiry: Theories, Methods, Evidence*. New York: Oxford University Press.

Babbie, E. R. 1997. *The Practice of Social Research*. 8th edn. Belmont, CA: Wadsworth.

Bailey, Kenneth D. 1999. *Methods of Social Research*. 5th edn. New York: McGraw-Hill.

Becker, Howard S. 1977. "Whose Side Are You On?" In *Journal of Social Problems*, 14:239–247.

Durkheim, Emile. 1895. *The Rules of Sociological Method*. 1964 edn. Trans. Sarah A. Solovay and John H. Mueller. New York: Free Press.

Gouldner, Alvin W. 1968. "The Sociologist as Partisan." In *American Sociologist*, 3:103–116.

Lofland, John. 1976. *Doing Social Life*. New York: John Wiley.

Lundberg, George. 1961. *Can Science Save Us?* 2nd edn. New York: McKay.

Mills, C. Wright. 1959. *The Sociological Imagination*. New York: Oxford University Press.

Turner, Stephen, and Jonathan H. Turner. 1990. *The Impossible Science: An Institutional Analysis of American Society*. Newberry Park, CA: Sage.

Weber, Max. 1919. "Science as a Vocation." In *Max Weber: Essays in Sociology.* 1969 edn. Trans. and ed. H. H. Gerth and C. Wright Mills. New York: Oxford University Press.

Wolfe, Alan. 1989. *Whose Keeper? Social Science and Moral Obligation.* Berkeley, CA: University of California Press.

The following works are good introductions to social theory and to some of the most important theorists in sociology.

Collins, Randall, and Michael Makowsky. 2004. *The Discovery of Society.* 7th edn. New York: McGraw-Hill.

Coser, Lewis A. 2003. *Masters of Sociological Thought.* 2nd edn. New York: Harcourt Brace Jovanovich.

Cuzzort, R. P., and Edith W. King. 1995. *Twentieth-Century Social Thought.* 5th edn. Orlando, FL: Harcourt Brace & Company.

Gamble, Andrew, David Marsh, and Tony Tant (eds.). 1999. *Marxism and Social Science.* Urbana: University of Illinois Press.

Ritzer, George, and Douglas J. Goodman. 2004. *Classical Sociology Theory.* 4th edn. Boston: McGraw-Hill.

Ritzer, George. 2007. *Contemporary Sociological Theory and Its Classical Roots: The Basics.* 2nd edn. Boston: McGraw-Hill.

Wallace, Ruth A., and Alison Wolf. 1998. *Contemporary Sociological Theory.* Upper Saddle River, NJ: Prentice Hall.

Winslow Homer—Four Boys on a Beach. *National Gallery of Art, Washington, DC.*

1979.19.1 (B-30701)/Dr. Homer, Winslow

Four Boys on the Beach, John Davis Hatch Collection, Andrew W. Mellon Fund, Image courtesy of the Board of Trustees, National Gallery of Art, Washington, c. 1873 graphite with watercolor and gouache on wove page. 141 x 340 (5 9/16 x 13 7/16).

✦ 2 ✦

Sociology as a Perspective: How Sociologists Think

Chapter 1 was a general introduction to the discipline of sociology. This chapter introduces the way sociologists think about the human being. It treats sociology as a "perspective," one approach to understanding the universe (specifically, society), one "window" to seeing the reality of human life.

How do sociologists think? What are the questions they ask? How do they try to unravel the mysteries of human existence? What are the qualities of the human being that are important to sociologists? This chapter introduces the general approach of the sociologist. Four topics are covered:

1. *The social nature of the human being.* Sociology attempts to understand the human being by focusing on the importance of our social life, from ongoing everyday interaction to the power of society. Human beings are thought to be social beings through and through. The sociologist wants to take this idea and see how this quality enters into every aspect of what we all are.
2. *The meaning and importance of social patterns.* Sociology treats society as more than a bunch of individuals. Instead, society begins with social interaction, and that interaction develops social patterns, rules, and agreements among people that direct and control future interaction. Humans exist within a world of social patterns, some of which are developed as they interact, but most of which were developed before they entered into the interaction, and some patterns have been in existence for hundreds—even thousands—of years.
3. *The meaning and importance of socialization.* Humans depend on socialization. Individuals must learn the patterns of society; those patterns become part of every individual. Society depends on individuals who are socialized, individuals who successfully internalize many of those patterns so that cooperation with one another becomes possible.
4. *An example of sociological thinking: Emile Durkheim.* In his work, Durkheim investigates all three of these themes: humans as thoroughly social, humans as embedded in social patterns, and humans as socialized into society. This is most illustrated by his book *Suicide: A Study in Sociology.*

HUMANS ARE SOCIAL BEINGS

Probably the central idea in sociology from which everything else develops is that human beings are *social*. We live in society. Our lives are affected by one another. Dependence on others is a central fact of life. To be social does not mean that we necessarily like one another (some of us do not), but that without interaction and society, human beings would be a different species of animal than we are.

Let us be slightly more systematic. It seems that humans are social in at least six ways:

1. *From the time we are born, we rely on others for survival.* Our physical and emotional needs are met only by relying on others. It takes others to feed us and to protect us from danger. It also takes others to give us affection, feelings of self-worth, warmth, and love — all of which seem essential for growth. This is certainly true of infants and small children; it is probably true of people throughout their lives.
2. *We learn how to survive from others.* We do not know how to survive at birth. Instinct does not carry us very far. We learn how to get along in our world. Our actions are learned; they arise from interaction with others: parents, friends, teachers, television heroes, strangers, books. We learn how and when to fight, to work, and to have fun. We learn how to speak up, to keep from getting stepped on, and how to cook food. Life is learning how to solve problems that face us in our world. This is a lifelong process: We must learn how to survive when we retire, and we must even learn how to die.
3. *We end up spending all our lives in social organization.* Every human being is born into a society, and rarely do we leave that society. We live our whole lives there. We live in an organized community; we work and play in many formal organizations and groups. Each has rules for us to follow; each socializes us; in many of them, it is where our lives take on meaning. Nature probably commands that we live our lives in social organization or perish, but if nature does not command it, we learn it very early.
4. *Many human qualities depend on our social life.* Most religions define us as human because of a God-given soul. Governments recognize our humanity through laws that declare the individual as human at conception, at three months, at birth, or at another point in time. However, if we recognize central human qualities such as language, self, conscience, and mind as the basis for all human action, at what point do we take these on? Whatever our potential for these qualities at birth, it clearly takes society to develop them. In a very basic sense, we become fully human through society. No stronger argument can be made for our social essence.
5. *Many of our individual qualities depend on interaction.* Each of us develops ideas, values, goals, interests, morals, talents, emotions, and tendencies to act in certain ways. These individual qualities are directed through interaction. Our society, community, family, and friends encourage some directions and discourage others. We are not perhaps exact copies of what others want us to be, but their expectations and teachings are important for our choices in life.
6. *Finally, human beings are social actors.* This means, like it or not, that we constantly adjust our actions to others around us. Yes, we try to impress others some of the time, but we also try to communicate to others, we try to influence them, avoid them, or at the very least, adjust our acts so that we can do what we want without being bothered by them. However, because we live around other people, our acts are formed with them in mind, and as social actors, we must take their acts into account when we act. We do not live in isolation — what we do results in part in what others around us do.

The centrality of this social nature of the human being is where sociology begins. Our social nature was not always appreciated, and many people do not appreciate its importance today. For a long time, philosophers debated the state of the human being before society existed. Students in introductory classes in sociology still want to know what would people look like if they never existed in a society. Some argued that we would be noble and good; others have argued we would be savage and evil. Some claim that we would be the same as we are now; others posit that we would be unrecognizable as humans.

Society precedes us all, argues the sociologist. All human beings are born into society; society is an important prerequisite for acting human. Even the first humans were born into a society with rules; even the very earliest humans had to be socialized and depended on others for their very survival. We cannot conceive of the human being developing and existing apart from society. *Society precedes all of us.* Without society, we would not exist as human beings. Even our nearest relatives in the animal kingdom depend on society.

HUMANS EXIST WITHIN SOCIAL PATTERNS

The second idea that describes the sociological approach to understanding the human being concerns *social patterns*.

We are born into society. We live, we die. Society exists before we are born; it continues to exist after we die. But what exactly do we mean by "society"?

Long ago, Durkheim described society as made up of "social facts." By this, he wanted to tell us that society exists "out there," an invisible but real force that works on all of us in some manner or another. Today, we sometimes call this "social forces" or "social patterns." Just as our biological inheritance influences what we do, so do these real forces that exist out there. Just as there is a physical and psychological reality, so too there is a *social reality*, a new additional force that emerges from the interaction of individuals. To say that something is *social* is to recognize that something real has happened *between individuals*.

Take rates at which events happen, for example. Durkheim isolated suicide rates in society. Each society has a suicide rate different from every other society. In fact, these rates tend to stay stable from year to year. If they change, something else has changed and has caused these rates to change. You and I are born into a society; it has a suicide rate, a crime rate, a birth rate, and a death rate. We enter colleges that have dropout rates, and we marry in a society that has a divorce rate. These rates are important to all of us. They exist as a force on us; their existence encourages or discourages our choices in life.

Social class as an example of social reality is even easier to understand. We are born into a class society. We are each located in that class system. We might be able to change our class, but our chances depend on the mobility rate. If we are born poor, our chance for moving up is much less than if we are born middle-class. What does class mean? It means that our lives are part of a social pattern that influences much of what we think and do. It influences our power, lifestyle, opportunities in life, with whom we interact, and the organizations we join. Even if we do change class dramatically through luck, skill, and/or hard work, we will be subject to a new set of social forces operating on the new class position.

Culture is another important social pattern (or social fact). When we say that humans are cultural animals, we mean that society provides the individual with many ready-made answers to problems he or she will encounter in life. Many of our ideas exist in culture; we learn them, and they become important to us. Many of our values and morals arise from that social force called culture. We do not develop in a social vacuum; our views are influenced by a social pattern that goes back a long time, often centuries.

Societies are made up of institutions, too, and institutions are social facts that influence what we do. The fact that America is capitalistic, practices monogamy, and has a two-party political system makes a difference to all of us. Institutions are imperatives; they are developed patterns that direct all of us in our lives.

Most people do not readily recognize these patterns. After all, many argue, society is simply a conglomeration of individuals, and society is no more and no less than the people who make it up. Chemists, biologists, and psychologists do not usually bother with social patterns created among people because their concern is with the individual organism and its development. The closest most of us come to recognizing the power of our social life is to admit that "other people influence us," or that we are "products of our environment" to some extent. But here the idea is different: Humans are said to exist within social patterns, social forces, or social facts; this is a much more complex and profound idea.

HUMANS ARE SOCIALIZED

To understand the sociological view of the human being is also to consider the concept sociologists call "socialization."

For society to function without serious conflict, the human being must be socialized. *Socialization* is the process by which the society, community, formal organization, or group teaches its members its ways. The family and school socialize the child, the fraternity must socialize its freshman recruits, the football team socializes its players, and society, in many direct and indirect ways, socializes its citizens. A socialized person is one who has been successfully made a member of his or her group, formal organization, community, and/or society. A socialized person controls himself or herself, but this self-control comes from learning society's controls.

Socialization creates the qualities that make us fully human. We have potential for human action at birth, but we take on language, self, mind, and conscience as we become socialized. What would we be like without socialization? Some adults are not very well socialized; they exhibit a lack of self-control, an inability to cooperate, a tendency toward impulsive behavior. There are very few examples of humans who developed completely apart from others, but when they are discovered, all appeared very strange. It is almost impossible to imagine the human being without socialization.

The wild boy of Aveyron is probably the most famous case of a child who grew up without much human contact and therefore was not socialized. He was found roaming the woods and fields of Laune, France, in 1797. He was captured, turned over to governmental authorities, and studied by a number of scholars and physicians. He was about 11 or 12 years old; he did not have "the gift of speech," but instead used only "cries and inarticulate sounds." He rejected all clothing, could not distinguish real objects from pictures and mirrored objects, and did not weep. "He had no emotional ties, no sexual expression, no speech; he had a peculiar gait and would occasionally run on all fours" (Lane 1976, 101).

Other cases of humans who grew up without social contact have appeared in the news occasionally. What emerges is a consistent picture: beings who do not use language, react to others with fear and hostility, and exhibit a general apathy.

Cooperation with others becomes difficult because human cooperation demands controlling oneself in relation to the whole, knowing what to do by understanding what others are doing, what George Herbert Mead called "taking the role of the generalized other."

Charles Cooley wrote that human nature does not come at birth. The human "cannot acquire it except through fellowship, and it decays in isolation" ([1909] 1962, 30). In a very real sense, we are socialized to become human beings.

Durkheim captures well the meaning and importance of socialization. Society, he wrote, is able to exist only because it gets inside the human being, shaping our inner life, creating our conscience, our ideas, and our values. Society's rules become our own; its ways become ours. When people violate its rules, we are angered and seek to reaffirm its rules through punishment. Because of socialization, when society's symbols—its flags, leaders, and religious objects, for instance—enter our presence, we are moved and feel that we belong to something good. Because of socialization, our identities become embedded in and dependent on society.

Marx, too, sensitizes us to the role of socialization in society. How is it possible to have a society where a few people own the means of production and control great wealth, while the masses must work for these privileged few and barely survive? Marx's answer is that the masses are taught to accept their place. They come to believe that they too may become wealthy if they work hard enough. They come to believe that the wealthy are somehow more deserving and that this is the natural state of things, or that change is undesirable or impossible. Of course, Marx is at least partly right: Humans, no matter what position they have in society, are socialized to accept society; if socialization works well, the job of the police is made much easier. Socialization allows society to get inside our very being.

Sociologists attempt to understand just how significant socialization is to every aspect of the actor. Human differences and similarities are understood in this context. Crime, success, values, morals, accomplishments, and failures are understood in part as resulting from socialization. Differences between men and women are located in socialization, as are differences in class and ethnic groups.

Of course, biology too may play some role. People have different potentials, talents, levels of "intelligence," and so on. Even infants are in fact different from one another in temperament, size, looks, and sex. Yet immediately after birth, they interact with other humans who encourage, discourage, and direct these various qualities. Sociologists want to know, therefore, what happens to the child growing up in poverty or in the upper class, how being male or female influences how others socialize us, and how different groups and societies handle different temperaments, looks, talents, and so on.

The social patterns described earlier are learned through socialization. We learn our positions and role expectations through socialization. We learn culture through socialization: What the organization thinks is true, worthwhile, and right. We learn our *identities*—who we think we are—through socialization. Even something as basic as *self-awareness*, our ability to look back on ourselves as objects in the world, comes to us through learning from others that we exist as entities. Others are our "looking glass," writes Cooley. Our self is our "looking glass self."

Socialization makes society possible. We are not like ants or bees; that is, we are not born with instincts that direct us to cooperate. Instead, we are socialized to direct ourselves in relation to society. Without socialization, we would all be so different that there would be no possibility for cooperation or social order. Indeed, without socialization, we would act impulsively without any self-control. Self-control is social control, and social control arises from socialization.

Sociologists rightly see the concept of socialization as one of the central concepts in all sociology. It is a central part of our social nature and a good way to introduce the sociological perspective.

DURKHEIM: THE STUDY OF SUICIDE

Three ideas, all basic to the sociological perspective, have been introduced in this chapter. In the history of thought, these ideas were revolutionary—they challenged what many intellectuals and religious leaders believed. They introduced us to a unique way of understanding the individual. *Human beings are social*: To understand them without taking this fact into account is to miss much of their essence. *Human beings exist within social patterns; those patterns influence, shape, control, and direct their actions*: To forget about society and its patterns in trying to understand human action is to ignore a very basic cause of what we do, think, and are. *Human beings are socialized; we are not simply learners, but we are taught the patterns of our particular society, and internalizing these patterns makes us members of that society*: To recognize our ability to learn without focusing on the particular learning we call socialization is to miss what we really are.

Alan Wolfe (1993) writes that sociology is a perspective that is a sharp contrast to all that went before it. Wolfe sees it as a discovery of "society" and "self." Before sociology, political science and economics seemed to be enough: rulers controlled people, and economic laws shaped their economic decisions. If we add psychology, the study of the individual human being, what is the need for sociology? Sociology studies society, not the state; it sees humans as social beings, not simply as political beings; it sees society as made up of and held together by social patterns, not simply by the commands of its political leaders. It focuses on social patterns, not simply economic ones, and regards all human relationships, not simply economic relationships, worthy of study. And, Wolfe argues, it is the "self" that sociologists insist on, not simply the individual, because with the self the individual is linked to society at all times and is socialized by society in what he or she does. Society creates the individual, and the individual is always influenced by socialization. Political science, economics, and psychology are all important. But to Wolfe—and most sociologists—so is sociology, the last social science to develop and the one that focuses on society—the human as a social being, the human as subject to a host of social patterns, and the human formed and reformed through socialization.

Probably more than anyone else, the work of Emile Durkheim represents the perspective of sociology. Durkheim's intellectual life was spent making a place for sociology in the academic world. Before he came along, sociology was fighting hard for recognition in a world that revered psychology and biology. After he died, it was generally recognized that human beings are social, affected by social patterns, and socialized. Because of him, it was also generally recognized that sociology was a science. Part of his success can be found in his most famous work *Suicide: A Study in Sociology*. Let us look briefly at this work to see how Durkheim introduced to the world the outline of the science of society.

Durkheim's Theory

Durkheim was interested in studying suicide rates because he thought such a study would help establish sociology as a scientific discipline. He wanted to show the importance of "social facts," his term for social patterns. Suicide, he argued, will always be a personal choice, and there are all kinds of psychological reasons one actor rather than another chooses it. However, even in this most individual of choices, social facts are at work—a society's suicide *rate* (high or low) influences the probability of an individual's suicide. This rate stays stable over time: We will find, for example, that one society might have 6 suicides per year for every 100,000 people, and another might have 12 suicides for every 100,000 people. This difference will hold true over a long period, so we might say that one society has a suicide rate twice as great as the other.

However, what causes high or low suicide rates? Durkheim believed the cause was another social fact, which he called "social solidarity," the degree to which a society is integrated, united, or held together as a solid whole. The opposite of high social solidarity is a high degree of individualism: If people are highly individualistic, then social solidarity is low. This is what modern times bring, he thought.

Low social solidarity (a social fact) will lead to a high suicide rate. Individualism will lead to greater reliance on self and less direction from an anchorage in group standards for guidance and meaning, with suicide becoming a more realistic option for many.

Durkheim's Evidence

Durkheim was a scientist. He wanted to test his idea carefully and systematically.

Durkheim had suicide data from government records for several European countries and provinces. He first divided these countries into Catholic and Protestant groups. He believed that because Protestantism emphasizes the individual's relationship to God and that Catholicism emphasizes the Church as an integrated community worshipping together, the Protestant countries and provinces would have higher suicide rates. This is exactly what he found. The probability of suicide was significantly higher in Protestant than in Catholic communities. Durkheim's theory was supported, but not proved: There is not enough evidence here to conclude that social solidarity was the real influence. After all, perhaps Catholics have lower suicide rates than Protestants for reasons besides solidarity.

Durkheim continued to test his theory. He argued that if his theory was correct, small communities (having higher social solidarity) would have lower suicide rates than cities. Examining his data, he found that this too was true. He went further: It follows, he reasoned, that married people would be more integrated into community than single people, women more than men, people with children more than those without, people who do not have a college education more than those who do (because college tends to break ties with groups and encourages individualism). Marriage, family, and lack of a college education are more likely to mean being part of a group, tradition, and society; being single, without children, and having a college education discourage embeddedness in group, tradition, and society. In every one of these cases, he found that his theory was supported: Single people, men, those without children, and those with a college education had higher suicide rates.

Durkheim kept going. How about the Jewish community? Will it have a high or low suicide rate? On the one hand, Jewish people in Europe were the most educated. On the other hand, their community was characterized by very high social solidarity. He found what he expected: The Jewish community had a lower rate of suicide than either the Protestants or Catholics. It is also easy to see why education did not make a big difference: Education took place *in the community*, and the purpose of education was to learn the traditions and ideas of the community. Instead of higher education encouraging individualism, it actually encouraged social solidarity.

What is the significance of this? Durkheim is doing two important things at once. First, he is establishing the existence of social facts (social forces, social patterns) that influence individual action. We do not, it seems, make our decisions solely on the basis of individual personality factors; rather, our decisions are made in a larger social context, influenced by social forces we are not even aware of. Our society, if it is low on social solidarity, will influence more of us to choose suicide.

Second, for his day, Durkheim's study is also good science. It shows how a scientist thinks and then tests his thinking creatively and systematically. Further, the study is published in a book for all of us to see. His data can be analyzed and criticized by others. We do not have to take Durkheim's word for either his conclusions or his evidence.

Extending His Theory

Durkheim showed another characteristic of the good scientist. He added to his theory, showing that social solidarity has a much more complex relationship to the suicide rate. Where there is very little social solidarity, a high rate of *egoistic suicide* results. However, Durkheim also believed that very high levels of social solidarity also lead to high suicide rates, which he called *altruistic suicide*.

Altruistic suicide, Durkheim reasoned, results from the fact that the individual comes to feel personal worth only through the group, gaining personal meaning only from something larger than self. Ego becomes nothing; giving up one's life to the group becomes honorable. Personal failure means that one lets down the group; dishonor and shame result, leading to a high probability for suicide. Durkheim again tested his theory. The army has very high social solidarity; the army also has a high suicide rate. Within the army, career officers, volunteers, and old-timers (the most highly integrated) all had higher suicide rates than the others. If Durkheim had been alive during World War II, he would have pointed to Japanese *kamikaze* pilots and Japanese officers who lost important battles as examples of altruistic suicide. Probably the best modern example is the mass suicide at Jonestown in Guyana: in November 1978, over 900 people, who had left the United States to follow Reverend Jim Jones, a charismatic religious leader, committed suicide by knowingly drinking Kool Aid poisoned with cyanide. The 1997 mass suicide of members of the Heaven's Gate commune in San Diego is also an example of what Durkheim described as altruistic suicide. The fact is that suicide is made easier for people who lack any individuality, who dedicate themselves to a society or community in a full sense, believing themselves to have honor, meaning, and purpose only as long as they exist together.

Durkheim's theory is interesting because it tells us that the relationship between social solidarity and suicide rates is *curvilinear*, that rates are higher at both ends of the scale in societies where there are either very high or very low levels of social solidarity.

Durkheim went further. He tried to isolate another social fact: the degree of change in society. This too, he argued, will affect the suicide rate. Societies that undergo rapid change will upset the social worlds of the individual, who will find that the groups of which he or she is a part no longer give appropriate guides to action. The old standards no longer work; the individual will have to make more and more decisions on his or her own, with increasingly less anchorage in social life. Here Durkheim is not describing social solidarity, but whether one's society is an appropriate guide to the present. In times of rapid change, the individual will reach a state of *anomie*, a term Durkheim used to mean without norms, without guides, a "state of normlessness." He appropriately called suicides that resulted from this state *anomic suicide*.

Durkheim again tested his idea. If his theory was right, then in periods of revolution, a society's suicide rate would go up. He found that it does. He also found higher suicide rates during times of economic depression and in times of rapid prosperity. He applied his idea to categories of people whose lives change suddenly: to those who become suddenly poor or suddenly rich, those who quickly become famous or drop into obscurity, who are released from prisoner-of-war camps, or who suddenly lose a close friend or family member.

To complete his theory, Durkheim described a fourth type of suicide caused by too much control by society's norms. The extreme example is a slave society in which life for the slave is characterized by too little change, too little hope for a better life, where the society is all controlling, and where change is minimal. This type of suicide he called *fatalistic*. He did not test this idea beyond mentioning a few examples.

Figure 2-1 shows the four extremes of social change and social solidarity in Durkheim's theory. A society without any of these extremes will have the lowest suicide rate. Remember: What Durkheim is trying to do is to isolate social forces, or what he

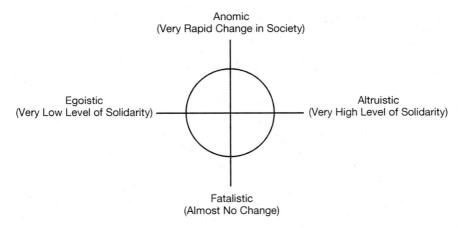

FIGURE 2-1   The Conditions of Society Under Which Suicide Is Most Prevalent

calls "social facts," and to show that these make a significant difference in our lives. We all live within a social context that includes a rate of social change, a level of social solidarity, and a suicide rate. What we do in our own personal lives is linked in many complex ways to this social context.

Durkheim's Influence

Durkheim's study of suicide has inspired much useful work. The concept of anomie has been applied to a number of theories and has inspired research in the area of deviance. Durkheim's study of suicide has influenced an important tradition in sociological research: that which uses careful statistical analysis for testing ideas. His study of suicide rates has opened doors to those of us interested in birth rates, death rates, divorce rates, and so on. He shows us that science can be applied to an understanding of society and shows us the reality and the importance of social forces.

Durkheim's work encourages others. Many sociologists have taken his theory and applied it to their own society and their own times. His theory still works. We can test it today with data from the United States. Do the categories of people Durkheim predicted would have the highest rates still have the highest rates today? Single people? Men? Recently divorced? Newly widowed? Protestants? Urban? Based on what has occurred in American society over the past 30 years, which categories of people might we predict have rapidly rising rates? Jewish people (because they are less integrated into a Jewish community)? Women (as they become more independent and less integrated into family and community)?

His study has also inspired criticism, leading some sociologists to go in directions he did not pursue. Jack Douglas, for example, criticized Durkheim for ignoring how people perceive suicide, saying that the way groups of people think about suicide — how they define it — is more important than the abstract social facts of social solidarity and social change that Durkheim isolated. Others do not like his heavy use of statistics, and still others criticize the bias of governmental data.

Still, we have no better theory of suicide rates than Durkheim's. Although his data may not be as good as we would like, and although some of his research and thinking might not be consistent with modern standards, *Suicide* remains a lasting contribution to the field of sociology. And it represents very well three of the ideas contained in Chapters 1 and 2: Human beings are social, we live within social patterns, and sociology is a scientific discipline.

Suicide does not focus on socialization, however. Recall that socialization is one of the other ideas discussed earlier. In his book, Durkheim attempted to uncover social forces and their importance — that which exists in society rather than how those forces get inside us. However, Durkheim's other work recognizes the great importance of socialization. He writes about the "collective conscience," the morality that exists outside in society entering into each individual in that society and becoming central to each individual's conscience — all a result of socialization. He writes about how certain objects in society — a cross, a flag, a certain song, a baseball star, or a U.S. President — can come to represent the society, and how these special representations become objects that individuals respond to emotionally and that bring a feeling of loyalty and belongingness to members of society when those objects enter our presence — through the power of socialization. Society, to

Durkheim, is possible largely because the solitary savage individual is socialized to become a full-fledged, committed member of society.

SOCIOLOGY: A SUMMARY

These first two chapters have introduced the discipline called sociology. Several ideas were presented:

1. Sociology is an academic discipline that began in the nineteenth century. It is the study of the human being as a social being. It is a scientific discipline; from its beginnings, it has been characterized by disagreement and debate. These ideas were emphasized in Chapter 1.
2. Sociology begins with the idea that human beings are social in very basic ways. We described six: relying on others for survival, learning how to survive, living our lives in organization, developing human qualities, developing our individual qualities, and being social actors.
3. Sociologists emphasize that humans exist within social patterns and that these patterns make a great difference to what we all do.
4. Sociology is also the study of socialization, the process by which the individual learns the ways of society. There are many examples of the importance of socialization to what we all are.
5. Emile Durkheim's work highlights the ideas described in this chapter and exhibits the power of the sociological perspective. His study, *Suicide*, underscores the power of society on the life of the individual, the possibility for a science of sociology, and the need for the individual to be a part of society. Durkheim's other works emphasize the importance of socialization to what we all become, especially our moral character and our loyalty to society.

It is time now to add meat to the skeleton. The next several chapters will build on these first two chapters and will show the many ways in which individual and society are intimately linked.

QUESTIONS TO CONSIDER

1. What is human nature? What do you think human nature consists of? How important is our "social nature"?
2. Human beings exist within social patterns. What exactly does this mean? Is this true? Is it exaggerated by the author of the text?
3. Human beings are socialized. Can you explain this? How important do you think socialization is?
4. What are Durkheim's major points in *Suicide*? Do his ideas make any sense to you?
5. Suppose that you were interested in testing Durkheim's theory of suicide today. What populations would you choose to study?

REFERENCES

Lane, Harlan. 1976. *The Wild Boy of Aveyron*. New York: Bantam Books.
Cooley, Charles Horton. 1909. *Social Organization* 1962 ed. New York: Schocker Books.
Wolfe, Alan. 1993. *The Human Difference: Animals, Computers, and the Necessity of Social Science*. Berkeley, CA: University of California Press.

RECOMMENDED READING

The following works discuss socialization, social patterns, and the general perspective of sociology. They are good representations of how sociologists think about the human being and society.

Bellah, Robert N., Richard Madsen, William M. Sullivan, Ann Swidler, and Steven M. Tipton. 1985. *Habits of the Heart: Individualism and Commitment in American Life.* New York: Harper & Row.

Berger, Aruthur A. *Dukheim Is Dead! Sherlock Holmes Is Introduced to Sociological Theory.* New York, NY: AltaMira Press.

Berger, Peter. 1963. *Invitation to Sociology.* Garden City, NY: Doubleday.

Berger, Peter L., and Thomas Luckmann. 1966. *The Social Construction of Reality.* Garden City, NY: Doubleday.

Blau, Peter M., and Marshall W. Meyer. 1987. *Bureaucracy in Modern Society.* 3rd edn. New York: Random House.

Blumer, Herbert. 1969. *Symbolic Interactionism: Perspective and Method.* Upper Saddle River, NJ: Prentice Hall.

Brim, Orville G., Jr., and S. Wheeler (eds.). 1966. *Socialization After Childhood.* New York: John Wiley.

Collins, Randall, and Michael Makowsky. 1998. *The Discovery of Society.* 6th edn. New York: McGraw-Hill.

Cooley, Charles Horton. 1902. *Human Nature and the Social Order.* 1964 edn. New York: Schocken Books.

Davis, Kingsley. 1947. "Final Note on a Case of Extreme Isolation." In *American Journal of Sociology*, 52:432–437.

Durkheim, Emile. 1895. *The Rules of the Sociological Method.* 1964 edn. Trans. Sarah A. Solovay and John H. Mueller. New York: Free Press.

Durkheim, Emile. 1897. *Suicide.* 1951 edn. Trans. and ed. John A. Spaulding and George Simpson. New York: Free Press.

Durkheim, Emile. 1915. *The Elementary Forms of Religious Life.* 1954 edn. Trans. Joseph Swain. New York: Free Press.

Elkin, Frederick, and Gerald Handel. 1989. *The Child in Society: The Process of Socialization.* 5th edn. New York: Random House.

Gilbert, Dennis, and Joseph A. Kahl. 1997. *The American Class Structure in an Age of Growing Inequality: A New Synthesis.* 5th edn. Belmont, CA: Wadsworth Publishing Co.

Goffman, Erving. 1959. *The Presentation of Self in Everyday Life.* New York: Doubleday (Anchor).

Goode, Erich. 2000. *Deviant Behavior: An Interactionist Approach.* 6th edn. Upper Saddle River, NJ: Prentice Hall.

Goode, Erich. 2000. *Paranormal Beliefs: A Sociological Introduction.* Prospect Heights, IL: Waveland Press, Inc.

Harrington, Michael. 1963. *The Other America.* New York: Penguin Books.

Henslin, James M. 2000. *Social Problems.* 5th edn. Upper Saddle River, NJ: Prentice Hall.

Jenkins, Richard. 1996. *Social Identity.* New York: Routledge.

Johnson, Allan G. 1997. *The Forest and the Trees: Sociology as Life, Practice, and Promise.* Philadelphia: Temple University Press.

Kanter, Rosabeth. 1977. *Men and Women of the Corporation.* New York: Basic Books.

Kerbo, Harold R. 1999. *Social Stratification and Inequality.* 4th edn. New York: McGraw-Hill.

Keister, Lisa A. 2005. *Getting Rich: America's New Rich and How They Got That Way.* New York: Cambridge University Press.

Lenski, Gerhard. 1987. *Human Societies: An Introduction to Macrosociology.* 8th edn. New York: McGraw-Hill.

Liebow, Elliot. 1967. *Tally's Corner.* Boston: Little, Brown.

Marx, Karl, and Friedrich Engels. 1848. *The Communist Manifesto.* 1955 edn. New York: Appleton-Century-Crofts.

McCall, George J., and J. L. Simmons. 1978. *Identities and Interactions.* New York: Free Press.

Mead, George Herbert. 1934. *Mind, Self and Society.* Chicago: University of Chicago Press.

Merton, Robert K. 1968. *Social Theory and Social Structure.* New York: Free Press.

Mills, C. Wright. 1956. *The Power Elite.* New York: Oxford University Press.

Mills, C. Wright. 1959. *The Sociological Imagination.* New York: Oxford University Press.

Myrdal, Gunnar. 1944. *An American Dilemma.* New York: Harper & Row.

Rose, Peter I. (ed.). 1979. *Socialization and the Life Cycle.* New York: St. Martin's Press.

Ryan, William. 1976. *Blaming the Victim.* Rev. ed. New York: Vintage.

Tocqueville, Alexis de. 1840. *Democracy in America.* 1969 edn. New York: Doubleday.
Weber, Max. 1905. *The Protestant Ethic and the Spirit of Capitalism.* 1958 edn. Trans. and ed. Talcott
    Parsons. New York: Scribners.
Wheelan, Susan A. 1994. *Group Processes: The Developmental Perspective.* Boston: Allyn & Bacon.
Wilson, William J. 1973. *Power, Racism, and Privilege.* New York: Macmillan.
Wilson, William J. 1987. *The Truly Disadvantaged: The Inner City, the Underclass, and Public Policy.*
    Chicago: University of Chicago Press.
Zimbardo, Philip. 1972. "Pathology of Imprisonment." In *Society*, 9:4–8.

John. H. Howard, The Bar at the Casa Verde (Painting for Mural). *Newborn Group.*

✦ 3 ✦

Humans Are Embedded in Social Organization

We hear words like "group," "organization," and "society" all the time. Most of us have some notion about what they mean. The purpose of this chapter is to try to define these terms carefully and to show their usefulness in the perspective of sociology.

To say "organization" is to say "routine," "pattern," "continuity." *Let's get organized!* really means let's put things into place, let's have some order, let's establish a pattern we can all use, let's get together so that we know what each person is doing. That is the basic meaning of organization—the patterns that develop among people over time. Sociologists study these patterns, how they are created, and how they come to influence, direct, or control the actors—ourselves.

Almost every person is born into social organization. Many of the social patterns we discover in our family, community, and society have been developed long before we enter them. Characteristically, individuals become part of social organization and are subject to its patterns. Only once in a while do they participate in creating social organization.

Where do social patterns come from? How do they arise in the first place? How are they reaffirmed? Altered? Done away with? The simplest answer is *social interaction*. As people interact, they develop social patterns—organization. Where interaction stops, social patterns die out. Where interaction is segregated, more than one set of patterns develop separate social organizations. Where interaction is interrupted, where many new actors enter in, where new problems arise for those in interaction, the social patterns are altered.

Social interaction is the key to understanding social patterns and social organization. The key to understanding social interaction is *social action*, to which we now turn.

ORGANIZATION BEGINS WITH SOCIAL ACTION

We all act—that is, we do things, we exhibit movement toward the world around us. Indeed, to fail to act is to be dead. Max Weber argued that the best way to define the subject matter of sociology is as the study of one kind of action—social action.

31

Of course, humans are not only social actors, but social action dominates much of what we do. It is central to understanding what human beings are.

Social action had a special meaning to Weber. For some people, *social* means having a lot of fun at parties, "socializing," being friendly, being nice to others. Others recognize that *social* has something to do with groups and society, that individual action is somehow influenced by other people. Weber, too, argued that humans are influenced by other people, but his analysis went beyond this.

Social action, according to Weber ([1922]1964, 88), takes place when the actor "orients his acts" to others and is thus influenced by these others. The actor takes account of others, or acts for others, or acts toward others, or acts against others, or acts in spite of others. The actor forms his or her acts in order to influence others, or to communicate to them, or to compliment or criticize them, or to fool them, or to make them laugh or cry, or to do all the various things people do in relation to others. *Wherever others make any difference to what we do, wherever we think of others as we act, there is an example of social action!*

Examples are everywhere. In a sense, I am writing this sentence for an audience even though there is no one in the room with me. When I see you and say "Hi!" my speech is aimed at you and is therefore a social act. When you turn your head and keep walking, ignoring me, you are acting with me in mind. When I talk to you, whistle, give you the peace sign, hit you, embrace you, hold your hand, sing to you, throw a baseball to you, I am engaging in social action. When I dress in the morning and imagine what I look like to others (even people I may not know personally), this is social action. When I move off into a corner so that I can escape being noticed at a party, I am a social actor because others in the situation make a difference in what I do. When I conform so that I do not look like a fool to others, and when I refuse to conform and tell others that they are the fools, I am a social actor. Alone in my room, sitting at my computer, what I do becomes a social act when I send an e-mail, when I consider the e-mail delivered to me, when I compose a request for a book, or when I plan my strategy for a final exam.

The key to social action is *acting with others in mind*. All intentional communication is social action, but communication is not essential to social action. (If I am a thief, I will act with police in mind so that I do not get caught, yet I may not necessarily want to communicate anything.) Sometimes, the people we have in mind are part of our current lives; sometimes, they are part of our past (people we know who have died) or our future (future generations of Americans); and sometimes, they are even imagined (I am writing this book for an imagined audience). Sometimes, we act with an individual in mind, and sometimes, with a group (our friends) or even a society (the United States).

Not all action is social action. If it is raining and I put up my umbrella, I am obviously not acting for the benefit of anyone but myself. Even if someone else puts an umbrella up and I see it and do the same, that is not social action either—it is imitation. It is only when I open up my umbrella in part for others, for an audience, that that action becomes social. If it is pouring, and others look at me holding an umbrella in my hand, and I decide that I had better open it up so that they do not consider me a fool, my act becomes a social act. Or if I offer to share it with the person next to me who is getting soaked, the act becomes social.

Social action is *intentional action*. I think of others as I act, I intend my acts for others, or I at least take account of others. This means that actions that are purely emotional or habitual are not social actions. Of course, there are probably no purely emotional unthinking acts, because even in our most emotional moments, we act with others in mind to some extent. If I bang my head on a doorpost and take my anger out on a friend by yelling at him, my act is not primarily a thinking one and it is not significantly social; yet there is at least a small element of thought in my act and it is certainly oriented to another person, so the act is social to some extent. And when I do something habitually and I do not carefully consider anyone else in the situation, there is also an exception to social action. This too, though, is quite rare, because most situations demand that we take into account other people. Driving may be habitual, but hopefully it is also social because every situation must take account of other drivers. So almost all our actions, even emotional and habitual responses, have an element of "taking others into account." We are almost always social actors.

Social action is important to what we are. We live our lives around others, and these others come to make a difference to what we do because we usually must consider them. Therefore, what we do at any moment is to some extent shaped by the situation, by the presence of particular others. Our action changes as others around us change. I will act differently depending on whom I am acting for at that moment. Sometimes my parents, my friends, a professor, a clerk, or a class of students will be important to me, and I will be influenced by their presence. It is not that we are only trying to impress each other—although this is a part of it—but we are also trying to influence each other, and what we do depends on what is appropriate in the situation we find ourselves in. Social action, then, means that we humans adjust from situation to situation—not drastically, perhaps, but we change nevertheless. And when we stay the same, it is generally because our audience has also stayed the same. What we do largely depends on the particular social world we are acting in. The importance of social action to what we are underlines once again the fact that we are social beings.

MUTUAL SOCIAL ACTION IS SOCIAL INTERACTION

Much of what humans do results from their interaction. Sometimes, I take you into account when I act; likewise, you take me into account when you act. The presence of each makes a difference for the other's acts. This is *mutual social action* or simply *social interaction*: Each person is both subject and object; that is, each person acts toward the others and is in turn considered an object by the others. The presence of each and the actions of each make a difference to the others' actions. This happens between you and me when I ask you to dance and you say "No!" It also happens when you say "Yes," when we dance (unless we only imagine the audience around us, or we respond only to the music and not each other), and also when we sit down for a drink. And we can imagine the many ways that interaction might take place through the evening, start again the next week, or continue for a whole year or even for a lifetime. Some social action never becomes interaction, some social interaction lasts only for a second, and some continues over time.

Sometimes, we act toward each other and do not understand what the other is really intending by his or her act. I act to impress you; you think I'm being foolish. You laugh at me, and I interpret your laughter as interest in me. We continue to misunderstand each other's actions and intentions, and our interaction might lead to conflict or to a quick end to the relationship. We can correct each other's interpretation, and interaction will continue.

Social interaction is what occurs *between* and among people. It is not simply what person A or person B does. It is what they do in relation to one another. Each forms his or her action as the other is acting; action unfolds over time as each takes into account the presence and actions of the other. Action cannot simply be predicted by knowing who the actors are or what their intentions are at the beginning of the interaction.

An instructor begins a lecture. A student asks a question. The instructor now alters what she intended to do in the lecture. She backs up and repeats what she said the day before. Another student becomes confused and asks a question. No one intended the class to go in this direction, but it does: The social acts of various actors direct the flow of action. So it is in conversations, buying and selling, playing chess or cards, driving a car, fights, sexual encounters, and any action that involves others. What we do becomes an important consideration for others; what they do becomes an important consideration for us. The actions of each one of us are directed by the social interaction as they develop back and forth. None of us can fully control the social situation, and none of us can easily escape its influence.

Clearly, *interaction is very important as a cause for human action*. Actors adjust to each other and are thus affected by each other's acts. As interaction unfolds, plans are altered, and actions are evaluated, altered, and aligned. People find themselves doing things they never imagined they could or would do, simply because the interaction leads them to a certain point. We are all potentially saints or sinners, and we become either or both depending in part on our interaction. Life is like a continuous stream of action going one way, then another, due, in part, to the influence of our encounters with others, their actions, our actions in return, and their actions taken in relation to ours.

Interaction is also very important because it is the source of our socialization. To some extent, every time we interact, we are being socialized. Interaction forms what we are—gives us new ideas; poses new options; and influences our values, self-image, identity, attitudes, and general personality. We are formed, reaffirmed, and altered as we interact. We learn to steal in interaction; we learn to value school in interaction. We learn that we are intelligent or beautiful in interaction; we learn prejudice or openness in interaction. We become a traditional woman or a feminist in interaction; we become religious, patriotic, or revolutionary in interaction. To some extent at least, we become a problem drinker or drug abuser in interaction, and to some extent, we control our addiction through interaction.

Finally, *social interaction is important because it leads to social patterns*. It is the very basis for all social organization. Imagine what happens in interaction over time. We develop relationships. We know more about what to expect from each other; we come to understand more clearly each other's meanings and intentions; we can agree on a number of matters; we develop routines of action; and we are less and less surprised by others' actions. We have developed *social patterns*, and these create a *social organization* of which we become a part.

In summary, social interaction is central to human life. It influences what we all do, what we all become, and how the social patterns that become the basis for our organized life develop.

SOCIAL ORGANIZATION IS PATTERNED SOCIAL INTERACTION

Patterned social interaction is what sociologists call interaction where action becomes more organized, less spontaneous, less accidental, or different, and we come to know what others will do and what we are supposed to do in relation to them. We do not have to start over; we do not have to explore how to act with each other whenever we come together. We have not necessarily changed as individuals, but we have changed when we are around each other. We have entered into social interaction governed by a body of rules, most of which are neither written nor explicitly stated. Interaction becomes regularized. We all come to know what to expect from one another and from ourselves.

Patterns are more than the individuals who comprise them; they are like new, additional forces that have arisen among people and now exert influence on each individual. They are not explainable just by adding up the individuals involved; they are social facts above and beyond the individuals themselves. Thus, when people interact over time, they are influenced not only by each other's specific acts, but also by the patterns that have developed among them. Two individuals on a date are influenced not only by each other, but by the rules and the ideas they have both come to accept in the relationship: for example, no outside dating; an openness in sharing personal problems; casual dress; a certain kind of humor; a right mixture of seriousness and humor in situations; a specific code of behavior around parents, adults, friends, employers, and other people whom they know personally or encounter for the first time.

Patterns are even more obvious when there are more than two people interacting over time. When children are added to a family, patterns will develop among all the actors so that all will know what to expect from each other. Sometimes, social patterns are written down: Families develop contracts between parents and children; committees and boards develop by-laws; churches and businesses establish in writing what the rules shall be; communities and societies write laws and documents that affirm a body of principles people are expected to believe in.

It might be easier to understand and appreciate social patterns if we recognize that, in general, they are a "body of rules" and that they are an agreed-on "view of reality" (what sociologists sometimes call "norms" and "perspective"). In effect, as people interact, they come to agree on rules that govern the interaction and a set of general ideas that those in the interaction use to see reality.

Individuals who continue interacting are expected to accept these patterns; people in the interaction are able to cooperate to the extent that these patterns work. Social patterns make it possible for social interaction to continue with less and less difficulty; they take the guesswork out of what people are supposed to do and think. Patterns bring organization, consistency, predictability, stability, and routine to our everyday existence. Without social patterns, cooperation on an ongoing basis would be impossible.

Most of the time, the social patterns we follow have been established by others who have interacted and developed the patterns. We enter the interaction, learn the patterns, and do what we are supposed to do. We know how to act in a movie theater because the patterns have been established and parents or friends have taught us what to do in such places. Teachers establish rules and students are taught them the first day of class. Indeed, if the rules are not clear, we ask. We are born into families whose patterns are already formed to a great extent; when we enter a fraternity, a business, a grocery store, or a new job, we have little to say about the patterns we follow. A *society* is a social organization that has existed for a long time; we live according to its social patterns, we are born into it, and we normally accept it as part of our taken-for granted world.

Start up a softball team. The game of softball has social patterns you inherit: positions on the team, a body of rules, and even the right ways to field ground balls, catch flies, and bat. The league you join also has social patterns—rules, schedules, places to play—that others have developed for you. The team might develop its own social patterns about how matters are decided—for example, who plays where, who bats when, how the captain is chosen—but there is no great room for originality. Playing together establishes social patterns in that people know what to expect from each other in the outfield, infield, and so on. As such, matters are "set," they become social patterns that all follow so that there can be a cooperative team. New situations arise; old rules are applied. "That's not fair," is the cry of the individual who feels a social pattern is being violated. Once developed, social patterns take on a life of their own: "That's just how we do things around here. If you don't like it, it's tough." And when the umpire steps onto the field, hundreds of additional rules now govern the team.

In summary, we have emphasized so far that when human beings act around others, they become social actors, they interact, and they form social patterns. All of these become important to what human beings do.

1. *We are social actors.* When we act, we take others into account—they matter for what we do. Our action depends on adjusting our actions to them in some way.
2. *We interact.* As we act with others in mind, they too act with us in mind. We affect one another. Action builds up over time as we adjust our acts to one another. This social interaction influences the flow of action on each actor's part, it socializes us, and it leads to the development of social patterns.
3. *We develop social patterns* through social interaction. Once created, these patterns come to exert themselves on us as we continue in the interaction.
4. *Most situations we enter have social patterns already set for us,* which we learn—and these patterns influence what we do.

THE FORMS OF SOCIAL ORGANIZATION

Social organization takes five forms: dyads, groups, formal organizations, communities, and societies. In each form, the basic elements of organization are the same: social interaction that has developed social patterns. Organization is made possible because individuals accept the patterns as guides to their thinking and acting. Such acceptance facilitates social control over the individual actor and cooperation among the actors in the social organization.

When we identify any *social organization,* two qualities must be in evidence: (1) *ongoing social interaction*—actors regularly interact with one another—and (2) *social patterns*—a set of rules and perspectives are to some extent characteristic of that particular organization. Actors in the organization are influenced by these patterns.

Dyads Are Twos

Dyads are formed when there is patterned social interaction between two people—friends, lovers, doctor–patient, mother–son, husband–wife—over time. The patterns come into play whenever the two people interact, whether face to face or apart (as by letter, telephone, or e-mail).

Groups Are More

The most common word used to refer to numbers of people is *group*. In sociology, a group is not just a number of people who are alike (such as people with blond hair or people who live on Third Street); a group, like a dyad, is made up of people who interact and form patterns, but a group is made up of three or more individuals.

When the individuals get together, they act according to the patterns. We may smoke all we want when we are with Helen and Edith, but when we are with Martha and Mary, we know that smoking is out. We talk up a storm around our friends, but we keep quiet in class. I remember how important it was in my junior high days to be "cool" at parties with mixed (boy–girl) company, how silly I acted when I was with George and Dave, and how serious I was in my interaction with Mike. In my family, I kept quiet; when I was with only my brother, I had to establish my superiority. In each group and dyad, the patterns were different. I knew what they were, and I adjusted my action accordingly. I'm not unique—we all do this it seems.

Groups are everywhere. A family is a group and has its own social patterns: for example, agreement over bathroom use, privacy, holiday celebration, the scheduling of meals, the relationship between husband and wife, as well as views of dating, marriage, cleanliness, punishment, religion, and education. The gang that gets together at Louie's Café Thursday night is a group, as is the Sunday afternoon baseball team and the committee appointed by the Chamber of Commerce or by the student senate. These are all examples of groups that are continuous and last a fairly long time. The patterns become taken for granted, and we become most aware of them when someone decides to violate them.

Often, however, dyads and groups exist for no more than a few minutes or perhaps an hour, a day, or an evening. When people gather at a party, they form a group (indeed, probably several groups), which changes as new people enter and others leave. These short-lived groups are still groups; there is interaction (mutual social action) and patterns emerge. The patterns are simple and slight at first, but after several minutes or an hour, more and more understanding about what one is to do and how the others see our acts is shared and affects all participants. And the more the group becomes isolated from other groups, the more its patterns become established and unique. Some sociologists have done extensive research on small-group discussions and have discovered that patterns emerge very early and remain fairly stable over time.

At first glance, there may not appear to be much of a difference between a dyad and a group, but size does indeed affect the nature of the patterns. Georg Simmel (1858–1918), a famous German sociologist, analyzed how dyads and groups differ.

1. In a dyad, there is instability and insecurity not characteristic of the group because the dyad is faced with dissolution if one person leaves. A group is capable of survival if a member leaves or is replaced because the group has a "collective identity" that does not depend on any one individual.
2. In a dyad, an individual can veto collective action. In a group, the individual, if he or she wants to remain in the group, may have to do things contrary to desire because the possibility exists that he or she will be outvoted. No longer does the individual have the power to veto action.
3. A dyad cannot have a coalition (an alliance), but in groups, coalitions will inevitably occur, and this makes the group qualitatively different from the dyad. Such coalitions can

be predicted beforehand. According to the work of Theodore Caplow, for example, in the triad (three-member group), the two weaker members will usually try to balance the power of the strongest.

4. Dyads are usually more intense, exhibit more emotional involvement, and are less impersonal than groups.

One more difference is implied in Simmel's discussion. The third party brings a "collective unity" not evident in the dyad. This has something important to say about social patterns, the central topic of this chapter. Although the dyad develops its own patterns, it is only when a third party enters that the patterns become truly independent of the actors. Although patterns are developed in dyads, and although they influence action, only in the group do the patterns take on a life of their own, apart from the actors who create them. This is one reason why dyads—more insecure, more personal, and less dependent on social patterns—will try to add a third force to the relationship: for example, a ring, a child, a treaty, a written vow.

Most of us are members of a wide variety of groups. We are born into a family group; we form friendship groups; we learn in a schoolroom that is made up of one, and often several, groups. We work in groups, we play in groups, and we are socialized in groups. We discuss our concerns in groups, and it is in groups that we test out our ideas about the world and we come to share perspectives about the world.

Charles Cooley (1909) called certain groups "primary groups." These are *small, relatively permanent, intimate, and unspecialized.* Individuals feel a close attachment to such groups, and they fulfill a wide range of personal needs. Cooley called these groups primary because they are *important to both the individual and the society.* These are the groups from which individuals receive their early socialization; thus, they are the groups that are most responsible for imparting those qualities that make us all human: language, self, mind, conscience. They provide individuals with close emotional ties important for general well-being. Such groups also are important for society because they influence individuals to see the world as those in society do and to control themselves as those in society wish.

Of course, many groups in modern society are not primary; indeed, our groups increasingly tend to become larger, temporary, impersonal, and specialized. Such groups are called *secondary*. A business organization is a secondary group; a college class is, and so too are most of the social clubs to which people belong. Our religious, educational, and leisure-time activities are filled with examples of groups that are secondary. Often, secondary groups become so large and complex that their social patterns must be made very explicit, often in written form. Such groups are a third form of social organization, the *formal organization*.

Formal Organizations Write Down Their Rules

As groups become larger, they generally become more formal and impersonal; patterns are made more explicit and are formally stated, so that members clearly understand what is expected. Face-to-face interaction occurs but less predictably; if patterns are to continue, they must depend on more than continuous interaction. *When a group makes patterns explicit through written rules, it becomes a formal organization.*

A formal organization may be small, but usually it is large. It is difficult for large numbers of people to know how to deal with each other in an orderly way without some written guidelines. Sometimes, a dyad becomes a formal organization to establish itself on a more secure level—for example, through a blood pact, a marriage, or a business contract—but usually it is characteristic of a larger group—a fraternity, a business corporation, a college, the army, the state department. Formal organizations characterize modern society—everything is written down; we rely on rules that can be read. Our relationships are impersonal to a great extent, organizations are large, and we are often one small actor in a very large formal organization where not many people know our name but where people know us by the positions we fill.

Interestingly, formal organizations inevitably inspire the formation of informal patterns that often become more important than the formal patterns. The way things are supposed to be on paper is balanced by patterns that actors negotiate on their own in face-to-face interaction. Formality aids people when they interact—it makes it relatively easy for new members to know very quickly what to do—but it is usually more important to alter the written patterns and bend them to fit our own situation because those who wrote the rules could not possibly have known our situation exactly. Indeed, most people in formal organizations seem to understand that written rules are guides that are not usually strictly adhered to. Sometimes, a problem occurs when it is not clear to actors to what extent the formal patterns are to be followed. Doctors know what they should do in hospitals; nurses know what they can do. The formal rules, however, are often bent because the real situation demands negotiated patterns: The doctor's lack of time, the nurse's willingness to take responsibility, and the patterns negotiated between them become more important than the formal rules. On the other hand, as lawsuits against doctors and hospitals increase, formal rules may take on even greater importance because following the rules helps protect people in courts of law. Health maintenance organizations (HMOs) and the increased power of insurance companies make medical care more and more formal, less and less personal, situational, spontaneous, and diverse.

Communities Are Self-Sufficient Units of Organization

Sometimes, the group or formal organization becomes relatively self-sufficient or independent of other social organizations. It takes care of all the basic needs of its members—economic, social, cultural, educational, political. People are able to live their whole lives within this social organization, carry out most of their activities within it, and only occasionally leave it. This is called a *community*, and it is the fourth form of social organization.

A family could be a community if its members interact primarily with each other in the basic activities of life—if, for example, it produces its own food, it supplies the leisure-time activities of its members, and it takes care of its members' health and education. Usually, however, the family is located in a larger community—a Hutterite settlement; Baudette, Minnesota; New York City. Harlem is a community within New York City, and a commune in Virginia is also a community. A prison is a community, as is a monastery.

Whenever there is patterned social interaction among people who have established a self-sufficiency—where interaction with outsiders is much less common than with insiders, and where the social organization itself fulfills the diverse needs of the individuals—then we say, "Here is a community." Communities normally have physical boundaries, but not always. So, for example, we sometimes describe American Jews as a community, or African Americans as a community. We mean by this that within the United States there exist interaction and social patterns among Jewish people that simultaneously unite them and to some extent set them off from others in many areas of life. This is also what we mean by an African-American community.

Whether or not a given group is a community is often debatable, but to the extent that we can establish it as a self-sufficient social organization, we can so designate it.

Societies Are the Most Inclusive Form of Organization

The last form of social organization is society, and it is also the most difficult to describe and to understand because it is the most distant and complex of all social organizations. We can define *society* simply as the largest social organization whose patterns make a significant difference to the individual's actions. It is the social organization within which all other social organizations exist. Within society, we will find a host of dyads, groups, formal organizations, and communities, each affected in part by its location in society. Society is a social organization with a long history, longer than any of its actors, and usually longer than other social organizations. It is embedded in its past; it is enduring.

Usually, sociologists go further and make society even more complex. Some, like Marion Levy (1952), point out that to be a society, an organization must have the characteristic that recruitment of new members comes through sexual reproduction, at least in part. The boundaries of societies are sometimes difficult to pinpoint. Are they defined by borders, by language, by religion, by history? In the modern world, society is usually the same thing as the nation-state (a political entity), but even here there are problems. Some nations, such as Cyprus the former Yugoslavia, Sudan, Iraq, China, and Lebanon, are clearly two or more societies, and the nation is an artificial attempt to forge one new society by increasing interaction among the several societies and by establishing formal patterns for all to follow. The Soviet nation was really several societies forged into one. Its collapse in the 1990s attested to its failure to unite into one nation several societies that maintained their own identities.

Some sociologists have developed an elaborate description of societies. Talcott Parsons and others describe societies as *systems of interrelated parts* such as structures or institutions. Societies develop parts to meet the requirements for survival. Society, therefore, is made up of political, economic, familial, religious, and military structures, each necessary for survival, each developed to meet the complex and diverse set of circumstances that confront it. The increased complexity of society described by some, however, should not keep us from recognizing the fact that society is like all other forms of social organization: It is made up of individuals who interact and develop social patterns.

It has become increasingly obvious to most people that we live in a *world order* as well as in society. Sociologists are all too aware of this. People interact all over the world. Representatives of societies meet, interact through letters or the press, and make agreements. Economic matters are increasingly worldwide: Labor problems in the United States are caused in part by decisions made in corporations that know no societal boundaries. The prosperity of the farmer in the United States is linked to worldwide economic patterns. Probably, the time has come to recognize that the world itself is becoming a society. Think of this in a matter of degree: The world will become a society to the extent that laws, customs, class structures, travel, trade, communication, language, culture, and institutions become established worldwide and make what we now call societies less and less important to people. Globalization may bring a common society, but the societies of the world are also looking at their own identities; "local" and "small" are also trends in our world.

SOCIAL ORGANIZATION SEEMS TO SIT RIGHT ON TOP OF THE UNITED STATES

Let us first summarize what we know about social organization: Humans act sometimes without others in mind, sometimes with others in mind (*social action*). Sometimes as they act, others act back, and action is built up back and forth (*social interaction*). Sometimes interaction is brief, and sometimes interaction goes on for a while and regularities are established (*social patterns*). Social interaction that is patterned is called social organization; *social organization* can be described as a dyad, a group, a formal organization, a community, or a society.

We are all part of a number of dyads and groups.

Usually, however, each of these dyads or groups is embedded in a larger social organization, such as larger groups and formal organizations.

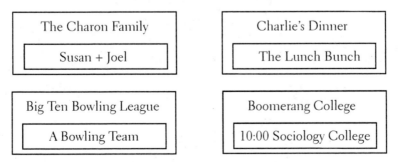

These dyads, groups, and formal organizations are part of communities, which are in turn located in society. The patterns that develop in each are influenced by the larger social organizations of which it is a part. Each one of us is in the middle of a large number of circles located within larger and larger circles (see Figure 3-1).

Dyads and societies are alike: They have patterns established through people interacting over time. Humans are constantly developing and learning the various patterns. We are all located within a large number of social organizations, and the patterns of each affect what we do. Some sociologists will argue that we are prisoners in these patterns, that we take them for granted or do not even realize they are there, and that our social action becomes almost completely habitual because of the routines they impose. This is the argument put forth in the next few chapters as we look at the nature of these patterns. The argument will be made that these patterns are powerful forces, that they control and shape us, and that the individual has almost no freedom because of them. This kind of determinism in fact represents what many sociologists see. We see humans as *caused* by social organization. If we are free, then our freedom can be understood only after considering the ways we are determined.

"Determinism" is a word given by philosophers and scientists to perspectives that see human action as caused—determined—by something other than free choice. Religion is a deterministic perspective when it emphasizes an all-powerful God who destines our actions; science is a deterministic perspective because it emphasizes natural and social forces as cause; astrology is a deterministic perspective when it argues that our actions and personalities are determined by the stars. Although most of sociology leans toward determinism, many sociologists believe that humans are

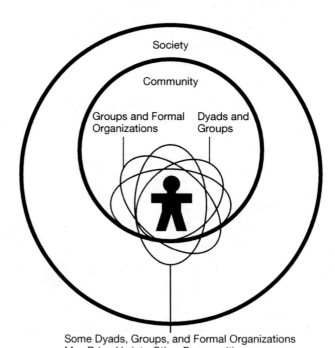

Some Dyads, Groups, and Formal Organizations
May Bring Us into Other Communities.

FIGURE 3-1   The Individual Within Social Organization

more than simply caused, that they do in fact make free choices in their lives. We think our own ideas and control our own directions to some extent, we create our own organizations, we question and rebel from organizations we enter and societies we are born into, and we build our own lives in spite of the power of society. This less deterministic view that characterizes many sociologists will be discussed in Chapter 11. That chapter is entitled "Symbols, Self, and Mind," and these are the qualities that make possible what freedom we have; these qualities, like most of the rest of our qualities, arise from social interaction. Yes, even the freedom we sometimes exhibit has its origin in our social nature.

QUESTIONS TO CONSIDER

1. What is the meaning of the following concepts? Can you give an example of each: social action, social interaction, patterned social interaction, dyads, groups, primary groups, secondary groups, formal organizations, communities, societies?
2. Are we in fact almost always social actors? Give some instances in which people act without taking others into account. What difference does it make anyway that human beings are social actors?
3. Can you think of a situation in which you acted contrary to the way you normally do because of others in the situation? Can you think of an instance in which interaction did in fact lead you down a path you never thought you would go? Is there an organization you belong to in which social patterns contradict your belief system?
4. According to this chapter, what is the human being? Why do we act the way we do?

REFERENCES

Cooley, Charles Horton. 1909. *Social Organization.* 1962 edn. New York: Schocken Books.
Levy, Marion J. 1952. *The Structure of Society.* Princeton, NJ: Princeton University Press.
Weber, Max. 1922. *Theory of Social and Economic Organization.* 1957 edn. Ed. A. M. Henderson and Talcott Parsons. New York: Free Press.

RECOMMENDED READING

The following works introduce the meaning and importance of social interaction and social organization. They also introduce the meaning and importance of dyads, groups, formal organizations, communities, and societies.

Anderson, Elijah. 1999. *Code of the Street: Decency, Violence, and the Moral Life of the Inner City.* New York: W.W. Norton & Company.
Anderson, Eric. 2005. *In the Game: Athletes and the Cult of Masculinity.* New York: State University of New York.
Aronson, Elliot. 1998. *The Social Animal.* 8th edn. New York: W.H. Freeman.
Barnes, Sandra L. 2005. *The Cost of Being Poor: A Comparative Study of Life in Poor Urban Neighborhoods in Gary Indiana.* New York: State University of New York Press.
Berger, Peter. 1963. *Invitation to Sociology.* Garden City, NY: Doubleday.
Blau, Peter M., and William R. Scott. 1962. *Formal Organizations.* San Francisco: Chandler.

Bowles, Samuel, Gintis Herbert, and Melissa Osborne-Groves. 2005. *Unequal Chances: Family Background and Economic Success*. New Jersey: Princeton University Press.

Caplow, Theodore. 1968. *Two Against One*. Upper Saddle River, NJ: Prentice Hall.

Danziger, Sheldon, and Ann Chih Lin (eds.). 2000. *Coping with Poverty: The Social Contexts of Neighborhood, Work, and Family in the African-American Community*. Ann Arbor: University of Michigan Press.

Davis, Kingsley. 1949. *Human Society*. New York: Macmillan.

Dohan, Daniel. 2003. *The Price of Poverty: Money, Work, and Culture in the Mexican American Barrio*. Berkeley, CA: University of California Press.

Durkheim, Emile. 1915. *The Elementary Forms of Religious Life*. 1954 edn. Trans. Joseph Swain. New York: Free Press.

Erikson, Kai T. 1966. *Wayward Puritans: A Study in the Sociology of Deviance*. New York: John Wiley.

Erikson, Kai T. 1976. *Everything in Its Path*. New York: Simon & Schuster.

Festinger, Leon. 1956. *When Prophecy Fails*. Minneapolis, MN: University of Minnesota Press.

Fine, Gary Alan. 1984. "Negotiated Orders and Organizational Cultures." In *Annual Review of Sociology*, 10:239–262.

Fine, Gary Alan. 1987. *With the Boys: Little League Baseball and Preadolescent Culture*. Chicago: University of Chicago Press.

Fischer, Claude. 1984. *The Urban Experience*. 2nd edn. New York: Harcourt Brace Jovanovich.

Forschi, Martha, and Edward J. Lawler (eds.). 1994. *Group Processes: Sociological Analysis*. New York: Nelson-Hall.

Gans, Herbert J. 1982. *The Urban Villagers*. 2nd edn. New York: Free Press.

Goffman, Erving. 1959. *The Presentation of Self in Everyday Life*. New York: Doubleday (Anchor).

Goffman, Erving. 1961. *Asylums: Essays on the Social Situation of Mental Patients and Other Inmates*. New York: Doubleday (Anchor).

Gouldner, Alvin. 1954. *Patterns of Industrial Bureaucracy*. New York: Free Press.

Horowitz, Ruth. 1983. *Honor and the American Dream: Culture and Identity in a Chicano Community*. New Brunswick, NJ: Rutgers University Press.

Hostetler, John A. 1980. *Amish Society*. Baltimore, MD: Johns Hopkins University Press.

Hull, Kathleen E. 2006. *Same-Sex Marriage: The Cultural Politics of Love and Law*. Cambridge, UK: Cambridge University Press.

Jenkins, Richard. 1996. *Social Identity*. New York: Routledge.

Jones, Ron. 1981. *No Substitute for Madness*. Covelo, CA: Island Press.

Kanter, Rosabeth. 1977. *Men and Women of the Corporation*. New York: Basic Books.

Keiser, R. Lincoln. 1979. *Vice Lords: Warriors of the Street*. New York: Holt, Rinehart & Winston.

Kephart, William M. 1993. *Extraordinary Groups: The Sociology of Unconventional Life-Styles*. 5th edn. New York: St. Martin's Press.

Lenski, Gerhard. 1987. *Human Societies: An Introduction to Macrosociology*. 8th edn. New York: McGraw-Hill.

Liebow, Elliot. 1967. *Tally's Corner*. Boston: Little, Brown.

Lofland, John. 1966. *Doomsday Cult*. Upper Saddle River, NJ: Prentice Hall.

Lynd, Robert, and Helen Lynd. 1929. *Middletown*. New York: Harcourt Brace Jovanovich.

Lynd, Robert, and Helen Lynd. 1937. *Middletown in Transition*. New York: Harcourt Brace Jovanovich.

McCall, George J., and J. L. Simmons. 1978. *Identities and Interactions*. New York: Free Press.

Mills, Theodore M. 1967. *The Sociology of Small Groups*. Upper Saddle River, NJ: Prentice Hall.

Olsen, Marvin E. 1978. *The Process of Social Organization*. 2nd edn. New York: Holt, Rinehart & Winston.

Perrow, Charles. 1986. *Complex Organizations*. 3rd edn. New York: Random House.

Peters, Thomas J., and Robert H. Waterman, Jr. 1982. *In Search of Excellence*. New York: Warner Books.

Shibutani, Tamotsu. 1961. *Society and Personality: An Interactionist Approach to Social Psychology*. Upper Saddle River, NJ: Prentice Hall.

Shils, Edward S., and Morris Janowitz. 1948. "Cohesion and Disintegration in the Wehrmacht in World War II." In *Public Opinion Quarterly*, 12:280–294.

Simmel, Georg. 1902–1903. "Metropolis and Mental Life." In *The Sociology of Georg Simmel*. 1950 edn. Ed. Kurt Wolff. New York: Free Press.

Simmel, Georg. 1902–1903. "The Isolated Individual and the Dyad." In *The Sociology of Georg Simmel*. 1950 edn. Ed. Kurt Wolff. New York: Free Press.

Sullivan, Maureen. 2004. *The Family of Woman: Lesbian Mothers, Their Children, and Undoing of Gender*. Berkeley, CA: University of California Press.

Wallerstein, Immanuel. 1974. *The Modern World-System*. New York: Academic Press.
Warriner, Charles K. 1956. "Groups Are Real: An Affirmation." In *American Sociological Review*, 21:549–554.
Warriner, Charles K. 1970. *The Emergence of Society*. Homewood, IL: Dorsey Press.
Weber, Max. 1924. *The Theory of Social and Economic Organization*. 1964 edn. Ed. A. M. Henderson and Talcott Parsons. New York: Free Press.
Wheelan, Susan A. 1994. *Group Processes: The Developmental Perspective*. Boston: Allyn & Bacon.
Whyte, William Foote. 1955. *Street Corner Society*. Chicago: University of Chicago Press.
Whyte, William H. 1956. *The Organization Man*. New York: Simon & Schuster.
Williams, Robin. 1970. *American Society: A Sociological Interpretation*. New York: Alfred A. Knopf.
Wirth, Louis. 1938. "Urbanism as a Way of Life." In *American Journal of Sociology*, 44:3–24.
Young, Alfred A. 2004. *The Minds of Marginalized Black Men*. New Jersey: Princeton University Press.

Opening Night. *Doree Loschiavo, Illustrator.*

✦ 4 ✦

Social Structure

When humans act toward one another over time, they get used to one another, they develop agreements, expectations, rules, regulations, and what we call "social patterns." Predictability enters our interaction; instead of always trying to figure out what to do around others, we know what to do. When we enter organizations already established, we learn the patterns already established; and when we are born into society, we are taught patterns developed long ago by nameless numbers of individuals who have interacted. Most of the time, we come to take on these patterns without even realizing it, and we come to be determined by forces outside our control.

WE ALL FILL POSITIONS IN SOCIAL STRUCTURE

One of the patterns in social organization is called *social structure*. Social structure refers to the fact that individuals act toward one another according to their *position* in the interaction. Over time, actors are located in relation to one another in the interaction—they have a "place"—and others act toward them according to their place, and they act toward others according to their place. These positions or places create a network or what we might describe as a social map; this network or map is called the social structure.

Social structures arise in every organization from dyads to societies. They constitute the skeleton of the organization and organize the interaction. Because they exist, each actor knows what to do in relation to others and the others know what to do in relation to the actor. If we form a friendship relationship, our positions are *friends* to one another. We know what to expect from each other: "Well, Marty, a real friend doesn't just rip into me but tries to help me work out my problem." We usually do not have the same expectations for each other: I may expect you to make more of the decisions, and you may expect me to protect you from "toughies"; I may expect you to be the funny guy, and you may expect me to be cool in the face of adversity. As friends, we might expect each other to be loyal, to share beliefs, concerns, and problems, but even here my expectations of you will probably differ from yours of me because of the way the relationship develops. If you are female and I am male (which by the way are positions in our society) we will often affect the structure that develops between us.

In groups, formal organizations, communities, and societies, we may be assigned positions already developed for us; when we are in those positions, people will act toward us accordingly. We will do approximately what is expected in our positions, and we will expect others to act right in their positions. Part of our socialization, part of learning within any social organization, is to learn our place or position and the relevant positions of others. My boss, my secretary, the janitor who cleans my office, my office partners, the planning people down the hall, the boss's son, the top advertising executive all are positions I learn to relate to.

Often, we want to learn these positions to know what to do around others and what to expect from the others with whom we interact—and also to know how much we can bend the rules and do what we want. For example, both teacher and student learn their own and others' positions within the college. In relation to each other, a teacher in a classroom may expect from the student good performance on an exam, a certain amount of respect, a seeking, questioning attitude (but only perhaps to a certain point), no cheating, and agreement to abide by the rules set up by the teacher (or by the class). The teacher in turn is expected to prepare for class, to give fair exams and grades, and to teach at a level that the students understand. This describes the social structure that develops between teacher and students. We might also describe the similarities among the social structures that develop in all university classrooms, and we might isolate some unique things in each structure caused by the interaction among actors. We might describe a general teacher's position that students learn as a result of being in a few classrooms, as well as the particular position of each teacher. So although many structures are made up of positions the individual learns elsewhere, each structure is in some ways unique because each develops through particular interaction.

A *social structure*, then, consists of an interrelated set of positions within the social organization. Positions form a network—they all are places in relation to all other positions—and they cannot be described as isolated entities. Thus, a teacher is someone who exists in relation to students, a husband in relation to wife, a boss in relation to employees, a colonel in relation to those under his or her command, and an upper class in relation to a lower class. We can identify two positions in a social structure as in a dyad or even in a simple group (teacher and students, for example), or we can identify several positions, even hundreds or thousands, that exist in a social structure within a community or society.

A position is like a slot. This is an impersonal word, perhaps an exaggeration, but it still emphasizes the fact that people are placed in positions whenever they interact with others, and certainly whenever they join an established organization. As we interact with others, we focus our perceptions and actions and expectations on where others are in relation to us. The more technical name for position is *status position*. Some sociologists prefer the term "status" or "role," but *position* or *status position* is more descriptive for our purposes here.

A street gang might have a social structure consisting of "leader," a leader's "right-hand man," a "clown," a "defender," and a "runner." A baseball team will have a structure consisting of "catcher," "pitcher," and all the other usual positions, and a family will have a structure that might include "wife–mother," "husband–father," "oldest child," and "youngest child."

ROLES ARE ATTACHED TO POSITIONS

Over time, people within the interaction come to focus on positions, and they develop expectations of behavior related to positions, not persons. Expectations are also called *norms*. Norms can be informal and simply agreed upon in the interaction, or they can be formal, written down, even becoming a body of rules, a constitution, charter, or contract. Norms can be stated, or they can be picked up by us watching other people's actions. Norms can be violated and met with only mild disapproval (you are foolish; I am going to pretend I didn't see that; stop it!), or its violation can be met with fines, imprisonment, or even death.

The norms focusing on a position together are called a role. A role should be thought of as a set of expectations, a script to be followed, a set of behaviors and thoughts a person is expected to follow in a position. *Think of a position as a part in a play; think of a role as a script handed to the actor in the position.* A role is a guide for what actors are supposed to do: "Here is what people in your position are supposed to do!" When someone acts according to the expectations—or role—we say that he or she is "enacting the role" like an actor on a stage. No actor follows all the expectations, but it is important to recognize that once a person is in a position, he or she is pressured to learn the part and act accordingly. Always some spontaneity and looseness is allowed, but too much of it violates the expectations of those in other positions and often upsets the interaction and is not tolerated.

Most of the time, we are barely aware of the script attached to our position. The norms are accepted without consciously thinking about it. We are expected to wear clothes in public, to be polite to people we meet, not to embarrass people we do not know, to drive on the correct side of the street, to use utensils when we eat. In a given day we will enter many roles and act appropriately without thinking twice. Some roles on the other hand are made very explicit and are very much part of our conscious life. For example, professors, parents, financial aid officers, and roommates continuously tell us how to act as a student. A marriage ceremony and certificate spells out what is expected in the positions. A catcher on a baseball team, a police officer on the street, the driver in a getaway car, and a private in the army tend to be clearly defined and understood roles.

A specific family group is a good example for illustrating norms, roles, status positions, and social structure. Let us keep it simple here: Let us imagine that Charlie and Alice become husband and wife and exist in a traditional family structure. Charlie has certain expectations (norms) for Alice that have developed between them over time. She is his wife (status position), and he expects her to have the primary responsibility for childrearing and for dealing with relatives. She is expected to listen to his gripes about his boss, to give him encouragement concerning his professional life, to be nice to his friends, to be patient with his impatience, and to spend the family funds carefully. Alice, on the other hand, expects Charlie, her husband (status position), to share in housework, to prepare the meals, to play with the children, to listen to her gripes about her boss, to encourage her to pursue her professional growth, and to know what to do in a weather emergency or when the plumbing breaks down.

Each set of expectations between Alice and Charlie constitutes a role, and the role is located within a dyad. Yet the children are also part of the social organization (the family group) within which the dyad is located. Charlie must also conform to their expectations of him as father (a status position), such as putting them to bed, being kind, reading to them, taking them to the movies occasionally, bragging about them to others, punishing and rewarding them for certain kinds of behavior. Charlie fills two separate status positions—husband and father—and the role expectations between them may be partly the same, may be different but complementary, or may be in direct conflict.

Charlie's roles in the family are also defined by many people outside the family. His parents may have expectations, such as that he be nice to his wife, does not spank his children, and is sure to bring his family to see them every Sunday afternoon. Charlie's roles in the family are also defined by neighbors, friends, maybe his employer, the community, and the society. There are even written laws governing his roles (concerning physical abuse, for example, or neglect, or the education of his children). So each of Charlie's roles in the family is a cluster of norms, which come from people both within and outside the group. And, of course, if Charlie and Alice break up, their expectations of one another will change dramatically; if they form family groups with others, a new structure with new roles and expectations will arise there.

So it is with the other social organizations of which Charlie is part: his office staff, his bowling team, his night-school class, his church, his friendship group, and the dyad (best friend) relationship he has with Maurice. Within each organization, he plays a role—acts according to the expectations of others—defined by those within and outside the social structure.

It is not difficult to understand why individuals in positions are attracted to following the script. In fact, we often seek a script when we enter a position: We want to know what to do as a student, a male, a new employee, a president in a corporation. We want to know how closely we have to follow the script and how much nonconformity is to be tolerated. Perhaps it is because we want to succeed in most positions we enter that we seek to learn the expectations of that position and how to act. Or perhaps it is because we seek the acceptance of those in the organization, or respect from those below us, or rewards from those above us. It is difficult for us to fill a position and not act according to the role associated with the position because so much pushes us to conform. Other people socialize us to learn and enact our role, and others depend on us to do this. In fact, we may even come to realize that the success of the organization depends on our conformity. As we come to believe in that organization, we face another force acting on us: loyalty.

ROLES ARE NOT AS SIMPLE AS A SCRIPT IN A PLAY

Somehow, we realize that the world is much more complex than this description implies. The example of Charlie and Alice is only meant as a beginning for understanding what happens to the actor because of position in social structure. Yes, when we interact, we form social structure with various positions, and each of us is placed there, and expectations direct what we are supposed to do. Yes, when we enter any existing position in an existing structure, we are taught how to act, we seek to be guided, and we conform to some extent. But roles are more; in the real world, roles are often *ambiguous*, *contradictory* in many ways, and always *negotiable*.

Roles cannot ever control everything we do in a position. There are too many new situations that arise and we must make it up as we go along. If all actions were determined for us in our positions, we would probably not be so willing to fill them, we would be bored without feeling any sense of worth, we would not try new things, and we would not bring our individual skills and ideas developed elsewhere to the position. *Roles are always ambiguous to some extent*, sometimes because it is impossible to make them perfectly clear, but more often because they are meant to be ambiguous so that people can deal with specific situations as they arise.

Roles are sometimes contradictory. They do not give a clear message to the actor, and the actor must decide what to do. For example, sometimes the same people have contradictory expectations of the actor. The congregation of the First Lutheran Church expects its minister to be a moral leader, to take sides, and to work for justice and equality, but at the same time it does not want him to get involved in migrant labor issues (because members of the congregation use migrant labor). My wife and I expect our children to keep their rooms spotlessly clean but to have a lot of fun playing, too. Students expect instructors to be personal, to show interest in them, to treat them as individuals. Yet instructors must also grade everyone impersonally—otherwise they are charged with having "favorites."

Individuals who are faced with contradictory expectations may not realize it. However, if they do, they must decide between those expectations—to ignore some, to try to satisfy both expectations to some extent, or to develop some strategy that may involve cheating or at least secrecy. Sociologists normally call this situation one of "role conflict." If all else fails, the actor may have to leave the position.

Role conflict is also caused by the fact that *many different people define the role, and they disagree with one another.* Daniel's dad expects him to fight back, but Daniel's mom expects him never to get into fights. The president of the university expects the vice president to "get rid of deadwood," but the faculty expects the vice president to advocate for their interests. Meanwhile, the faculty union simply wants the vice president to follow what the union contract spells out. The individual in the position is again faced with role conflict, so that what appears on paper to be a clear role ends up being very messy and sometimes impossible.

Of course, sometimes role conflict arises from the fact that *the individual plays different roles that are contradictory in some way.* To be a housewife and a professional can sometimes be contradictory roles, such as soldier and Christian, social scientist and social reformer, student and working person, political radical and corporate lawyer, or world peacemaker and defender of one nation's security. Many of us are good at isolating these roles from one another, but the conflict becomes serious when performing one role interferes with another role. After all, we have only so much time in a day that if we spend it in one role, we cannot spend it in performing in the others.

Finally, we also experience role conflict when *the role does not fit us.* We can call this situation person–role conflict. I am not made for this role; the role is too demanding, too difficult, too boring, too unethical, or too time-consuming. Each individual has expectations and abilities he or she brings to the role, and although the role shapes the person to a high degree, some people find certain roles to be unsuitable for them.

Ambiguity and role conflict make roles complex. So does "role negotiation." When we enter a position and are given a role, we act. Others act back, and we, in turn, act again. Others define what we are supposed to do, but we tell them through what we do how we define the role; and through this interaction, the actual role is formed. Of course, too much creativity in defining roles may upset interaction, even to the point of our being expelled from the organization, but some creativity is inevitable, expected, and necessary for both the actor and the organization.

Role ambiguity, role conflict, and role negotiation mean that roles may exist but that each of us plays some part in determining how we actually act. It would be a mistake, however, to underestimate the power of role definition by others. Our roles are to some extent independent of us—the expectations are "out there," and when we enter a position, there are forces all around us telling us in clear (and sometimes unclear) terms, "You are expected to act a certain way in your position."

Whenever I slip and think that roles are not very important after all, I recall the experiment performed by Philip Zimbardo at Stanford University. Zimbardo (1972) tested the effects of isolating people from the outside world for a couple of weeks, putting them in a "prison situation" in which some of them were in the position of guard and some were in the position of prisoner. Would they actually be subject to role expectations, and would they really enact the roles in their positions? Would they take the experiment seriously? Would they enjoy themselves? Would they learn something about other people? After warning students that this experiment would happen soon, Zimbardo actually imprisoned some of them and made some guards. Within a few days, these people *became* their roles—that is, the guards actually came to act brutally, the prisoners really "wanted out." Something happened to everyone involved: A structure evolved, the situation demanded new behaviors from everyone, and the new roles took over. The situation became so nightmarish that the study had to be ended much earlier than planned. Remember, these were "mature, emotionally stable, normal, intelligent college students from middle-class homes throughout the United States and Canada. . . . None had any criminal record. . . ." Here is Zimbardo's description of what happened:

> At the end of only six days, we had to close down our mock prison because what we saw was frightening. It was no longer apparent to most of the students (or to us) where reality ended and their roles began. The majority had indeed become prisoners or guards. . . . There were dramatic changes in virtually every aspect of their behavior, thinking, and feeling . . . we saw some boys (guards) treat others as if they were despicable animals, taking pleasure in cruelty, while other boys (prisoners) become servile, dehumanized robots who thought only of escape, of their own individual survival, and of their mounting hatred for the guards.
>
> (p. 4)

STATUS POSITIONS FORM OUR IDENTITIES

Much of our socialization involves learning about the many status positions and roles in the world. The child learns how firefighters and dentists work, what grocery clerks and teachers do, and so on. The child learns what Mom and Dad do, what bad guys do, and what good students do. The child plays at these roles and, in playing them, displays a recognition that he or she knows the expectations attached to each.

We give names to each status position, and this makes it easier for us when we meet other people. We learn what a *friend* is, and we are influenced by our learning when we decide to interact with someone as a friend. We also may learn the status position of wife, son, teacher, plumber, president, secretary, man, woman, minister, clerk, listener, quarterback, assistant, convicted criminal, boss, or movie producer. All nouns we use for people that imply relationships with others are names we give to status positions. These labels help us identify others; we know who they are if we can label them. When we meet someone at a party and learn the person's identifying labels in the larger world, we immediately have images of the person according to his or her label or position: We may think to ourselves, "oh, she's a doctor" (probably rich and smart); "oh, he's a teacher" (teachers are awfully stuffy). Of course, we are often in error in assigning personal qualities on the basis of position, but initially, this is all we know about the individual and this is all we have learned about individuals in that position. We cannot help but use this to guide what we do. It is also one way that others are able to understand how to act toward us—their knowledge of our identifying labels impacts what they do.

The naming process associated with the positions of people brings us to a second quality associated with our positions. As others act toward us in our position, we are told *who we are* in the world; others label who we are in the interaction, and we come to take these labels to see ourselves. "You are my son." "You are my son's son." "You are your mother's son." "You are the son of my friend." The message is clear: You are a son, others see you as a son, and you come to see yourself as a son. "You are from a good family that goes back many years." "You are part of a privileged class of people." "You are more cultured than others." "People like you are supposed to lead others; people like you do not do those kinds of things." The message is clear: You are upper class, others see you as upper class, you come to see yourself as upper class. "You are a man, a college graduate, an accountant, an assistant to the vice-president of the company"; "You are a middle-aged worker"; "You are a minority in society."

This quality—created in social structure—is called *identity*. An identity is who we see ourselves as. *It is the name we call ourselves and the name we usually announce to others in our actions.* For most of us, gender is our most important identity, but class position and occupation are also very important. Identities are linked to our positions; to discover our own identities, all we really have to do is list our positions in social structure and to determine which positions are most important. I am husband, father, professor, sociologist, U.S. citizen, oldest son in my family, and upper middle class. We have many identities, and if we are honest about it, most of them are identities others see us as; this, in turn, influences who in the world we think we are. This view of ourselves influences us to act with the role; acting the role encourages even further definition by others and may lead us to seek out and to associate with others "like us." Over time, identity becomes solidified and stable (but not really rigid and unbending). Of course, we might also declare that we are honest, or intelligent, or loving, or good looking—and these qualities are important too—but they are personal qualities, not identities. Interestingly, these qualities are often associated with our identities: I am loving, moral, knowledgeable because I am a member of the clergy; I am brave, aggressive, tough because I am a soldier; I am beautiful, thin, neat, a cool dresser because I am a model. It is true that all these examples sound like roles (others expect us to act these ways because we are in these positions), but more than this: As we come to see ourselves in these positions, we increasingly expect these attributes from ourselves.

The identity I have situates me in relation to others. I see who I am in relation to them. Their acts remind me of who I am; my acts toward them continue to tell them who I am. Identity, like role, is attached to my status position; it is my "social address" in social structure.

Peter Berger describes an individual who has just become a commissioned officer in the army. He plays the role, but at first, he is distanced from it:

> [He] will at first be at least slightly embarrassed by the salutes he now receives from the enlisted men he meets on his way. Probably he will respond to them in a friendly, almost apologetic manner. The new insignia on his uniform are at that point still something that he has merely put on, almost like a disguise. Indeed, the new officer may even tell himself and others that underneath he is still the same person, that he simply has new responsibilities. . . . This attitude is not likely to last very long. In order to carry out his new role of officer, our man must maintain a certain bearing.
>
> (1963, 98)

Over time, the actor *becomes the role*. As he acts as an officer, and as others act toward him as an officer, he increasingly comes to think of himself as an officer. He eventually takes on the identity:

> With every salute given and accepted (along, of course, with a hundred other ceremonial acts that enhance his new status), our man is fortified in his new bearing. . . . He not only acts like an officer, he feels like one. Gone are the embarrassment, the apologetic attitude, the I'm-just-another-guy-really grin. If on some occasion an enlisted man should fail to salute with the appropriate amount of enthusiasm or even commit the unthinkable act of failing to salute at all, our officer is not merely going to punish a violation of military regulations. He will be driven with every fiber of his being to redress an offense against the appointed order of his cosmos.
>
> (1963, 98)

Each of us is therefore many people, each associated with a status position. We *become* our status positions, we think of ourselves in terms of those positions, and we announce these positions to others in how we act in the world. "This is who I am!" And as others know "who we are," they are influenced to act toward us accordingly. In a sense, who we are arises from how others address us over time. Identity, like action, is socially created in social structure.

We have, up to now, described two qualities that arise from our status positions. These are *role* (how we are expected to act in relation to others) and *identity* (who we think we are in relation to others). There is more to positions than this, however.

POSITIONS ARE UNEQUAL

It is probably obvious by now that status positions are not usually equal. Inequality seems to be inherent in almost all social structures, at least to some degree. Even in a dyad there is inequality as a rule, and this is certainly true of all groups, formal organizations, communities, and societies. As people interact, some will almost always emerge with more of the valued things than the others. It was that way with Elaine and me. Our relationship started with my courting her, with my wanting her more than she wanted me, and with her calling the shots and getting her way. It had to be that way at first: She had so many people in love with her, and I was lonely. Gradually, the relationship shifted. She liked me! As she broke her friendships with others and became more dependent on me, we became more and more equal, and we probably retained a delicate balance of equality for a short time. Eventually, I became more powerful in the relationship. This may sound crude and oversimplified, but still that relationship, like almost all relationships, has elements of inequality, with some status positions more privileged and more powerful than the others. If we try to diagram social structures, we end up organizing them in a hierarchy of higher/lower positions (see Figure 4-1).

Friendship may be the only social structure that is characterized by equality. Indeed, there is actually a strain toward equality. When inequality threatens, friends try to balance the relationship to reach a state of equality. If you do something for me, I am ready to do something for you. If I tell you what to do, I expect you to tell me what to do later on. If I treat you, you'll want to treat me. Friends try to give and take equally so that no one becomes either powerful or dependent. We count on one another if we are friends. We are equals.

Of course, some friendships are not characterized by perfect equality. Beyond friendship, all social structures imply inequality, and all structures develop status positions that are higher than some and lower than others. What do we mean by

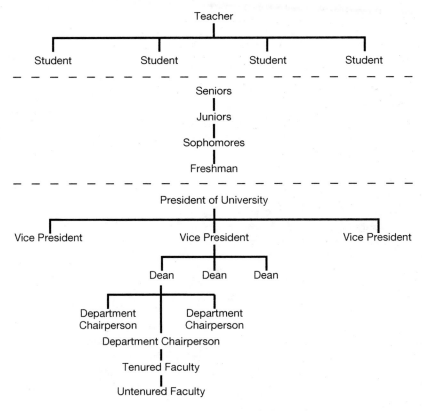

FIGURE 4-1   Status Positions Within Three Social Structures

inequality? Sociologists identify three different qualities arising from positions that cause inequality. These are *power, prestige*, and *privilege*. People in a social structure have various degrees of these qualities, all attached to their positions.

Unequal Power

One position can be higher in power than other positions. A president gets high power in his or her position, and conversely, an enlisted person in the army has low power attached to position. *Social power refers to the ability one actor has for achieving his or her will in relation to others in the social organization.* Some positions allow the actor to direct others in the organization according to his or her will. Some positions require that their holders must obey others. "Get elected to office, then make changes in the city council." "Get promoted and you won't have to take orders anymore—you will give them." Indeed, many of us seek promotion to have more control over our own lives and to have more say in the direction of others in the social organization and in the direction of the social organization itself.

In society, the governmental positions of Supreme Court justice and U.S. president mean a great deal of power. So, too, do positions of cabinet officer, FBI director, and White House chief of staff. Certain members of Congress have great power, especially if they have high positions in key committees or in their political parties. In business, corporate executives are in especially key positions to determine the direction of society and various communities. Officers in labor unions and the American Medical Association (AMA), American Rifle Association, and the American Bar Association (ABA) are very influential. Imagine society as having thousands of positions, some far more powerful than others. If a person achieves a powerful position, then he or she will have an advantage over others—power to achieve his or her will. Although some individuals bungle it and others have personal qualities that allow them to achieve their will even in a low position, it is most important to see real social power anchored in positions. *In any organization, position is almost always the most important resource that the actor can use to achieve his or her will.*

It is critical to recognize that class, gender, and race are structures with positions, and these positions also have power attached to them. In general, although it is not necessarily right, the wealthy have greater power in society than the poor, men have more power than women, whites have more power than nonwhites.

Unequal Prestige

The positions in social organization also differ in the amount of prestige associated with them. Being a senior at college probably has little power, but it does carry a lot more prestige than does the freshman's position. *Prestige refers to the honor that people in social structure accord the position.* We defer to others according to their position; we may ignore, expect deference from, and even act in an insulting way to those who are in lower positions than our own. If you become a U.S. Supreme Court Justice, you are honored because of your position. If you are rich or the president of a corporation or university, people generally see you in a position worthy of honor. Many of us seek positions that give us honor by others. Self-respect may be personal to some extent: I am good, intelligent, honest, capable. However, self-respect also comes from "who we are" in relation to others. It is associated with the position we fill in social structure. It seems odd that this is so if you think about it, but that seems to be the way it is, and we all seem to recognize it.

In most societies, men have more prestige than women, and in almost all societies, being upper class brings more prestige than being poor. One is honored or dishonored for race and religion, too. All of these are positions in society's social structure.

Prestige can change over time. If Americans no longer respect the police or the president or Supreme Court justices, it means those positions have declined in prestige. It is often easier to list positions that do not carry great prestige: private in the army, prostitute, freshman, the "baby" of the family, the nontenured instructor on a college faculty. Prestige is subjective. If most of us do, not regard a certain position as having high prestige, that does not mean all of us agree; nor does it necessarily mean that people who fill that position cannot be good at it or gain a great deal of satisfaction (or money) from doing it. Prestige cannot be ignored, however. It is real. In every social organization, prestige is one of the qualities associated with all positions.

Unequal Privileges

Finally, positions also bring with them certain *privileges*, the good things, so to speak, the benefits, the opportunities that come to those filling the position. These privileges may be high income and other material benefits, opportunity to choose one's own office furniture, choice of home, long vacations, a secretary, quality schooling, an expensive car, and so on. Even dyads and groups have privileges associated with positions: being able to call on other people for assistance, skills, or loyalty; being in the position to demand continuous compliments, service, or favors.

Nothing seems more obvious than all the privileges that go with class position in society. Not only comfort, but health, good education, opportunities for children, and greater choices in every aspect of life go with high class position; hardship, lack of economic and educational opportunity, and poor health go with low class position. Being male or female, black, red, or white also make significant differences in privileges. Discrimination on the basis of race or gender attest to the fact that such positions are unequal in terms of opportunity, that is, unequal in privilege.

In addition to a *role* and an *identity* then, each status position also has a certain amount of *power*, a certain degree of *prestige* and *privileges* attached—or denied. Different amounts of power, prestige, and privilege create the inequality within the social structure. Usually, but not always, these three qualities are interrelated. That is, the greater the power associated with a position, the greater the prestige and privileges. An actor high in one of these attributes in a position will normally find himself or herself high in the others. Positions that have high power can generally reap high privileges and prestige. Positions with high prestige have been used to gain power and privilege, and positions with high privileges have been able to gain more power and prestige. The opposite is also generally true: Those with low privileges, such as the poor in society, also will have low power and low prestige in society.

OUR POSITIONS ALSO GIVE US OUR PERSPECTIVES

Not only do our positions within social structure provide us with our roles, our power, our prestige, our privileges, and our identities, they also create our *perspectives*: They give us the eyeglasses through which we look at the world. People define the world according to where they are located. A boss and an employee may both value the business (an organization), but for different reasons. Each will have a different view of it (and perhaps also of American business in general). Teachers and students see school differently (after all, teachers gain their livelihood from their position; students may see their position as a hurdle to overcome). Rich and poor people differ in their outlooks or perspectives, and seniors and freshmen are far from the same in how they view the university.

Our status position may also influence how we look at the world in general. Not only does a corporate executive see the corporation differently from the man or woman who works on the assembly line, but the executive probably has a different view of government, capitalism, foreign policy, American education, and perhaps even religion. What we think is true, what we value, and what we believe is wrong or right in the world arise from our position.

There are many reasons position is so important to perspective. First of all, we are *socialized* into our positions: not only in how to act and who we are but also in how to think, how to approach understanding reality. Teachers interact and share a view of their profession, the school, students, and American education. Principals socialize teachers how to look at reality, as do teachers' colleges, novels, and students.

The second reason that positions give rise to perspectives is that each position is in fact a location in organization, a point within it, and thus an *angle of perception* used to understand what is taking place in and outside the organization. Each position is a place *from* which we look, causing us to see reality at that particular *angle*. In truth, the president of the United States must see foreign policy differently from the rest of us. If nothing more, he or she knows that his or her decisions will have lasting influence. The rest of us can talk a good game without having to care about consequences. Rich and poor, man and woman, boss and employee, quarterback and running back—each must necessarily see the world from a different perspective.

The third reason we are influenced to see the world through our position has to do with our desire to *successfully enact* the position. If we want to act like a lawyer, we have to think like one; if we want to be a successful student, we have to think like one; if we are going to survive in a prison, we have to think like a prisoner. Success in position means that we have to understand how people in that position think. We have to understand how others who are somehow linked to that position expect us to think in that position.

It is important to remember that this is a very complex process. Positions do not simply stamp themselves on the actor; perspectives are not simply swallowed up by the actor. Instead, it is important to recognize that each position puts a strain on the actor, pushing the actor to see the world in a given direction, influencing the actor to understand and believe things about reality because he or she is in that particular position. Not all poor people see reality in exactly the same way—nor do all students, soldiers, or first-chair horn players. But there is pressure exerted by each position that, if ignored too much, has consequences for both the actor and others in social structure.

This is a very simple point. However, it is also very profound and should tell us all something about human similarities and differences. I am like other professors and unlike corporate executives because my place in social structure shapes the way I see my world. I am like others from the middle class, and I am different from the poor, the unemployed, or the wealthy because my middle-class position causes much of what I see and think.

SUMMARY: THE MEANING AND IMPORTANCE OF STRUCTURE

Social structure is an integral part of people's lives and it is an integral part of every social organization. Structure positions people in relation to one another, and thus brings predictability and control to their lives. We all become actors who fill *positions*—either developed by our own social interaction or already defined for us as we enter the organization. Once in these positions, we are given *roles* (scripts), *identities* (names), *perspectives* (guides to understanding), and a *rank* (usually unequal) with a certain amount of *power* (ability to achieve will in relation to others), *privilege* (opportunities), and *prestige* (honor/dishonor). We can refuse to accept the identity, the role, or the perspective, but doing so is not easy because the forces are great once we are in the position. We can reject the power, but efficiency, predictability, and even cooperation may suffer. Over time, most of us come to gladly seek the privileges and prestige that come from position because we realize that others are more unfortunate and that we "deserve" what we get. Even those low in a social structure are pressured to accept their low prestige and their almost dearth of privileges because so much in society tries to justify their lowly place.

Position matters. From position arise roles, identity, power, privilege, prestige, and perspective. From the qualities that arise from position, the actor is shaped. We are influenced to act, think, and be what our positions demand.

Chapter 5 is a continuation of this chapter on social structure. It focuses on society's structures—especially class structure, gender structure, and dominant-minority group structure. In many ways, these are the most important structures of all.

QUESTIONS TO CONSIDER

1. What is the meaning of social structure? What happens to the individual who exists in social structure? Do you think the author goes too far in describing the importance of social structure?
2. What is the meaning of role conflict? Give some examples of role conflict from your own life.
3. What is the human being, according to this chapter? Is this accurate? Is it appealing to you?
4. Does equality ever exist in social structure?

REFERENCES

Berger, Peter L. 1963. *Invitation to Sociology.* Garden City, NY: Doubleday.
Zimbardo, Philip. 1972. "Pathology of Imprisonment." In *Society*, 9:4–8.

RECOMMENDED READING

The following works make use of the concepts introduced in this chapter. Each is an attempt to understand the human being in the context of social structure.

Anderson, Eric. 2005. *In the Game: Athletes and the Cult of Masculinity*. New York: State University of New York Press.

Arendt, Hannah. 1958. *The Origins of Totalitarianism*. Cleveland, OH: Meridian Books.

Barnes, Sandra L. 2005. *The Cost of Being Poor: A Comparative Study of Life in Poor Urban Neighborhoods in Gary Indiana*. New York: State University of New York Press.

Beeghley, Leonard. 1995. *The Structure of Social Stratification in the United States*. 2nd edn. Needham Heights, MA: Allyn & Bacon.

Beeghley, Leonard. 1996. *What Does Your Wife Do?: Gender and the Transformation of Family Life*. Boulder, CO: Westview Press.

Blau, Peter M. 1955. *The Dynamics of Bureaucracy*. Chicago: University of Chicago Press.

Blau, Peter M., and Marshall W. Meyer. 1987. *Bureaucracy in Modern Society*. 3rd edn. New York: Random House.

Blauner, Robert. 1964. *Alienation and Freedom: The Factory Worker and His Industry*. Chicago: University of Chicago Press.

Blauner, Robert. 1972. *Racial Oppression in America*. New York: Harper & Row.

Bottomore, T. B. 1966. *Classes in Modern Society*. New York: Pantheon Books.

Bowles, Samuel, Gintis Herbert, and Melissa Osborne-Groves. 2005. *Unequal Chances: Family Background and Economic Success*. New Jersey: Princeton University Press.

Carmichael, Stokely, and Charles V. Hamilton. 1967. *Black Power*. New York: Random House.

Dahrendorf, Ralf. 1959. *Class and Class Conflict in Industrial Society*. Stanford, CA: Stanford University Press.

Durkheim, Emile. 1893. *The Division of Labor in Society*. 1964 edn. Trans. George Simpson. New York: Free Press.

Dye, Thomas R. 1986. *Who's Running America?* 4th edn. Upper Saddle River, NJ: Prentice Hall.

Emerson, Michael O., and Rodney M. Woo. 2006. *People of the Dream: Multiracial Congregations in the United States*. New Jersey: Princeton University Press.

Feagin, Joe R., and Clairece Booher Feagin. 1986. *Discrimination American Style: Institutional Racism and Sexism*. 2nd edn. Malabar, FL: Kreiger.

Foner, Nancy. 2005. *In a New Land: A Comparative View of Immigration*. New York: New York University Press.

Gans, Herbert J. 1993. *People, Plans, and Policies: Essays on Poverty, Racism, and Other National Urban Problems*. New York: Columbia University Press.

Goffman, Erving. 1963. *Stigma: Notes on the Management of Spoiled Identity*. Upper Saddle River, NJ: Prentice Hall.

Gouldner, Alvin. 1954. *Patterns of Industrial Bureaucracy*. New York: Free Press.

Harrington, Michael. 1963. *The Other America*. New York: Penguin Books.

Jacobs, Nancy T., Mark A. Segal, and Carol D. Foster. 1994. *Into the Third Century: A Social Profile of America*. Farmington Hills: Gale Group.

Jones, London Y. 1980. *Great Expectations: America and the Baby Boom Generation*. New York: Coward, McCann & Geoghegan.

Jones, Ron. 1981. *No Substitute for Madness*. Covelo, CA: Island Press.

Kanter, Rosabeth. 1977. *Men and Women of the Corporation*. New York: Basic Books.

Keiser, R. Lincoln. 1979. *Vice Lords: Warriors of the Street*. New York: Holt, Rinehart & Winston.

Keller, Suzanne. 1963. *Beyond the Ruling Class: Strategic Elites in Modern Society*. New York: Random House.

Kelman, Herbert C., and V. Lee Hamilton. 1989. *Crimes of Obedience*. New Haven: Yale University Press.

Lenski, Gerhard E. 1966. *Power and Privilege: A Theory of Social Stratification*. New York: McGraw-Hill.

Liebow, Elliot. 1967. *Tally's Corner*. Boston: Little, Brown.

Lipset, Seymour Martin, Martin Trow, and James Coleman. 1956. *Union Democracy: The Inside Politics of the International Typographical Union*. New York: Free Press.

Lynd, Robert, and Helen Lynd. 1929. *Middletown*. New York: Harcourt Brace Jovanovich.

Manning, Christel J. 1999. *God Gave Us the Right: Conservative Catholic, Evangelical Protestant, and Orthodox Jewish Women Grapple with Feminism.* New Brunswick, NJ: Rutgers University Press.

Marger, Martin N. 1987. *Elites and Masses.* 2nd edn. New York: Van Nostrand Reinhold.

Marx, Karl, and Friedrich Engels. 1848. *The Communist Manifesto.* 1955 edn. New York: Appleton-Century-Crofts.

Merton, Robert K. 1968. *Social Theory and Social Structure.* New York: Free Press.

Michels, Robert. 1915. *Political Parties.* 1962 edn. Trans. Eden Paul and Cedar Paul. New York: Free Press.

Milgram, Stanley. 1963. "Behavioral Study of Obedience." In *Journal of Abnormal and Social Psychology,* 67:371–378.

Mills, C. Wright. 1956. *The Power Elite.* New York: Oxford University Press.

Mintz, Beth, and Michael Schwartz. 1985. *The Power Structure of American Business.* Chicago: University of Chicago Press.

Myrdal, Gunnar. 1944. *An American Dilemma.* New York: Harper & Row.

Olsen, Marvin E. (ed.). 1970. *Power in Societies.* New York: Macmillan.

Olsen, Marvin E. 1978. *The Process of Social Organization.* 2nd edn. New York: Holt, Rinehart & Winston.

Phillips, Kevin. 1990. *The Politics of Rich and Poor.* New York: Random House.

Sullivan, Oriel. 2006. *Changing Gender Relations, Changing Families: Tracing the Pace of Change Over Time.* New York: Rowman & Littlefield.

Turner, Ralph H. 1968. "The Role and the Person." In *American Journal of Sociology,* 84:1–23.

Useem, Michael. 1984. *The Inner Circle.* New York: Oxford University Press.

Van den Berghe, Pierre. 1978. *Race and Racism: A Comparative Perspective.* New York: John Wiley.

Whyte, William Foote. 1949. "The Social Structure of the Restaurant." In *American Sociological Review,* 54:302–310.

Whyte, William Foote. 1955. *Street Corner Society.* Chicago: University of Chicago Press.

Williams, Christine L. 2006. *Inside Toyland: Working, Shopping, and Social Inequality.* Berkeley, CA: University of California Press.

Wilson, William J. 1973. *Power, Racism, and Privilege.* New York: Macmillan.

Wilson, William J. 1987. *The Truly Disadvantaged: The Inner City, the Underclass, and Public Policy.* Chicago: University of Chicago Press.

Wrong, Dennis. 1980. *Power, Its Forms, Bases and Uses.* New York: Harper & Row.

Young, Alfred A. 2004. *The Minds of Marginalized Black Men.* New Jersey: Princeton University Press.

The Escalator Mari-Louise Van Esselstyn, 1942. Egg tempera on masonite. *Museum of the city of New York, Gift of the Artist.*

+ 5 +

Inequality in Society

It is part of the American way of thinking that the United States is a land of opportunity for all—that all have a roughly equal chance to succeed. It is difficult for us to see that inequality is built into the very nature of society, that we are in fact all part of social structures that work against equal opportunity. Most of us spend much of our lives trying to "make it" in a society we perceive to be open.

Yet we have always had inequality in society. We have always had a few privileged people and a large number of poor. We have always had class inheritance within families, and we have always had opportunities limited by class in virtually every aspect of life: government, education, health care, choice of neighborhood, and the law and the courts, to name a few.

There are several reasons why this is difficult for us to see. First, equal opportunity has been a central part of the heritage we have been taught. Second, many people have come to the United States from societies with much less opportunity and have been able to succeed here where they would not have had the opportunity to succeed in their homelands. Third, because of the tremendous industrial growth in the United States throughout most of our history, almost everyone's position has improved over that of his or her parents. Finally, inequality is easily hidden, especially at the extremes of poverty and wealth.

Inequality in both income and wealth has characterized the United States since its beginnings. To appreciate the extent of this inequality, consider Table 5-1, which describes family income in 2004. The top fifth, in terms of income, received 47.9 percent of the total income in the United States. This means that this top fifth earned almost as much as the other four-fifths of the population. Table 5-2 shows

TABLE 5-1   Share of Income Received by Each Fifth of Families in the United
States, 2004

Lowest Fifth (%)	Second Fifth (%)	Middle Fifth (%)	Fourth Fifth (%)	Highest Fifth (%)
4.0	9.6	15.4	23.0	47.9

TABLE 5-2   Income Distribution in the United States Since 1947

Year	Lowest Fifth (%)	Second Fifth (%)	Middle Fifth (%)	Fourth Fifth (%)	Highest Fifth (%)
1947	5.1	11.8	16.7	23.2	43.3
1953	4.7	12.5	18.0	23.9	40.9
1963	5.0	12.1	17.7	24.0	41.2
1973	5.5	11.9	17.5	24.0	41.1
1983	4.7	11.1	17.1	24.4	42.7
1986	4.6	10.7	16.8	24.0	43.7
1997	4.2	9.9	15.7	23.0	47.2
2004	4.0	9.6	15.4	23.0	47.9

Source: U.S. Bureau of the Census, Share of Aggregate Income Received by Each Fifth and Top 5 Percent of Families, 1947–2004. Washington, DC: U.S. Government Printing Office.

that the income distribution did not change very much since 1947 until 1997, when the top fifth rose significantly to 47.2 percent.

These figures describe the inequality in *yearly income*. An even better assessment of inequality is the total wealth of U.S. families—property, savings, investments, business assets, and so on. It is much more difficult to get reliable data on wealth. We know that in 1962, about 20 percent of American families owned 76 percent of the total wealth; the bottom 20 percent of families owned less than 1 percent of the wealth; and 60 percent owned 8.5 percent of the wealth (see Figure 5-1).

Michael Harrington described a similar picture in 1980:

The bottom quarter of the society has no wealth at all—or, more accurately, has nega-tive wealth since many of its members are net debtors. The next 55.9 percent of the people have 23.8 percent of the wealth. Adding those two groups together, the cumu-lative figure shows that 81.3 percent of the Americans hold 23.8 percent of the wealth. In short, four-fifths of the people own somewhat less than the top 0.5 percent. Moreover, the wealth of the "ordinary" (nonrich) citizen takes the form of homes

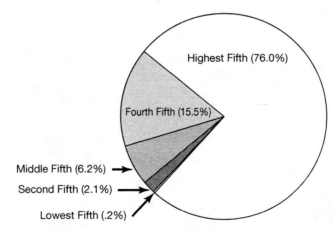

FIGURE 5-1   Distribution of Wealth Among U.S. Families in 1962
(*Source:* U.S. Office of Management and Budget, Executive Office of the President, 1973.)

(which are, as has just been noted, heavily mortgaged), automobiles (purchased on credit) and other consumers' durables, like washing machines and television sets. In other words, most of the "wealth" of four-fifths of the population does not itself generate income or wealth.

(1980, 155)

In 1983, data were compiled for the Federal Reserve (U.S. Congress, 1986). Here are some of their findings:

1. The top 10 percent owns 90 percent of the stock in the United States. (The top 1 percent owns 60 percent.)
2. The top 10 percent owns 73 percent of the total wealth. (The top 1 percent owns 42 percent.)
3. Between 1963 and 1983, the top 0.5 percent went up in its average wealth by 147 percent. The next 9.5 percent went up by about 65 percent, the bottom 90 percent by 45 percent.

Another attempt was made to document wealth distribution in 1994. It is very close to the 1962 data (see Table 5-3).

In June 2007, William N. Wolff wrote a working paper for The Levy Economics Institute of Bard College, to probably be published soon, focusing on some important details concerning the upper 10 percent from 2004 data. Wolff is an Economics Professor from New York University, who has spent much of his academic career studying, researching, and publishing economic inequality in the United States.

1. The top 10 percent of the U.S. population owns 85.4 percent of all stock and mutual funds (down from 90 percent in 1983).
2. The top 10 percent of the U.S. population owns 60.9 percent of all deposits in the United States (up from 52.9 percent in 1983). The 1 percent holds 20.8 percent.
3. The top 10 percent of the U.S. population owns 58.3 percent of all pension accounts.

Although details sometimes vary, the general picture that emerges is consistent and clear:

1. Income and wealth are highly concentrated in the United States, and taxes have not significantly altered that concentration.
2. The inequality that exists today is highly consistent with the inequality that has existed at least since the U.S. Civil War.
3. Although there is opportunity to change one's position in the system of inequality, most of that change in the past occurred when everyone moved up because of economic opportunity. *Relative position* does not change easily, and when it does, it is usually slightly above or below one's parents.

TABLE 5-3   Wealth Distribution in the United States, 1962 and 1994

Year	Lowest Fifth	Second Fifth	Middle Fifth	Fourth Fifth	Highest Fifth
1962	0.2%	2.1%	6.2%	15.5%	76%
1994 estimate	−0.7	2	7.1	16.6	75.2

Source: Hurst et al. "Wealth Economics of American Families," 1984–1994.

4. Beginning in the 1970s, the occupational system has changed considerably from what it was—fewer jobs in industry, more service jobs, less opportunity in various professions—causing less opportunity for upward mobility than characterize this society from its beginning.
5. In the late twentieth century, opportunity for many increased as the computer and communications revolution took place. Many college graduates entered newly created positions in society and found even more affluence than their parents, while the vast majority of young people found employment in occupations that offered little chance for affluence, often facing the prospect of accepting a lower position in the class structure than the position held by their parents.

THE MEANING OF SOCIAL CLASS

One's *class* is most easily understood as one's position in the class structure in society. One's *class position* depends on economic criteria, the two most easily understood being income and wealth. Any class structure has many positions or ranks. Sociologists differ about the number of classes in the United States—some dividing everyone into 2 classes, and others distinguishing as many as 12. Where one draws a line and declares "Here is a class!" depends on what one wants to understand. For example, Rossides (1989) identifies five classes: upper, upper-middle, lower-middle, working, and lower. Michael Harrington, on the other hand, is interested in three: the poor, the nonrich, and the rich. Some sociologists examine class as occupational levels: business executives, professionals, managers, white-collar workers, blue-collar workers, and unskilled workers, for example. Sometimes Karl Marx will emphasize two classes: bourgeoisie and proletariat, the capitalist class and the working class. At other times, Marx identifies several other classes in order to more carefully distinguish people: financial capitalists, industrial capitalists, petty bourgeoisie, the working class, and lumpenproletariat (unemployed, nonproductive, those without skills to sell).

No matter how it is defined, class has rich meaning in sociology. It is similar to all other positions in social organization. The higher one's class, for example, the more *power* one has. Having high rank means that one can influence the economic and political order more regularly than can those who hold low rank or live in poverty. When economic resources matter in interaction with others, the higher one's class, the greater the probability of achieving one's will. Research since the 1950s has documented how much power those who sit at the top of U.S. corporations have, from determining futures of whole communities to influencing American foreign policy. At the other end of the spectrum, one thing we know about the poor in all societies is that they are powerless to control their economic destiny, they are dependent on others for survival, and they have almost no impact on the direction of the economic and political order. They are least likely to vote, and they are most likely to believe their vote does not really matter.

Class also brings *prestige*—or lack of it. High position brings admittance to the "right" clubs and neighborhoods, the admiration of others, and public recognition. It brings the opportunity to buy goods that symbolize importance (expensive cars, diamonds, designer dresses, large homes). Low position in the class structure elicits contempt from many, dishonor from some, and sympathy from still others. Low class position in society is not usually sought, except by those few individuals who do not care about such matters. In a society where class is so important, competition for class position "sets up a contest for dignity," a struggle to win over others to gain "self respect" (Sennett and Cobb, 1972, 147–148).

Of course, class position influences the *privileges* one has in life, or what Max Weber called "life chances" or opportunities. Class influences educational opportunities, life expectancy, health, occupational placement, marital satisfaction, nutrition, level of economic hardship, and occupational and geographical mobility. Class influences all of these matters for our children, and it influences the quality of life we will have after we retire. Class also influences whether a person is arrested for a crime and, once arrested, the likelihood of being denied bail, going to trial, being found guilty, and getting a heavy sentence.

Class position also brings *role expectations*. We tend to marry those in approximately the same class position we are in. Poverty brings lower educational expectations than being in the upper class does. Indeed, whether one goes to college, which college one goes to, what one's major is, and whether one goes on to graduate school are influenced by expectations of family and friends that are largely class based. How one is supposed to act around others; how one is supposed to speak; what one is supposed to like in food, drink, and music are also tied to class. Weber described such expectations as the *lifestyle* associated with class position.

Class position also tells the individual who he or she is. It is one of our central *identities*. Others label us by class, we think of ourselves in terms of class, and through our actions and dress, we announce our class to others. Like all our identities, class identity makes a difference in how we act around others.

Class position helps determine our *perspective* and the actions that arise from perspective. For example, if we are in the upper class, we are more likely to believe in the political system and we are more likely to be active politically. We are also much more likely to be conservative on economic matters. We are more interested in how to save money rather than how to pay our bills and more likely to judge harshly those who are unable to pay theirs. Class influences what we think about gender roles, religion, education, and child-rearing practices.

The class structure, therefore, is like all other structures of which we are a part: It is made up of status positions (classes), each of which influences the actor's actions by giving him or her power, prestige, privilege, identity, role, and perspective.

GENDER AND RACE

In our society—and in most—race and gender act in the same way as class. We are born boys or girls, and this places us in a social position, with role, identity, power, privilege, prestige, and perspective attached. For a long time, the position of woman in society had a particular set of expectations attached. Men expected women to act like housewives and mothers (roles), and many women assumed these as their identities. This, combined with other factors, brought women a lower position in relation to men, with less power in everyday interaction and in society, fewer privileges (in educational, sexual, and occupational choices, for example), and lower prestige (traditionally the women's prestige was tied to her husband's).

Of course, most of us no longer accept this gender structure without question. Both men and women see that gender differentiation into positions (as well as the roles and ranking that comes with them) is, after all, a *social structure*, a social pattern that has emerged over many years. Biology does not command it, and thus, like all else human, it remains the same or it changes as people interact over time. Such patterns, however, are embedded in history and are difficult to alter overnight. Although it is clear that our thinking about male and female differences has changed, it is also clear that in the beginning of the twenty-first century one's gender is still important for a host of matters, from occupational and political opportunities to role expectations and identity. Structure has a tendency to hang on.

We also fill positions in society based on race. A racial structure has always characterized the United States: Those who have come here from Europe conquered the Native American, enslaved the African, and eventually used the Asian and Mexican as cheap labor. In each case, a social structure was built in which nonwhite status remained low. Segregation was written into the law, and segregation between races was embedded in neighborhood patterns. Role expectations, power, prestige, privileges, identity, and perspective arose from such positions. Like the gender structure, the racial structure has had a long time to develop and is very difficult to change. We might change our ideas about what is just, but it is far more difficult to ensure greater opportunities for racial minorities. Where significant change is tried—such as affirmative action or busing students to achieve more equal education—cries of outrage and distress are heard from many quarters. Many whites, like many in the upper classes, do not welcome losing their favored position in society.

CLASS, RACE, AND GENDER STRUCTURES ARE SPECIAL SOCIAL STRUCTURES

Class, race, and gender, then, are all social structures in society, but they are also very special structures, characterized by the following qualities:

1. *The individual is placed in all three at birth.* One's initial position depends on biology or family.
2. *The individual's position in all three is perpetuated by the family.* That is, the family directly places the individual (for example, by determining race or bestowing wealth), and the family teaches the position to the individual (for example, how to act "like a man" or how to be a "young lady" or the way that "people like us" are supposed to act).
3. *The individual's position in these structures influences placement in most other structures.* In government, in business, in the military, or in education, what one can achieve is influenced by class, race, and gender positions.
4. *The individual's position in these structures is generally fixed.* We cannot, of course, change race or gender. Class position may be less fixed, but for the vast majority of people, class placement at birth has a strong influence: The rich generally stay rich, the poor stay poor, and those in between move slightly above or below where they were born. Class position at birth acts as a constraining force: It does not determine where one ends up, but it does act as an important influence.
5. *Various institutions in society cooperate to protect and perpetuate the structures as they have developed.* Political, legal, economic, educational, religious, and kinship institutions socialize us, encourage us, and reward us to accept the existing social patterns and our place in them. Often, the structures are presented as just, moral, and natural; opposition to them is condemned as immoral or unpatriotic and is subject to punishment.
6. *These structures are embedded in a long history.* They are therefore difficult to challenge or alter. We are used to them. They are less open to challenge than structures created in other forms of organization such as groups and formal organizations. It is difficult for most

of us to see realistic alternatives to them because they seem so much an integral part of our taken-for-granted world. Even for those of us who want to do away with them (or at least to alter them), it is often difficult to make sound suggestions about how to institute workable changes.

The term *social stratification* or *stratification system* is generally applied to social structures that are relatively fixed, such as class, race, and gender. Stratification, of course, is a concept borrowed from geology, where it refers to the layering of rocks beneath the earth's surface. A system of *social stratification* is similar to layers of rock: It is ageless and relatively permanent, and individuals in each layer are embedded. Yet, of course, earthquakes sometimes occur — they are relatively rare but powerful — and foundations are shaken. Profound change can then occur.

SOCIAL STRATIFICATION AFFECTS PLACEMENT IN OTHER SOCIAL ORGANIZATIONS

Social stratification is evidenced in everyday interaction. It is woven throughout the concrete situations in our lives as well as in the organizations we join. For example, how a woman's position is defined in society affects her position in the family. If, in society, women are expected to be housewives and mothers, and if they are excluded from full participation in the occupational system, then we can expect that John will be influenced to treat Mary, his wife, as well as Betty, his daughter, in that way. This will affect his actions toward them, the opportunities he provides for them, and the privileges he is willing to grant them. As society changes, however, and as women enter into the occupational order and rise in it, Mary will be encouraged to gain more power for herself in relation to John, privileges will be more negotiable, and John will be influenced to change how he acts.

As African Americans pulled together in the third quarter of the twentieth century, they changed their relative position in society to some extent. Their positions improved in communities, businesses, government, groups, and schools. A larger middle class developed, economically prosperous, more educated, and occupationally placed in various communities, businesses, governments, and groups. But for most African Americans, racial inequality continued, and for various changes in our society, their outlook for success is not very probable. The racial and ethnic stratification system is changing dramatically because of immigration in this century, but its existence is intact. It is just more complex than it was.

Class, race, and gender affect placement of the individual in almost every social organization. An interesting study by Rosabeth Kanter published in 1977 examined how sexual stratification affected relationships in formal organizations. First of all, the jobs people held were influenced by their sex, with women holding almost none of the supervisory and managerial jobs and almost all of the clerical jobs, which had "low status, little autonomy or opportunity for growth, and generally low pay." The images of men were rational, efficient, and objective and of women were emotional, irrational, and concerned with helping others. Thus, the images of men had worked to exclude and justify the exclusion of women from the centers of power and responsibility. Management had been defined as "masculine" and more routine office jobs as "feminine." The corporation therefore had masculine and feminine status positions, and the sex stratification in society carried over into the corporation. Indeed, Kanter also pointed out that women often gained their job satisfaction, rewards, and prestige through the men on whom they were dependent. They judged themselves and each other in terms of whom (the men) they worked for and not the skills exhibited and tasks performed.

Kanter also noted the emphasis managers placed on social similarity in their circle of power, hiring and promoting people on the basis of "who fits in," who they can "trust," who is "their own kind." The result was that men developed a closed world, promoting and hiring other *men*. As Kanter wrote: "Men reproduce themselves in their own image." This, of course, excluded most women from the status positions of power. Managers in the corporation that Kanter observed felt "uncomfortable having to communicate with women," whom they saw as not sharing "masculine" social qualities. Women, unlike men, were also seen as lacking the loyalty necessary to the organization ("since they also have loyalties to family"). Finally, Kanter pointed out that even if women were promoted to high positions, they encountered the burden of overcoming the stereotype of the "woman boss" that both men and women have come to share. In short, women in the corporation tended to be placed according to the stratification system that was developed throughout society.

Kanter's work is important. She highlighted how the society's stratification system impacted gendered distinctions in corporations up to the 1970s, and she examined the issues that had to be confronted if the stratification in the corporation was to be changed. We have seen that much has been done to make gender equality less stratified both in society in general and in the corporation. However, her description is also relevant today; where inequality exists, these still are many of the issues.

THE ORIGIN OF SOCIAL STRATIFICATION SYSTEMS

No one really knows exactly how or why stratification systems have developed in almost every known society. We can argue, of course, as we did in Chapter 4, that social structure is simply an inevitable pattern and that one characteristic of social structures is that they are almost always unequal. Sociologists have tried to better understand the dynamics involved in the rise of stratification systems. Usually the explanation revolves around the interplay of conflict and power.

If we define *conflict* as the struggle for whatever is valued among people, we can realize that whenever something is valued that cannot equally belong to everyone, there will be conflict—struggles over what is valued. Some win, some lose. As some win, they will try to consolidate their position as best they can; those who lose are placed in a position that makes it difficult for them to win in the future. The power of those who win increases over time, and the social patterns that emerge in society (which the powerful encourage) tend to favor their interests. Gerhard Lenski (1966, chapter 3) most clearly describes this process:

1. In any society, whatever is valued will always be in short supply. When this occurs, humans will pursue these values for themselves, and some, because of personal or group advantage, will be more successful than others in obtaining them.
2. Obtaining and keeping material goods through the successful application of personal or group power brings an accumulation of goods (privileges). Both power and privileges in turn bring prestige.

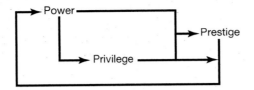

FIGURE 5-2 The Interplay of Power, Privilege, and Prestige: The Origin of Stratification

3. Both prestige and control over valued goods bring, in turn, more power. The circle is complete (see Figure 5-2).
4. The system of distribution, created out of personal power or group advantage, is eventually justified; it becomes "legitimated," or regarded as right. Inequality is protected by the power of a few, and eventually by the ideas developed in society.
5. Finally, advantages are passed down to offspring. Possession of goods is not associated with person but with family. A class system is thus created and perpetuated.

Lenski's description is aimed at the class system. Similar arguments have been applied to the origin of both racial and gender stratification. When people (who are different in race, ethnic group background, or gender) come together, there will be conflict, unequal power, winners, losers, and the emergence of an unequal structure. In the history of the United States, whites dominated Africans, Native Americans, Asians, and Mexicans; took land or cheap labor from these groups; and then created a society that systematically excluded them from full participation. There was conflict among groups with unequal power, and a social structure developed that has been perpetuated throughout American life.

Inequality between men and women goes back even further. We can imagine that men won in relation to women where there was conflict; they accumulated power and established a system of perpetuated inequality. Winning might have been based on physical strength or just the fact that women were at a disadvantage because of continuous pregnancy, but men emerged at the top of society, women at the bottom.

Whatever its origin, however, social stratification is real, and its effects are the same as in any social structure. New members are assigned positions, and those positions have important consequences for the lives of those members.

SOCIAL MOBILITY

Social mobility refers to change in the individual's class either in relation to his or her parents or during his or her own lifetime. We say that a society has high mobility where individuals are likely to change their positions.

We cannot change our gender or race. These are called *ascribed* qualities (rather than *achieved* qualities) and cannot be escaped. Individual blacks or women can achieve much in society in spite of the fact that it is more difficult for them, but they will always remain black or women. As long as these qualities are important for placing people in society, the individual will be affected.

Class is slightly different. Because it is based on economic criteria, it is *achieved*, at least to some degree. Societies differ in the extent to which class mobility is possible. Realistically, however, there is not very much movement for the vast majority of people in the class system. In the United States as well as in other Western industrialized societies, inherited wealth, family socialization, and family contacts (or lack of them) place real limits on mobility. To rise out of the depths of poverty and acquire wealth is not possible except for the very few, and to lose family fortune and upper-class position is highly unlikely except for the very reckless. Working-class and middle-class children are generally satisfied with improving their position over that of their parents, but few have realistic expectations of making it into the ranks of the upper class. Poverty imprisons people, and it is difficult for those caught up in it to do much more than survive. There is no question that people can move up in the class system in America, but movement is very limited. It also seems to be true that opportunity is no greater in the United States than it is in other industrialized nations.

One of the reasons it *seems* that there is a great deal of mobility in the United States is that we have experienced high prosperity and rapid economic change for so long. This has meant that almost all people have been able to improve their positions relative to that of their parents, and over their own lifetimes, people have been able to improve their positions relative to where they began. Yet this has not meant great opportunity for the individual to improve his or her position relative to others in the class structure. Movement up the social structure is predictably small.

STRUCTURAL CHANGE

Nothing stays the same. Over time, structures change. As they do, opportunities open up for people long deprived, and those who have always had privileges are forced to surrender some. For example, since World War II, there has been a steady change in the relationship between men and women. As women have entered the paid labor force, expectations have changed about what women's roles are, and their power, privileges, and prestige have all become more equal to those of men. Widespread use of birth control, the women's movement, longer lifespans, and the increasing independence of children have all contributed to this changing gender structure.

The racial structure has also changed. Migration of blacks to urban centers and to the North since 1900 has increased their power in relation to whites, and this has been accompanied by increases in both privileges and prestige. Although it is a mistake to believe that the United States has achieved anything approaching racial equality, there have been many improvements since 1900. Organization and protest, legislation, executive action, and Supreme Court decisions, as well as achievements by individual blacks, have all worked to alter the social structure.

Change in the class structure is more difficult and complex. The relative numbers, power, privilege, and prestige of the upper class have remained fairly stable since the Civil War, perhaps fluctuating in short periods. The number of those in the poverty class has probably declined since the Civil War, yet since World War II, this class has also remained stable. This class was and is a powerless class without prestige, and although its privileges have increased, those privileges have not increased to nearly the extent they have for other classes.

When we define class in terms of *occupation*, the class structure has changed considerably. In 1900, farm workers constituted 37.6 percent of the population; in

1987, they were 3 percent. In the same period, those in white-collar occupations went from 17.6 percent to 50.9 percent. The whole nature of work and the occupations necessary for the work force have dramatically changed, but it is not clear that the class structure (measured in income or wealth) has changed very much. It is probably accurate to maintain that the jobs of the working class, the jobs of the middle class, and the type of wealth that the upper class controls have all changed, as has the relative size of the classes (smaller middle class, larger affluent class, and larger working class, depending on one's definition). Class structure changes in a highly affluent society such as ours, but a class structure remains, and power, privilege, and prestige remain unequal, and perhaps the inequality we see today is greater than we have ever had as a society, if we examine the differences between the top and the bottom. There is also a lot of evidence that the middle class is becoming less in numbers and in power, and the opportunities for mobility by those below the middle class are much less.

MARX'S VIEW OF SOCIAL STRATIFICATION

Karl Marx (1848), more than any other social thinker, emphasized the central importance of social structure to our lives. Most sociologists do not accept all of Marx's perspective, but like Durkheim's *Suicide*, Marx's writings have spurred research, debate, and important directions of analysis.

Marx believed that *economic* class was central to society because all other systems of inequality were dependent on it. Within economic class, there were basically two possible positions for each person: owner or worker. Marx understood that ownership of the means of production (the land or the factories or the slaves, depending on the historical period of society) confers many benefits, especially power in relation to others. No resource is more important to the individual than control over property that produces the valued goods of the society, because that means control over people's jobs as well as all the things they need for survival. That position, he argued, also makes it possible to control all other institutional systems in society, such as the police, the courts, the army, the government, religion, and the educational system. People who had the land or factories or slaves could thus control people's lives directly (through jobs and goods produced) and indirectly (by controlling the various institutional systems of society). The workers, on the other hand, were powerless, lacking the resources (at least until they decided to unite and overthrow the owners) to change their position in relation to the propertied class. Indeed, Marx argued, the workers would become more and more poor, less and less powerful.

Marx also argued that the powerful determined the *ideas* that prevailed in the society. They were in the best position to teach what they considered the truth, and the ideas they taught would be in their own interests—for example, competition is a law of nature, poverty is inevitable, protection of private property is more important than protection of workers' rights or people's lives. With the army, police, government, law, religion, and ideas as tools, the wealthy can perpetuate a system from which they gain many privileges.

Marx saw that those who have the power also have the privileges in the society. They have longer lives; better health care; higher educational opportunities; more leisure time, comfort, and security. The workers, he believed, are doomed to poverty. Their dependent position places them at the mercy of the propertied; they are exploited, used as tools, and granted only those privileges that will keep them dependent.

Marx predicted an eventual end to the class structure in society and its replacement by a structure of equality. Because class position is so important in determining how people act, Marx believed that real social change can come only when the old class structure is destroyed. Marx did not believe it is possible to reform the class structure through laws or education because in the long run such reforms only serve to protect the powerful. Eventually, however, the workers will become conscious of their exploited position and realize that they can do something to change society. They will organize, overthrow the existing social structure, and create a society of equality.

Although Marx has many critics, sociologists as well as others, in a way this testifies to his importance. Marx's ideas, like those of the other classical sociologists, have been the focus of many important debates in sociology and have encouraged a great deal of theoretical and empirical work. Marx long ago saw what many of us understand all too well today. Our *position* in the economic order is central to determining much of who we are, what we do, and what we think. It is central to our power and privilege in society. And this social structure, built over many generations and centuries, is very stable. Few share Marx's belief that it will eventually be overthrown and replaced with a nonstratified society, although many people take the spirit of Marx and try to work for a less stratified society. The insights of Marx as well as the continuing experience of sociology tells us that the stratification systems—around for a long time, accepted as right by most, defended in a number of subtle ways by those who gain from them, perpetuated through the family—are highly resistant to change.

SUMMARY

Humans are located in society by class, race, and gender. The individual's location, or position, brings role, identity, perspective, power, privilege, and prestige.

Class, race, and gender are part of special social structures called *social stratification systems*. The individual's position within such structures arises from birth and family. Position is impossible or difficult to change, and the structures change slowly.

Social stratification systems arise out of conflict and power, and they are protected by society's institutions and the ideas that most of society's people learn to believe.

Social structure in society is one of the most central concepts in all of sociology. Sociologists have long documented the lack of privileges among the poor, the power of the wealthy, the role expectations and lack of privileges that constrain women, and the lack of privileges and power of racial minorities. This research has established the continuing importance of position in America's social structures.

Social structure arises in all interaction over time and is part of every social organization, from dyads to societies. Our status positions include not only class, race, and gender—discussed in this chapter—but also student, eldest son, friend, clerk, and mayor—discussed in Chapter 4.

In addition to social structure and its tendency to make people unequal in society, there is another social pattern that emerges when people interact over time. That pattern is *culture* and is the topic of the next chapter. Before turning to that topic, however, take a moment to recall the larger picture:

- Social action among actors brings about social interaction; social interaction creates social patterns over time.
- We call social interaction that is patterned *social organization*.
- There are five types of social organizations: dyads, groups, formal organizations, communities, and societies.
- One of the social patterns is *social structure*, a set of status positions in which each status position acts as a controlling force over the actor who exists within the position.
- Each status position controls the actor because it has attached to it a role, an identity, a perspective, and a certain amount of power, prestige, and privileges. Each position thus shapes what the actor does, who the actor is, and how the actor views reality. Each status position also ranks the actor in relation to others.
- Society has very special structures called *stratification systems*.

In Chapter 6 we will turn our attention to culture, a second pattern that also exercises control over the human being in every social organization.

QUESTIONS TO CONSIDER

1. What is class? What is social stratification? What is social mobility? What is inequality?
2. If class, race, and gender are positions within social structures, we should be able to describe them in terms of power, prestige, privileges, role, identity, and perspective. Can you do this?
3. What are the most dramatic changes taking place in American society in relation to inequality? Compare and contrast changes taking place in class, gender, and race.
4. In your opinion, do circumstances at birth make a very big difference in what people achieve—or is it hard work, or luck, or intelligence, or . . . ?

REFERENCES

Erik Hurst & Ming Ching Luoh & Frank P. Stafford, 1998. "The Wealth Dynamics of American Families, 1984–94," Brookings Papers on Economic Activity, Economic Studies Program, The Brookings Institution, vol. 57 (1998–1) pages 267–338. [Downloadable!]
Marx, Karl, and Friedrich Engels. 1848. *The Communist Manifesto*. 1955 edn. New York: Appleton-Century-Crofts.
Lenski, Gerhard E. 1966. *Power and Privilege: A Theory of Social Stratification*. New York: McGraw-Hill.
Harrington, Michael. 1980. *Decade of Decision*. New York: Simon & Schuster.
Rossides, Daniel W. 1989. *Social Stratification*. Englewood Cliffs, NJ: Prentice Hall.
Sennett, Richard, and Jonathan Cobb. 1972. *The Hidden Injuries of Class*. New York: Random House.
U.S. Bureau of the Census. 1986. *Household Wealth and Asset Ownership, 1984*, P70–7.

RECOMMENDED READING

The following works are some of the best analyses of inequality in society. They focus primarily on class, race, ethnic groups, and gender.

Anderson, Elijah. 1999. *Code of the Street: Decency, Violence, and the Moral Life of the Inner City*. New York: W.W. Norton & Company.

Anderson, Eric. 2005. *In the Game: Athletes and the Cult of Masculinity*. New York: State University of New York Press.

Auletta, Ken. 1982. *The Underclass*. New York: McGraw-Hill.

Baldwin, James. 1963. *The Fire Next Time*. New York: Dial Press.

Barnes, Sandra L. 2005. *The Cost of Being Poor: A Comparative Study of Life in Poor Urban Neighborhoods in Gary Indiana*. New York: State University of New York Press.

Bauman, Zygmunt. 1998. *Work, Consumerism and the New Poor*. Philadelphia: Open University Press.

Beeghley, Leonard. 1995. *The Structure of Social Stratification in the United States*. 2nd edn. Needham Heights, MA: Allyn & Bacon.

Beeghley, Leonard. 1996. *What Does Your Wife Do?: Gender and the Transformation of Family Life*. Boulder, CO: Westview Press.

Bell, Derrick. 1992. *Faces at the Bottom of the Well: The Permanence of Racism*. New York: Basic Books.

Bensman, David, and Roberta Lynch. 1987. *Rusted Dreams: Hard Times in a Steel Community*. New York: McGraw-Hill.

Bernard, Jessie. 1987. *The Female World from a Global Perspective*. Bloomington, IN: Indiana University Press.

Blauner, Robert. 1972. *Racial Oppression in America*. New York: Harper & Row.

Bottomore, T. B. 1966. *Classes in Modern Society*. New York: Pantheon Books.

Bowles, Samuel, and Herbert Gintis. 1976. *Schooling and Capitalist America*. New York: Basic Books.

Bowser, Benjamin P. 2006. *The Black Middle Class: Social Mobility–and Vulnerability*. Boulder, CO: Lynne Rienner.

Braun, Denny. 1997. *The Rich Get Richer*. 2nd edn. Chicago: Nelson-Hall.

Brown, Michael, Martin Carnoy, Elliot Currie, Troy Duster, David B. Oppenheimer, Majorie M. Shultz, and David Wellman. 2003. *Whitewashing Race: The Myth of a Color-Blind Society*. Berkeley, CA: University of California Press.

Cannadine, David. 1999. *The Rise and Fall of Class in Britain*. New York: Columbia University Press.

Carmichael, Stokely, and Charles V. Hamilton. 1967. *Black Power*. New York: Random House.

Cashmore, E. Ellis. 1987. *The Logic of Racism*. London: Allen & Unwin.

Chambliss, William J. 1973. "The Saints and the Roughnecks." In *Society*, 11:24–31.

Chin, Margaret M. 2005. *Sewing Women: Immigrants and the New York City Garment Industry*. New York: Columbia University Press.

Coles, Robert. 1977. "Entitlement." In *The Atlantic*, September.

Collins, Randall. 1979. *The Credential Society: An Historical Sociology of Education and Stratification*. New York: Academic Press.

Cookson, P. W., and C. H. Persell. 1985. *Preparing for Power: America's Elite Boarding Schools*. New York: Basic Books.

Coontz, Stepanie. 2005. *Marriage, a History. From Obedience to Intimacy or How Love Conquered Marriage*. New York, NY: Viking.

Cose, Ellis. 1993. *The Rage of a Privileged Class*. New York: HarperCollins.

Curtis, James, and Lorne Tepperman (eds.). 1994. *Haves and Have-Nots: An International Reader on Social Inequality*. Upper Saddle River, NJ: Prentice Hall.

Dahrendorf, Ralf. 1959. *Class and Class Conflict in Industrial Society*. Stanford, CA: Stanford University Press.

Danziger, Sheldon, and Ann Chih Lin (eds.). 2000. *Coping with Poverty: The Socail Contexts of Neighborhood, Work, and Family in the African-American Community*. Ann Arbor: University of Michigan Press.

Della Fave, L. Richard. 1980. "The Meek Shall Not Inherit the Earth: Self-Evaluation and the Legitimacy of Stratification." In *American Sociological Review*, 45:995–971.

Dohan, Daniel. 2003. *The Price of Poverty: Money, Work, and Culture in the Mexican American Barrio*. Berkeley, CA: University of California Press.

Duneier, Mitchell. 1992. *Slim's Table*. Chicago: University of Chicago Press.

Edin, Kathryn, and Maria Kefalas. 2005. *Promises I Can Keep: Why Poor Women Put Motherhood Before Marriage*. Berkeley, CA: University of California Press.

Ehrenreich, Barbara. 2001. *Nickel and Dimed: On (Not) Gewtting By in America*. New York, NY: Metropolitan/Owl Books.

Ehrenreich, Barbara. 2006. *Bait and Switch: The (Futile) Pursuit of the American Dream*. New York: Metropolitan Books.

Emerson, Michael O., and Rodney M. Woo. 2006. *People of the Dream: Multiracial Congregations in the United States*. New Jersey: Princeton University Press.

Engels, Friedrich. 1884. "The Origin of the Family, Private Property, and the State." In *Karl Marx: On Society and Social Change*. 1972 edn. Ed. Neil J. Smelser. Chicago: University of Chicago Press.

Fanon, Frantz. 1963. *The Wretched of the Earth*. New York: Grove Press.

Farley, John E. 1999. *Majority-Minority Relations*. 4th edn. Upper Saddle River, NJ: Prentice Hall.

Feagin, Joe R. 1975. *Subordinating the Poor: Welfare and American Beliefs*. Upper Saddle River, NJ: Prentice Hall.

Feagin, Joe R. 2000. *Racist America: Roots, Current Realities, and Future Reparations*. New York: Routledge.

Feagin, Joe R., and Clairece Booher Feagin. 1986. *Discrimination American Style: Institutional Racism and Sexism*. 2nd edn. Malabar, FL: Kreiger.

Feagin, Joe R., and Melvin P. Sikes. 1994. *Living with Racism: The Black Middle Class Experiences*. Boston: Beacon Press.

Freeman, Jo. 1999. *Waves of Protest: Social Movements Since the Sixties*. Lanham, MD: Rowman & Littlefield.

Freeman, Jo. 1995. *Women: A Feminist Perspective*. 3rd edn. Palo Alto, CA: Mayfield.

Friedan, Betty. 1963. *The Feminine Mystique*. New York: Norton.

Gans, Herbert J. 1993. *People, Plans, and Policies: Essays on Poverty, Racism, and Other National Urban Problems*. New York: Columbia University Press.

Gans, Herbert J. 1995. *The War Against the Poor: The Underclass and Antipoverty Policy*. New York: Basic Books.

Gilbert, Dennis, and Joseph A. Kahl. 1997. *The American Class Structure in an Age of Growing Inequality: A New Synthesis*. 5th edn. Belmont, CA: Wadsworth Publishing Co.

Glasgow, Douglas G. 1980. *The Black Underclass*. San Francisco, CA: Jossey-Bass.

Guillaumin, Collette. 1995. *Racism, Sexism, Power and Ideology*. New York: Routledge.

Hacker, Andrew. 1992. *Two Nations: Black and White, Separate, Hostile, Unequal*. New York: Scribner's.

Harrington, Michael. 1963. *The Other America*. New York: Penguin Books.

Healey, Joseph F. 1997. *Race, Ethnicity, and Gender in the United States: Inequality, Group Conflict, and Power*. Thousand Oaks, CA: Pine Forge.

Hill, Herbert, and James E. Jones, Jr. (eds.). 1993. *Race in America: The Struggle for Equality*. Madison: University of Wisconsin Press.

Hochschild, Jennifer L. 1995. *Facing Up to the American Dream: Race, Class, and the Soul of the Nation*. Princeton, NJ: Princeton University Press.

Irwin, John. 1985. *Jail: Managing the Underclass in American Society*. Berkeley, CA: University of California Press.

Jencks, Christopher. 1992. *Rethinking Social Policy: Race, Poverty and the Underclass*. New York: HarperCollins.

Johnson, Heather B. 2006. *The American Dream and the Power of Wealth: Choosing Schools and Inheriting Inequality in the Land of Opportunity*. New York: Routledge.

Kanter, Rosabeth. 1977. *Men and Women of the Corporation*. New York: Basic Books.

Keister, Lisa A. 2000. *Wealth in America: Trends in Wealth Inequality*. New York: Cambridge University Press.

Kelso, William A. 1994. *Poverty and the Underclass: Changing Perceptions of the Poor in America*. New York: New York University Press.

Kerbo, Harold R. 1999. *Social Stratification and Inequality*. 4th edn. New York: McGraw-Hill.

Kitano, Harry H. L. 1996. *Race Relations*. 5th edn. Upper Saddle River, NJ: Prentice Hall.

Kozol, Jonathan. 1988. *Rachel and Her Children: Homeless Families in America*. New York: Crown Publishers.

Kozol, Jonathan. 1991. *Savage Inequalities*. New York: Crown Publishers.

Lengermann, Patricia Madoo, and Ruth A. Wallace. 1985. *Gender in America: Social Control and Social Change*. Upper Saddle River, NJ: Prentice Hall.

Liebow, Elliot. 1967. *Tally's Corner*. Boston: Little, Brown.

Lorber, Judith. 2005. *Breaking the Bowls: Degendering and Feminist Change*. New York: Norton.

Lynd, Robert, and Helen Lynd. 1929. *Middletown*. New York: Harcourt Brace Jovanovich.

Lynd, Robert, and Helen Lynd. 1937. *Middletown in Transition*. New York: Harcourt Brace Jovanovich.

Malcolm X, and Alex Haley. 1965. *The Autobiography of Malcolm X*. New York: Grove Press.

Mann, Coramae Richey. 1994. *Unequal Justice: A Question of Color*. Bloomington: Indiana University Press.

Mann, Michael. 2004. *The Dark Side of Democracy: Explaining Ethnic Cleansing*. New York: Cambridge University Press.

Marchevsky, Alejandra, and Jeanne Theoharis. *Not Working: Latina Immigrants, Low-Wage Jobs, and the Failure of Welfare Reform*. New York: New York University Press.

Marger, Martin. 1999. *Race and Ethnic Relations: America and Global Perspectives*. 5th edn. Belmont, CA: Wadsworth.

Massey, Douglas S., and Nancy A. Denton. 1993. *American Apartheid: Segregation and the Making of the Underclass*. Cambridge, MA: Harvard University Press.

McMurrer, Daniel P., and Isabel V. Sawhill. 1998. *Getting Ahead: Economic and Social Mobility in America*. Washington, DC: The Urban Institute Press.

Myrdal, Gunnar. 1944. *An American Dilemma*. New York: Harper & Row.

Newman, Katherine S. 1993. *Declining Fortunes: The Withering of the American Dream*. New York: Basic Books.

Noel, Donald. 1968. "A Theory of the Origin of Ethnic Stratification." In *Social Problems*, 16:157–172.

Penn, Michael L., and Rahel Nardos. 2003. *Overcoming Violence Against Women and Girls*. New York, NY: Rowman & Littlefield Publishers, Inc.

Perrucci, Robert, and Earl Wysong. 2001. *The New Class Society: Goodbuye American Dream?* 2nd edn. New York: Rowman & Littlefield Publishers, Inc.

Phillips, Kevin. 1990. *The Politics of Rich and Poor*. New York: Random House.

Piven, Frances Fox, and Richard A. Cloward. 1979. *Poor People's Movements: Why They Succeed, How They Fail*. New York: Vintage.

Quadagno, Jill. 1994. *The Color of Welfare: How Racism Undermined the War on Poverty*. New York: Oxford University Press.

Rossides, Daniel W. 1996. *Social Stratification*. Upper Saddle River, NJ: Prentice Hall.

Rotenberg, Paula S. 2002. *White Privilege: Essential Readings on the Other Side of Racism*. New York, NY: Worth Publishers.

Ryan, William. 1976. *Blaming the Victim*. Rev. edn. New York: Vintage.

Sears, David O., Jim Sidanius, and Lawrence Bobo (eds.). *Racialized Politics: The Debate About Racism in America*. Chicago: University of Chicago Press.

Sewell, W. H., R. M. Hauser, and D. L. Featherman. 1976. *Schooling and Achievement in American Society*. New York: Academic Press.

Simpson, George E., and J. Milton Yinger. 1985. *Racial and Cultural Minorities: An Analysis of Prejudice and Discrimination*. 5th edn. New York: Harper & Row.

Steinberg, Stephen. 1989. *The Ethnic Myth: Race, Ethnicity, and Class in America*. 2nd edn. Boston: Beacon Press.

Steinberg, Stephen. 1995. *Turning Back: The Retreat from Racial Justice in American Thought and Policy*. Boston: Beacon Press.

Sullivan, Maureen. 2004. *The Family of Woman: Lesbian Mothers, their Children, and Undoing of Gender*. Berkeley, CA: University of California Press.

Sullivan, Oriel. 2006. *Changing Gender Relations, Changing Families: Tracing the Pace of Change Over Time*. New York: Rowman & Littlefield.

Terkel, Studs. 1972. *Working*. 1975 edn. New York: Avon Books.

Terkel, Studs. 1992. *Race: How Blacks and Whites Think and Feel About the American Obsession*. New York: New Press.

Tichenor, Veronica J. 2005. *Earning More and Getting Less: Why Successful Wives Can't Buy Equality*. New Jersey: Rutgers University Press.

Van den Berghe, Pierre. 1978. *Race and Racism: A Comparative Perspective*. New York: John Wiley.

Weitzman, Lenore J. 1985. *The Divorce Revolution: The Unexpected Social and Economic Consequences for Women and Children in America*. New York: Free Press.

West, Cornel. 1993. *Race Matters*. Boston: Beacon Press.

Wilson, William J. 1973. *Power, Racism, and Privilege*. New York: Macmillan.

Wilson, William J. 1978. *The Declining Significance of Race*. Chicago: University of Chicago Press.

Wilson, William J. 1987. *The Truly Disadvantaged: The Inner City, the Underclass, and Public Policy*. Chicago: University of Chicago Press.

Wilson, William J. 1999. *The Bridge Over the Racial Divide*. Berkeley: University of California Press.

Winant, Howard. 1994. *Racial Conditions: Politics, Theory, and Comparisons*. Minneapolis: University of Minnesota Press.

Wolff, Edward N. 2007. "Recent Trends in Household Wealth in the United States: Rising Debt and the Middle-Class Squeeze." Working Paper No. 502. The Levy Economics Institute of Bard College, (www.levy.org).

Yinger, J. Milton. 1994. *Ethnicity: Source of Strength? Source of Conflict?* Albany, NY: State University of New York Press.

Young, Alfred A. 2004. *The Minds of Marginalized Black Men.* New Jersey: Princeton University Press.

Zweig, Michael 2000. *The Working Class Majority: America's Best Kept Secret.* Ithaca, NY: Cornell University Press.

Thomas Hart Benton, The Arts of Life in America. *Arts of the West New Britain Museum of American Art, 56 Lexington St., New Britain, CT 06052–1412*

♦ 6 ♦

Culture

Culture is the second pattern of social organization. Like social structure, it is developed in interaction over time; it determines much of what the individual does; and it allows for continuity, stability, and predictability among people.

CULTURE IS A SHARED PERSPECTIVE ON THE WORLD

In the language of social science, *culture* does not mean violins, poetry, or art. *Culture is a perspective on the world that people come to share as they interact.* It is what people come to agree on, their consensus, their shared reality, their common ideas. The United States is a society whose people share a culture. And within the United States, each community, each formal organization, each group, and each dyad has its own culture (or what some social scientists call a *subculture* because it is a culture *within* another culture). Whereas structure emphasizes differences (people relate to each other in terms of their different positions), culture emphasizes similarities (how we agree).

To be part of the "youth culture" in the United States, for example, is to share with a number of people certain ideas about truth, politics, authority, happiness, freedom, and music. On the street, in print and speech, on college campuses, on the web, in concerts and movies, a perspective develops as people share experiences and become increasingly similar to each other on the one hand, while becoming increasingly different from those outside their interaction on the other hand. A common language develops among those who share the culture, reinforcing solidarity and excluding outsiders.

When Marsha and Henry interact, they form their own unique culture too, in a sense. They talk things out and come to share views about each other, parents, adults, children, China, life, work, and the future. They say things to each other that only they fully understand, because they have a common context within which to place those things. While others are straight-faced, they break out laughing at the same situation, funny only to them because they see it in a similar light.

In the sense we are describing culture here, culture is made up of what people come to share *in their heads*—their ideas about what is true, right, and important. Such ideas are guides to what we do, they determine many of our choices, and they have far more consequences than simply being carried around in our heads. We should think of *our culture as shared in interaction, constituting our agreed-on perspective of the world, and directing our acts in the world.*

This definition of culture is not the only definition, but it tends to be central to sociology. Some anthropologists may define culture in a similar way, but most anthropological approaches treat culture as a total way of life, including what people believe, what they do, and what they make. Each definition of culture has a different emphasis; sociologists tend to emphasize culture as the way a people think and treat. A people's way of life–their actions–as a product of culture.

Culture Is Learned

To argue that culture is important is to believe that learning about the world and how to act in it is a result of socialization in contrast to biology. It is also to believe that humans do not simply imitate, but they learn about the world from other people who teach them through language. Culture is that which we *learn* and come to *believe.*

For human beings ideas are anchored in group life. We seek group support for what we believe; we test our ideas with each other; we tend to accept the ideas that are supported by those people with whom we interact and are important to us. Sharing and agreeing is the basis of all culture. Interaction is so important that it becomes very difficult to think the same way as do people outside the interaction and outside the developing culture. We are born into a family and learn its culture, the larger community's culture, and society's culture. We enter a school, a gang, a sorority, or a corporation, and in each case a culture is presented, and we tend to learn that culture is "the right way to think," and if we want to belong, we are careful not to challenge that culture, eventually internalizing what is taught. Acceptance of culture is encouraged as the organization becomes important to our identity, to our meaning as individuals. The ideas shared in organization penetrate us; our minds are filled with these ideas, and our actions tend to be caused by these ideas. In truth, whatever else we are because of our biology, culture makes us much more flexible, much more changeable, and much more dependent on what is put into our heads through social interaction.

Culture distinguishes us from those with whom we do not interact. Isolation of a group, society, or other social organization creates a people's unique view of the world; as interaction moves outside the established organization, less uniqueness usually results. Our culture becomes more and more like those who surround us.

Culture Is a Social Inheritance

Many social organizations we enter have existed for a long time; people who have power within them teach us their long-established "truths" so that we may become good members and the social organization will continue. Culture is a social inheritance; it consists of ideas that may have developed long before we were born. Our society, for example, has a history reaching beyond any individual's life, the ideas developed over time are taught to each generation, and "truth" is anchored in interaction by people long dead. Examples of this are everywhere: Successful people must get a college diploma; women should get married and have children; romantic love should be the basis for marriage; making money is the best way to encourage people to work. Each child is taught this culture by the family, school, and church—those social organizations that are its carriers. We are socialized to accept the ideas of those in the positions of "knowing better," those who have many years of history on their side, a long tradition, rightness or God or science or whatever. Formal organizations have a history, too, as do communities and groups. We may contribute our ideas, but we are always confronted by a powerful force—a culture—that developed before we entered the scene and that we have little choice but to accept if we want to continue interacting in the social organization.

Witness the individual who tries to break away from the culture. To break out of the culture is to stand alone, to chance being thrust from the social organization, or in some societies to be penalized with imprisonment or death. To reject the organization's definition of truth is to reject the organization itself—and one must be prepared either to be isolated or to join other organizations that share the "right" views, which turn out to have, of course, another culture.

We may change social organizations and therefore trade one culture for another. Each organization, however, has a way of defining the world, a way of thinking, a set of rules, that it encourages its members to share, and we will be expected to join in, too. We may adopt a radical perspective at college, but when we go off to teach high school or to join in a business after graduation, our beliefs change because we are cut off increasingly more from the people with whom we interacted at college. Some of us may leave our community or even our society to enter a new one. Over time, the old culture will gradually be replaced with new ideas and rules. This is difficult for most of us. We hesitate to break away from one set of truths and learn a new way, a new culture. "I guess I'm just old-fashioned" is what many people feel.

A culture, then, is a shared perspective, a set of ideas that people develop and learn in social interaction. Actually, we might find it useful to divide this set of ideas into three categories: (1) what is true (our truths), (2) what is worthwhile (our values and goals), and (3) what is the correct way of acting (our rules). In this context, a culture is defined as a *people's shared truths, values, goals, and rules.* Let us examine each in turn.

CULTURE IS A BODY OF "TRUTH"

A culture is, first of all, a set of ideas concerning what is true or real. All people do not agree on what is true in the world. Each social organization develops a culture that contains a body of truths, and so will each community within society, each formal organization, group, and dyad. We share truths as we interact, and people with whom we do not interact have truths we often do not learn, usually do not understand, and rarely believe. In Fargo, North Dakota, we believe that farming is the backbone of the United States; in Chicago, we believe that farmers make too much money; and in Texas, we believe that farming is big business. In the United States, we believe that separation of church and state is right and democratic; in other societies, people are socialized to believe that a state church must be supported by all.

Sociologists share their own truths, as do students at the University of Chicago and, to some extent, students all over the United States. A group may share beliefs about the nature of God, life, and society; that is part of its culture. Baptists may hold that life is a testing ground for an afterlife existence, humanists may hold that the purpose of life is to seek goodness, and the National Association of Manufacturers may emphasize gaining powerful positions and increasing wealth. An automobile company's truth may be that its product is the mode of transportation that gives us the greatest independence, and an ecology group's truth may be that the automobile is responsible for poisoning us through air pollution.

Almost all of us like to think that our ideas about the world are true. Some of them probably are, but most of them we have come to accept not because of careful evidence but because of our interaction. If we are honest with ourselves, we will realize that our ideas, by and large, are *cultural*, that they are formed in social organization and taught to us as members of organization. Even if they are to some extent true, they are also limited in capturing reality because each is a focus, exaggerating certain aspects of reality and ignoring other aspects. Can anyone truly believe he or she would have the same set of truths as someone born in Russia or Switzerland or Mexico or Japan? Can psychology majors truly believe that their truths would be the same if they had majored in sociology and interacted with sociologists? Can New Yorkers truly believe that their ideas about living would be the same if they had grown up in Great Falls, Montana, or Dallas, Texas?

We all have different ideas about the world, about what is and is not true. Those of us who are very careful are probably going to capture some ideas close to the truth. Most of us, however, will accept those ideas our organizations teach; our interaction will influence what we believe. If we understand this, our disagreements with others will seem more like differences arising in interaction—cultural—than a matter of truth versus falsehood. My good friend, Larry, is a neuropsychologist. When he and I discuss human beings, we disagree a lot about why humans act as they do. He focuses on the brain, while I focus on our social life; neither of us focuses on early childhood training. That is because each of us has accepted a culture associated with our profession, different from each other, and different from other social scientists. Of course, we are going to disagree. Maybe he is in error; maybe I am; maybe we both are (How good is our evidence?). It is probably true, however, that we both have something important to say and that our disagreement is largely cultural.

There are good reasons why a given society develops one set of truths rather than another. People develop a philosophy, a belief system, a view of reality that is *useful* to them. It works for their organization. We tend to believe ideas that successfully guide us in our action, that help us make sense out of the experiences that confront us, and that support the organization. Social organizations develop truths over time as people work out ways of dealing with their environment. Truths are developed to solve the problems we face, to justify our actions, and to validate the structures we create. In the end, ideas that work for a people's situation become their truths; because every social organization is in a different situation and every social organization has a different history, cultures will be different.

"America is the land of opportunity. It is a just system. It is a place where all people can make it to the top. It is based on fair competition that brings out the best qualities of the human being. If someone makes it in this system, he or she should be able to keep what he or she makes. If someone does not make it, chances are that person did not try hard enough." These ideas are *cultural*. They work well to protect the economic system and the social inequality we have. They probably encourage people to try hard to improve their position in life. Wealthy people will certainly believe and try to teach these ideas to the rest of us. These ideas may or may not be true. Truth or falsehood depends on the evidence rather than on the fact that a majority may believe these ideas.

It is far from this simple, however. Although on the one hand, a people's particular body of truth may be functional for them, we must also remember the role of social structure in creating ideas. Power is an important aspect in all social structures; those who have the most power will have the most impact on creating the culture—and the ideas that prevail in social organization as part of its culture are usually ideas that most benefit those in power. It is not that these people necessarily lie and mislead others; it is that their truths, highly consistent with their position in society, tend to prevail as *the* truths.

CULTURE IS A SET OF VALUES

Culture is also made up of ideas about what is worth working for (ends). These ends are of two kinds: values and goals. Sometimes, the distinction between values and goals is difficult to make because both consist of ideas about what we should pursue, what purpose our action should have.

A *value* is a long-range commitment of the organization or individual. It is a strong preference and an organizing principle around which goals are established and action takes place. A *goal* is a short-range objective in a specific situation by an individual or social organization.

In most situations, our choice of action depends on our value commitments. Is honesty or a college degree a more important value to us? Is God or school; friendship or family; materialism or love; freedom or equality; courage or safety; doing right or doing what is popular; the future, present, or past; people or things; getting a good education or getting a good job? We are guided by such values, and they, in turn, are developed in interaction with others.

Often, situations arise in which we must choose among values, because if we follow one, we cannot follow the others. Most of us, for example, value freedom, equality, and life, but when we are faced with a real situation to work out, some of these values become more important to us than others. An individual may favor equality for all people, but may also desire a certain job that he or she is afraid will be given to a minority candidate, and must then commit himself or herself either to equality or to personal security. A person may value both a college education and an active social life, which may involve a choice on various occasions. Academic classes sometimes force us to choose between open-mindedness and the security that comes with certainty. Values are not simple guides because they are often contradictory. Even so, if we examine ourselves closely, we will see a core of values that influence us in many situations.

We learn our values in interaction. Groups, formal organizations, communities, and society direct our priorities by teaching us a set of values. Every social organization has slightly different values, and we change as we change organization. The values society teaches us are difficult to question because they normally seem like the only sensible ones. Organizations have a stake in teaching us to value certain things. If we become strongly committed to an organization, then its values become our own. If we spend all our time interacting within an organization (for example, a certain community), then its values tend to become our own. Alternative values are difficult to accept if they do not have some social basis, that is, if they do not arise from an organization of which we are a part. Strong value commitments normally reflect strong social commitments: to a religion, to a fraternity, to feminists, to a family, or to a political party, for example.

Strong commitment to a social organization means that the organization itself becomes an important value to the individual. We may be willing to give up time or money or even life for it; we may find our whole purpose in life tied to it. People sacrifice for families; they work hard for businesses; they volunteer for churches and charities; and they endanger their own lives for country. Sometimes it is because of what the social organization stands for; often it is because the organization itself has become a value.

Whatever values are developed in an organization will be largely functional for the organization. Like ideas about truth, values serve a purpose; they mobilize the individuals around desired ends and cause them to act in ways that aid the organization. It is no accident that corporations value profit and growth, the work ethic and capitalism, planning and noninterference by government. These values serve the corporation's stability and continuity, and employees are encouraged to acquire these as their personal values. In addition, values, like truths, are most likely to reflect the values taught by and beneficial to those at the top of the social structure.

Values Are Reflected in Action

Our values are not necessarily what we choose on a questionnaire or what we say we believe in to our children or friends. Our stated values may be only what we are supposed to believe in. Values are really reflected in what we do, not in what we say. Our goals, decisions, and actions reveal our values. I may tell others I value education, but others can see by my lack of interest in school that I do not. I may tell others I believe in love, but others can see that love is not reflected in my actions. The emphasis in this society on buying things, making lots of money, and judging each other on the basis of wealth reflects a value commitment to materialism by large numbers of people. Family life is less important today than it once was—no matter what we *say*, our decisions reflect the fact that other values have become more important to us. Yet, among many men today, family life has become a more important value than it was for their fathers, as their work becomes less important. Values shift in society, and as we see men spending more time with family, we see a shift.

The relationship between values and action is more complex than this. It may be that we act differently from what we say we believe in. Yet what we say still can have a long-range impact. It is probably better to say "I believe in democracy" than to say "I believe in white supremacy," no matter what the reality of our action is, for if we say (and think) that we believe in democracy, someone can point out how our action contradicts our value, and there is some chance for us to alter our acts and bring them in line with our stated values. Equality, for example, is a value that Americans often espouse but clearly have not followed in relation to racial minorities and women. The success of movements to alter society depends in part on their appeal to the value of equality. "If you really believe in equality, then show me through your acts that you are willing to do something to alter the unjust racial and gender stratification systems!" It would be much harder to appeal to those who espouse the natural superiority of whites and men and who say they value a society built on inequality.

There Is an American Value System, but It Is Complex and Often Inconsistent

The United States as a society has a value system we have come to share over a long history. It is made up in part of the values of individualism, equality, and material success. Yet the argument can be made that we also value conformity, a segregated society, and material security. Listing American values is a difficult task because there are so many exceptions and contradictions. I realized this when I first read the well-known study by Robin Williams (1970), which attempted to isolate and analyze the American value system. The values that Williams listed—success, materialism, work, progress, practicality, democracy—seemed to conflict with other values many Americans hold, such as leisure, tradition, even racial supremacy.

Yet, on a very general level, Americans do share a value system, especially when we look at the United States in contrast to other societies such as Holland or Mexico or Saudi Arabia. Dutch culture is far more secular than we are, values freedom and tolerance of personal expression, values the artistic, the creative, and less judgmental in the sexual activities of other people. Mexican culture is highly patriarchal (machismo), traditional in its religion, and more important to community and family. Saudi Arabia is an Islamic society that values tradition and family, strict division of gender, and religious education. Many would argue that the United States seems to be more and more individualistic, materialistic, goal oriented, seeking pleasure in life, maybe more secular, child centered in family, charitable, and practical.

Within the United States, each community also has a value system, influenced by the larger society but also unique because of the interaction that takes place in a particular community over time. Harlem, Minneapolis, Atlanta, Peoria, Harvard, Salt Lake City, and San Antonio are all communities in the United States. Each shares the dominant culture, yet each is somewhat unique in the values it emphasizes. Some will have high commitment to family, some to work, some to religion, some to "law and order," and some to radical change.

Each formal organization also develops a value system, as does each group and each dyad.

As complex and contradictory as an organization's value system may be, it is still different from other organizations, and it is still important to what people do. Although individualism is not held by all Americans as the most important value, it seems to have been an extremely important value from the very beginning of this society. It weaves itself throughout our history, and by the early first decade of the twenty-first century, its place had become very prominent. It is an individualism bonded to materialism, and it is an individualism that sometimes includes free thinking, and sometimes does not. It is an individualism that has all kinds of implications for our view of taxes, business, crime, athletics, and sex; it is an individualism that competes with values such as family, equality, responsibility to the poor and disadvantaged, and even commitment to a liberal arts education.

CULTURE IS A SET OF GOALS

Goals, like values, are the ends for which people work. Goals are practical ends; values are moral ones. Goals are to be achieved and then replaced by other goals; values are general guides for action. Goals are the specific ends we organize our action around, the ends that create the problems we try to solve. Humans are problem solvers. Individually, we establish goals to achieve, and we organize our efforts to achieve them; together in organizations, we share goals to achieve, and we cooperate to overcome the problems that may arise. A team cooperates to win a game or achieve first place. A corporation may try to increase profits by 5 percent in the first quarter of the year. A society may try to negotiate a peace treaty, lower inflation, or redistribute income through higher taxes for some. These are all goals.

Values are important for goals. They are our abstract long-range commitments that act to oversee our goals. We work for those goals that are consistent with our value commitments. My goals on Sunday might include going to church in the morning, working for the United Fund in the afternoon, and spending time in the evening discussing religious issues with my children, all of which are consistent with my value commitment to religion. I also might have longer-range goals consistent with this value: to become head of our church, to make the church a more meaningful experience for the congregation, to teach my children the value of religion. A person whose value is education might have the goals of graduating high school, graduating college, getting a graduate degree, teaching, encouraging his or her children to learn, and so on.

Values and goals are two components of culture. Like ideas about truth, they arise among people as interaction takes place over time. They are important for keeping the organization together, for transforming the individual into a cooperating actor—in a sense, for changing individual values and goals to organizational ones. Some sociologists emphasize the importance of common goals and values for the continuation of all organization. It is obviously difficult for cooperation to take place over time if there is not at least some agreement among the actors about what should be worked for.

Culture means agreement; individuals whose truths, values, and goals are contrary to those of the organizations in which they interact make it difficult for the organization to succeed. Think of the dyad relationships with parent, friend, teacher, or employer. Without some agreement on ideas about reality, values, and goals, these dyads will experience conflict, tension, and perhaps dissolution.

CULTURE IS A SET OF NORMS

The set of norms we share is the fourth component of culture. We have earlier described norms as *the expectations we have for each other*—how we are supposed to act—the rules, the laws, the right way. Norms are associated with one's position and are thus part of structure (remember, they make up a *role*), but they are also associated with membership in the group, irrespective of position (they make up the *culture*).

In interaction, we agree on the rules of the game (the means used to achieve the ends), and we agree to operate within the rules while in the social organization. These rules may be simple procedures to be followed, or informal expectations, or traditions, laws, or morals. We each obey the norms for different reasons—moral commitment, fear, expectation of reward, or simply because we believe rules are necessary—but most of us do obey them. In fact, most of us never really think about them. We simply accept most of the norms we learn because we are part of the organization. Often, we do not consider that alternative norms might be more rational or just.

Organizations need rules to function. A social organization can work only if members agree, at least to some extent, to give up personal beliefs about how people should act and accept the organization's beliefs. This need not involve moral agreement (and usually does not), but each organization expects that certain procedures, laws, and traditions will be followed. The extent to which rules are necessary is a subject for debate, but most of us would probably agree that some agreed-upon norms are necessary for all social organization. We expect each other to be on time, to help each other, to be faithful, to seek each other's company. The gang requires that new members go through initiation rites, demands personal bravery and loyalty to the gang above all other organizations, influences individuals to act "cool," and asks everyone to contribute time and money to the group and to take orders from the leader. The bank expects employees to be honest, friendly to all customers, and cheerful; it sets up elaborate procedures to guarantee accuracy and security; and it develops a set of criteria for promotion of employees. Communities and societies have customs and laws that all are expected to follow.

Every situation we enter is governed by norms. Eating, dressing, walking, driving, and even sleeping are governed by rules that have arisen over a long social history. The way we worship God, celebrate birth, mourn death, and even feel pain depends on society's norms. The range is almost endless: from simple procedures necessary for the functioning of an office to taboos whose violation is dealt with by execution.

Organization is built on the acceptance of norms to a great extent. We predict the actions of strangers on the street, on planes, and in stores. We expect that people will wait their turn, treat each other with respect, and act peaceably. One effect of violent random crime and hijacking is the undermining of long-accepted norms, leading to distrust and fear of others in situations once characterized by taken-for-granted trust.

These norms, then, exist in all social organizations and are part of the pattern called culture. They influence or shape or control (depending on the situation) the individual's action. Some rules (such as laws) are obeyed because we realize that if we do not obey, we will be punished or the society will be threatened; some rules, on the other hand, take on a moral significance, become our ideas of right and wrong; they become more than just rules because conscience and guilt play a strong part in enforcement. Most social organizations will attempt to make their rules seem morally right. Sometimes they are successful; sometimes they are not. For some individuals, a rule becomes a moral guide; for others, a rule remains just a rule.

CULTURE, SUBCULTURE, AND COUNTERCULTURE

Many sociologists reserve the term *culture* for the shared perspective of people in a whole society and then introduce other terms to refer to cultures within that society. They sometimes distinguish *subcultures, countercultures, group cultures,* and *dominant cultures.* Subcultures are part of any distinctive community or group in society. Adolescents are sometimes described as forming a subculture, and so are various ethnic groups, such as African Americans or Jews. Subculture does not mean that the community has an "inferior" culture. No sociologist uses the term to mean that. The prefix *sub* should be taken to mean "within" not "inferior to."

The concept of *subculture* is an important one because it reminds us that although there may be "an American culture," there are many highly distinctive groups and communities within America. At the same time, however, the term also implies that the subculture does not develop in a vacuum, that it is influenced by the larger culture in many complex and subtle ways. So, as Marvin Olsen points out, the juvenile gang that believes it is right to steal cars may appear to be very different from the dominant culture, yet it, too, emphasizes monetary success and peer acceptance, and to that extent has been influenced by the dominant culture's values (1978, 162–163).

The term *counterculture* is used to describe certain other cultures within the dominant societal culture. The counterculture, unlike the subculture, explicitly "rejects the norms and values that unite the dominant culture while the [subculture] finds ways of affirming the national culture and the fundamental value orientation of the dominant society" (Roberts, 1978, 114). The counterculture rejects the "central values of the culture, and a greater discrepancy exists *between* the culture and the counterculture than *within* either one of them" (115).

Like every society, America has had important countercultures. The Bohemians of the 1920s, the Beatniks of the 1950s, and the Hippies of the 1960s are the most important examples. In each case, communities separated themselves from the larger society and pursued radically different values, while offering certain people a real alternative to the dominant culture. These countercultures acted as an important critique of the dominant culture's ideas and values. In every case, these countercultures contributed to society by providing havens for the disenchanted—very often the most creative people in society. All societies have such countercultures, which often provide the setting for criticism that leads to social change.

The term *group culture* is sometimes used to refer to a culture that arises in a group or formal organization. Like subculture and counterculture, group culture is a useful concept. The Los Angeles Lakers has a group culture, as does the First Lutheran Church and the Student Senate. Although not as distinct as a subculture, a group culture still has its own emphases and makes its members at least slightly different from outsiders.

In spite of these distinctions, it is more important to see that there is a basic similarity among all cultures. All of these cultures are social patterns that arise in interaction. Every social organization has its own culture to some extent. Each is different from every other one, sometimes slightly, sometimes greatly so. Each has an important influence on the individual members.

CULTURE IS IMPORTANT

Culture is central to the individual and to social organization. First, *it influences what we do.* We worship God or gods or nothing because of our shared truths and norms and values: our culture. Americans may be materialistic, but that is not inherent to our nature. It arises from culture, which places a high value on material goods and causes us to make decisions that are materialistic. We marry, have children, get a job, buy a new home because that is what our culture causes us to do. And if we decide not to marry, not to have children, not to find a permanent job or buy a new home, that too can be linked to culture: to a culture that has changed over the past 30 years, causing many more of us to make such decisions. Not only are we influenced by American culture, but also by the cultures in our community, our formal organizations, our groups, and our dyads.

Second, *culture is important for social organization.* It is one of three patterns in all social organization (the other two are social structure and institutions). It means that those in interaction understand and agree with each other; they share a notion of what the world is all about and how they should work together in that world. We know what to expect from each other because of sharing a culture; we become accustomed to each other's actions and ways of thinking. As a result, we are able to cooperate, to solve problems together, and to work things out.

Most people do not appreciate the power of culture. This is because the worlds we find ourselves in seem natural, proper, right, normal. It becomes, as some call it, a world taken for granted. Our culture's truths become ours, and it is difficult to understand why others can be so different, why others do things that are strange, why others seem to not want the same things we do, or why they just "think funny." Indeed, it is easy to understand why organizations benefit from teaching that their cultures are right and that other ways of doing things are wrong or silly or unnatural or sinful.

THE REAL SIGNIFICANCE OF CULTURE: THE SOCIAL CONSTRUCTION OF REALITY

It is easy to get lost in the many details contained in this chapter. It is also easy to overlook the whole significance of culture when we try to memorize a number of subpoints.

The real significance of culture is that human beings come to believe in what they do through interaction. Our truths, morals, values, and goals are, to a very great extent, socially created. This is an important insight, and it is often difficult to grasp. This is because every social organization attempts to make it appear that its culture is right, is in fact the only way "good people" should think or act. Social scientists sometimes call this tendency *ethnocentrism*, the thinking that one's own culture (*ethno*) is central (*centrism*) to the universe, and that all other cultures are to be judged accordingly (usually as inferior).

In fact, once we appreciate the meaning of culture, it becomes difficult to be ethnocentric, to regard our own truths in absolute terms. Some of these truths may in fact be absolutely true, our values and morals may be absolutely right, but we can never know that for sure. All we can know for sure is that, to a great extent, what we have come to know and believe about the universe has resulted from interaction. It is cultural.

Reality may exist "out there," independent of how we see it. There may be something out there. However, how we see it, what we think about it, what we value in it, and what we regard as right have arisen from what Peter Berger and Thomas Luckmann (1966) have called "the social construction of reality." It is through our social life that we come to know what exists. It is through our social life that we learn what is real, what to call it, and how to use it. Between "reality as it is" and "reality as I see it" exists social organization and its culture, the social eyeglasses through which I look.

SUMMARY

In this chapter, we have emphasized that all social organizations develop the social pattern we have here called *culture*. Culture is a shared view of reality, a shared perspective, a shared agreement concerning what is true, right, and worthwhile. Culture, like social structure, arises in interaction, influences the individual actor, and helps ensure social organization.

One more social pattern should be explained. That is the social pattern called *institution*, and it is the subject of Chapter 7.

QUESTIONS TO CONSIDER

1. What are the most important ideas you believe in? What are the most important values? What are the most important norms? Are these cultural?
2. Most of us want to believe that the cultures we share are true and good and that other cultures are probably not as good. Is there any way of establishing that one culture is in fact better than another?
3. What are the most important ideas people in the United States believe? What are the most important values? What are the most important norms we follow?
4. Why does culture arise in the first place?
5. Why is culture a necessary part of all organized life?

REFERENCES

Berger, Peter L., and Thomas Luckmann. 1966. *The Social Construction of Reality*. Garden City, NY: Doubleday.

Olsen, Marvin E. 1978. *The Process of Social Organization*. 2nd edn. New York: Holt, Rinehart & Winston.

Roberts, Keith A. 1978. "Toward a Generic Concept of Counter-Culture." In *Sociological Focus*, 11:111–116.

Williams, Robin. 1970. *American Society: A Sociological Interpretation*. New York: Alfred A. Knopf.

RECOMMENDED READING

The following are approaches to the concept of culture from a sociological perspective.

Adler, Patricia A., and Peter Adler (eds.). 1994. *Constructions of Deviance: Social Power, Context, and Interaction*. Belmont, CA: Wadsworth.

Anderson, Elijah. 1999. *Code of the Street: Decency, Violence, and the Moral Life of the Inner City*. New York: W.W. Norton & Company.

Anderson, Eric. 2005. *In the Game: Athletes and the Cult of Masculinity*. New York: State University of New York Press.

Barnes, Sandra L. 2005. *The Cost of Being Poor: A Comparative Study of Life in Poor Urban Neighborhoods in Gary Indiana*. New York: State University of New York Press.

Barton, Bernadette. 2006. *Stripped: Inside the Lives of Exotic Dancers*. New York: New York University Press.

Bauman, Zygmunt. 1998. *Work, Consumerism and the New Poor*. Philadelphia: Open Universuty Press.

Becker, Howard S. 1976. *Boys in White: Student Culture in Medical School*. Rev. ed. Chicago: University of Chicago Press.

Becker, Howard S. 1982. "Culture: A Sociological View." In *The Yale Review*, 71:513–527.

Bellah, Robert N., Richard Madsen, William M. Sullivan, Ann Swidler, and Steven M. Tipton. 1985. *Habits of the Heart: Individualism and Commitment in American Life*. New York: Harper & Row.

Dohan, Daniel. 2003. *The Price of Poverty: Money, Work, and Culture in the Mexican American Barrio*. Berkeley, CA: University of California Press.

Durkheim, Emile. 1915. *The Elementary Forms of Religious Life*. 1954 edn. Trans. Joseph Swain. New York: Free Press.

Edin, Kathryn, and Maria Kefalas. 2005. *Promises I Can Keep: Why Poor Women Put Motherhood Before Marriage*. Berkeley, CA: University of California Press.

Eitzen, Stanley. D. 2001. *Sport in Contemporary Society: An Anthology*. 6th edn. New York: Worth Publishers.

Eliade, Mircea. 1954. *Cosmos and History*. New York: Harper & Row.

Emerson, Michael O., and Rodney M. Woo. 2006. *People of the Dream: Multiracial Congregations in the United States*. New Jersey: Princeton University Press.

Erikson, Kai T. 1966. *Wayward Puritans: A Study in the Sociology of Deviance*. New York: John Wiley.

Festinger, Leon. 1956. *When Prophecy Fails*. Minneapolis, MN: University of Minnesota Press.

Fine, Gary Alan. 1987. *With the Boys: Little League Baseball and Preadolescent Culture*. Chicago: University of Chicago Press.

Foner, Nancy. 2005. *In a New Land: A Comparative View of Immigration*. New York: New York University Press.

Gans, Herbert J. 1988. *Middle American Individualism: The Future of Liberal Democracy*. New York: Free Press.

Geertz, Clifford. 1965. "The Impact of the Concept of Culture on the Concept of Man." In *New Views of the Nature of Man*. Ed. John R. Platt. Chicago: University of Chicago Press.

Geertz, Clifford. 1984. "Distinguished Lecture: Anti Anti-Relativism." In *American Anthropologist*, 86:263–278.

Gehlen, Arnold. 1980. *Man in the Age of Technology*. New York: Columbia University Press.

Giddens, Anthony. 2000. *Runaway World: How Globalization Is Reshaping Our Lives*. New York: Routledge.

Goldhagen, Daniel Jonah. 1996. *Hitler's Willing Executioners: Ordinary Germans and the Holocaust*. New York: Alfred A. Knopf.

Hall, John A., and Charles Lindholm. 2000. *Is America Breaking Apart?* Princeton, NJ: Princeton University Press.

Herskovits, Melville Jean. 1972. *Cultural Relativism*. Ed. Frances Herskovits. New York: Random House.

Hostetler, John A. 1980. *Amish Society*. Baltimore, MD: Johns Hopkins University Press.

Johnson, Heather B. 2006. *The American Dream and the Power of Wealth: Choosing Schools and Inheriting Inequality in the Land of Opportunity*. New York: Routledge.

Jones, Landon Y. 1980. *Great Expectations: America and the Baby Boom Generation*. New York: Coward, McCann & Geoghegan.

Keiser, R. Lincoln. 1979. *Vice Lords: Warriors of the Street*. New York: Holt, Rinehart & Winston.

Keister, Lisa A. 2005 *America's New Rich and How They Got That Way*. New York: Cambridge University Press.

Kelso, William A. 1994. *Poverty and the Underclass: Changing Perceptions of the Poor in America*. New York: New York University Press.

Kluckhohn, Clyde. 1949. *Mirror for Man*. New York: McGraw-Hill.

Lee, Robert G. 1999. *Orientals: Asian Americans in Popular Culture*. Philadelphia: Temple University Press.

Liebow, Elliot. 1967. *Tally's Corner*. Boston: Little, Brown.

Lofland, John. 1966. *Doomsday Cult*. Upper Saddle River, NJ: Prentice Hall.

Mannheim, Karl. 1929. *Ideology and Utopia*. 1936 edn. New York: Harcourt Brace Jovanovich.

Manning, Christel J. 1999. *God Gave Us the Right: Conservative Catholic, Evangelical Protestant, and Orthodox Jewish Women Grapple with Feminism*. New Brunswick, NJ: Rutgers University Press.

Marchevsky, Alejandra, and Jeanne Theoharis. *Not Working: Latina Immigrants, Low-Wage Jobs, and the Failure of Welfare Reform*. New York: New York University Press.

Marcuse, Herbert. 1964. *One-Dimensional Man*. Boston: Beacon Press.

Merry, Sally E. 2005. *Human Rights and Gender Violence: Translating International Law into Local Justice*. Chicago, IL: University of Chicago Press.

Paap, Kris. 2006. *Working Construction: Why White Working Class Men Put Themselves—and the Labor Movement—in Harm's Way*. Ithaca, NY: ILR Press/Cornell University Press.

Postman, Neil. 1992. *Technopoly: The Surrender of Culture to Technology*. New York: Knopf.

Ritzer, George. 1993. *The McDonaldization of Society*. Newbury Park, CA: Pine Forge Press.

Roszak, Theodore. 1969. *The Making of a Counter-Culture: Reflections on the Technocratic Society and Its Youthful Opposition*. New York: Doubleday.

Shames, Laurence. 1991. *The Hunger for More: Searching for Values in an Age of Greed*. New York: Random House.

Shibutani, Tamotsu. 1955. "Reference Groups as Perspectives." In *American Journal of Sociology*, 60:562–569.

Shibutani, Tamotsu. 1970. "On the Personification of Adversaries." In *Human Nature and Collective Behavior*. Ed. Tamotsu Shibutani. Upper Saddle River, NJ: Prentice Hall.

Simmel, Georg. 1902–1903. "Metropolis and Mental Life." In *The Sociology of Georg Simmel*. 1950 edn. Ed. Kurt Wolff. New York: Free Press.

Steinberg, Stephen. 1995. *Turning Back: The Retreat from Racial Justice in American Thought and Policy*. Boston: Beacon Press.

Sullivan, Maureen. 2004. *The Family of Woman: Lesbian Mothers, Their Children, and Undoing of Gender*. Berkeley, CA: University of California Press.

Sullivan, Oriel. 2006. *Changing Gender Relations, Changing Families: Tracing the Pace of Change Over Time*. New York: Rowman & Littlefield.

Sumner, William Graham. 1906. *Folkways*. 1940 edn. Boston: Ginn and Company.

Thomas, William I., and Florian Znaniecki. 1918. *The Polish Peasant in Europe and America*. 1958 edn. New York: Dover.

Tocqueville, Alexis de. 1840. *Democracy in America*. 1969 edn. New York: Doubleday.

Turnbull, Colin. 1972. *The Mountain People*. New York: Simon & Schuster.

Walker, Beverly M. (ed.). 1995. *Construction of Group Realities: Culture, Society, and Personal Construction Theory*. New York: Pareger.

White, Leslie A. 1940. *The Science of Culture*. New York: Farrar, Straus & Giroux.

White, Leslie A. 1959. *The Evolution of Culture*. New York: McGraw-Hill.

Whorf, Benjamin Lee. 1956. *Language, Thought, and Reality.* New York: John Wiley.

Wolfe, Alan. 1998. *One Nation, After All.* New York: Penguin Books.

Wuthnow, Robert. 1987. *Meaning and Moral Order: Explorations in Cultural Analysis.* Berkeley, CA: University of California Press.

Yinger, Milton J. 1982. *Countercultures: The Promise and Peril of a World Turned Upside Down.* New York: Free Press.

Young, Alfred A. 2004. *The Minds of Marginalized Black Men.* New Jersey: Princeton University Press.

Zborowski, M. 1953. "Cultural Components in Responses to Pain." In *Journal of Social Issues,* 8:16–31.

Zellner, William W. 1995. *Countercultures: A Sociological Analysis.* New York: St. Martin's Press.

William Gropper. (1897-1977) (c) Copyright "The Senate", (1935). Oil on canvas, 25⅛" × 33⅛" : *The Museum of Modern Art,*
New York. Gift of A. Conger Goodyear. (108.1936) Photograph © 1995. The Museum of Modern Art,
New York. Digital Image (c) The Museum of Modern Art/Lincensed by SCALA/Art Resource, NY.

✦ 7 ✦

Social Institutions

INSTITUTIONS ARE SOCIAL PATTERNS

A *social structure* is made up of a set of positions, all of which relate to one another. A *culture* is a reality that actors come to believe in organization. A *social institution* is a very important tradition in society—a type of action, interaction, role, or organization that is especially important in society. It is an established way something is done. It is highly valued—regarded as very important to most of us—and we feel obligated to defend it, even fight for it. We see it as representative of what we all are. It is an important part of our environment, the ways we expect our world to be. Most of us even regard it as the only good way for normal people to act. Alternatives are difficult to imagine.

What characterizes American society? What exists here that makes us unique in the world? What are the basic ways we do things? We have a public school system, a plurality of religions, large corporations, federalism, capitalism, child-centered families, the automobile, and the computer. These are some of our most important institutions, some of our most important traditions, the social patterns that most of us regard as central to our society. A visitor will notice how we do such things in our society, and he or she will be able to identify such characteristic patterns as central to American life. "This is what Americans do! These are their institutions!"

The term "institution" is used in many ways. It is sometimes used to refer to the several spheres of society: economy, religion, the military, and government, for example. It is sometimes used to refer to a specific organization with which we want to impress others: Moorhead State University, Fergus Falls Hospital, or the St. Cloud State Prison. Both ways of using this term are acceptable, but in this book, we use the term a third way: as a certain type of social pattern. It is a pattern that exists in a sphere: an economic institution, a religious institution, or a political institution, for example. It is a pattern on which organizations such as Moorhead State University are modeled: "the state university," for example.

SOCIAL INSTITUTIONS ARE THE MOST
CENTRAL GROOVES IN SOCIETY

Think of an institution as a groove, an important pattern in society that we learn to follow and accept, something that directs many of our actions. Remember that society, as well as any other organization, is people interacting and forming social patterns (including social institutions). My family is a group, a social organization; *the monogamous family* is an *American institution*. General Motors is a formal organization; *the large corporation* is an *American institution*. The University of Arizona is a formal organization or perhaps a community; *the university* is an *American institution*, *the public university* is an *American institution*, and *the state university* is an *American institution*. These institutions are the various grooves in our society; they are influential in the types of organization we develop and actions we all take.

I sometimes like to think of dripping water or flowing rivers as having something to do with institutions. As water drips on the same spot continuously over a long period, or as water flows down mountains for a very long time, a groove is created and established; that groove becomes the guide for future drips and rains. Institutions are actions we perform in society over several generations; gradually, they catch on and establish themselves. Eventually, most of us simply accept them as the right and proper ways to live in this society. In fact, normally these grooves are defended by our culture, and all types of justifications are developed to explain the reason for their being.

INSTITUTIONS ARE THE CENTRAL WAYS A SOCIETY
FUNCTIONS AND SOLVES ITS ONGOING PROBLEMS

Institutions are the established, traditional, habitual, legitimate ways a society carries out its business. Something becomes an institution to the extent that it is central to society. Every society has a political system, but what are the institutions that characterize our particular political system? We have "separation of powers" between executive, legislative, and judicial branches. We have "federalism," the "two-party system," "a constitutional system," "voting," and "a federal income tax." The "presidency," the "Congress," and "the Supreme Court" are so important to us that they too are institutions. We have no kings or dictators, we do not welcome military control of foreign policy, nor do we have a tradition of rulers who come to power through *coup d'etats*.

Institutions are normally regarded by those in society as central to that society's continuation. Although there are always alternatives to institutions, we do not seriously consider using them.

It is useful to regard institutions as patterns designed to deal with the ongoing problems that face any society. All societies face problems of defense, producing goods and feeding the people, housing the population, making life secure, establishing order, socializing the young, keeping people loyal and satisfied, and protecting their own patterns (structure, culture, and institutions). Institutions are patterns developed in a society to deal with such problems, thus helping ensure the continuation of society. For example:

- Every society develops kinship institutions to socialize the young, to regulate sexual relationships, and to place individuals into social structure.

- Most societies develop judicial and police institutions to help maintain peace between actors, protect property, and settle disputes.
- Every society develops economic institutions to coordinate economic activities, encourage work, produce and distribute goods, and even maintain the inequality among classes in society.

Actually, institutions (1) serve most people's interests by preventing chaos, meeting personal needs, and cooperatively dealing with common problems, and (2) they are the instruments of the most powerful who use them to protect their own positions in society. We should be able to understand the collapse of the former Soviet Union and the Eastern European communist nations in large part because the institutions developed over the years no longer worked. Problems were not dealt with effectively. Corruption, inefficiency, reliance on force, and super government were all unable to deal with increasingly serious problems. Chaos reigned, people went without food and shelter, and those in power did not serve others, nor were they able to protect their positions. Indeed, in our own society, we seem to be questioning our own institutions as inadequate ways of dealing with serious problems associated with poverty, retirement, health care, violence, ignorance, crime, work, meaning, and family. Institutions are there to make sure that society functions (for everyone, not only for the wealthy and powerful); if they do not, they must change or the problems will become even more serious.

INSTITUTIONS ARE WIDELY ACCEPTED AND DEEPLY ENTRENCHED

We sometimes use the term "institutionalized" when we describe a pattern that has been around for any length of time. To become institutionalized means that the pattern has become formalized and deeply entrenched in organization. That is what an institution means: *a type of action, role, interaction, or organization that has become widely accepted and appears to be a natural pattern in society.* An institution seems the only sensible way for us to do something. "Of course we don't have kings." "Of course our parents do not decide whom we marry." "Of course we must give grades in college." "Of course we have checking accounts and credit cards." Institutions regulate people's behavior by determining courses of action for them that they follow without seriously considering alternatives. Most animals are governed by instincts; humans are governed by institutions.

Marriage is an institution. People do not have to get married—but in our society, that has been the accepted, legitimate, right, moral, even healthy way people are supposed to live. Even today, it is a widely followed institution; it is a central tradition, and alternatives are still considered less than desirable by most people. Cultural ideas embedded in religion have taught us that marriage is moral (indeed, a moral obligation in some religions), that it will bring happiness and meaning to our lives, and that it is the only moral way to have sex. Government used to encourage marriage by making sure that children born out of wedlock would be labeled as illegitimate, and governments encourage marriage through tax laws. Novels, magazines, movies, radio, and television have encouraged us to regard marriage between man and woman as central to what life is all about. In the past, most of us came to believe that women who did not marry could not live worthwhile lives and that they would become "old maids." Men were expected to marry if they were to rise in the corporate structure, and we believed children could be happy and secure only within a family where parents were married. Institutions change, of course, as do what we learn from culture. However, marriage remains an important institution in society, and it is still legitimated, protected, and accepted.

Marriage, like other institutions, has become part of our taken-for-granted world. We are taught to believe that "everyone does it this way," when indeed it is only because of shared agreement through interaction over time that people have come to adopt this particular alternative. Nothing in society really has to be the way it is. It only seems that way to those of us who are used to it and who have been taught to accept it.

Segregation, for example, has been an important institution in our society. It governs our schools, neighborhoods, businesses, and even religion. For a long time, it governed even more than these things, such as where people ate, played, swam, washed, walked, and even used the bathroom. For some people in society, segregation is still the way to deal with ongoing problems. It is, for some, a way of keeping nonwhites or other minorities from competing and living with the "rest of us," a way of "protecting our neighborhoods," and a way of maintaining a certain lifestyle. Indeed, segregation has helped create many of our most serious problems and is contrary to the basic principles of democracy. For much of our history, however, it has functioned as an important American institution. The famous author James Baldwin wrote a letter to his nephew concerning segregation in our society, and in it he successfully captured how institutions become embedded in all of our lives:

> Try to imagine how you would feel if you woke up one morning to find the sun shining and all the stars aflame. You would be frightened because it is out of the order of nature. Any upheaval in the universe is terrifying because it so profoundly attacks one's sense of one's reality. Well, the black man has functioned in the white man's world as a fixed star, as an immovable pillar: and as he moves out of his place heaven and earth are shaken to their foundations. . . .
>
> (1963, 23)

When an institution such as segregation begins to crumble, many people find their taken-for-granted world shaken. When the legal basis for segregation was eventually challenged, many fought hard to protect it. When segregated schools and lunch counters were challenged, many cried out that democracy itself was finally ending. When busing students to achieve integrated schools was instituted in various communities, and where organizations were forced to institute affirmative action procedures, many argued that real justice was on the way out. We are all used to institutions, and the institution of segregation is no exception. People fight to maintain what they are used to, and it is very difficult for them to understand that other ways of doing things may be more legitimate, rational, democratic, or humane. Institutions are like "fixed stars," or "immovable pillars."

When a pattern has become an institution, it seems important and right. Normally we regard it as central to our way of life, important for the continuation of our society. What would our society be without television, soap operas, Academy Awards, professional football, baseball, movies, and Google? These are some of the patterns we call *institutions*.

SOCIAL INSTITUTIONS ARE REAL FORCES
WORKING ON ACTORS

Institutions normally take a long time to develop. They are anchored in history. This gives them permanence, stability, general acceptance, and importance.

We should recognize that institutions are real forces that work on the individual even if the individual is not aware of them. Institutions exist just as physical things exist. Like structure and culture, institutions take on a life of their own. They exist apart from our consciousness. They influence and control us, often without our being aware of their power. An institution, Peter Berger and Thomas Luckmann write, normally comes into existence before we are born, and it will normally be there after we are dead. We die; it lives. Institutions cannot be wished away, and they resist our "attempts to change or evade them." They force us to act in certain ways, Berger and Luckmann continue, because we accept that which is there, and because, if we do not, we will be subject to "control mechanisms" that force our acceptance (1966, 60).

Like structure and culture, institutions arise as people interact over time. When people first encounter each other, they may say to themselves, "What is he doing, anyway?" Over time, the other actor's repeated action leads the individual to say, "There he goes again." Actions become institutions when new parties enter the relationship, and they must learn the established patterns. Things change dramatically. The pattern has a historical basis, developed by actors in the past, handed down in the present to new persons. What might have been simply something we all did becomes a very serious matter when a new person enters the organization. This makes the institution a thing in itself, an objective fact that confronts new actors in organization. Once institutions exist, people will say to themselves and to each other, "This is how things are done around here." They must either accept it or suffer the consequences (Berger and Luckmann, 1966, 58).

Institutions receive their objective character through time. Although all organizations may have them, institutions are most evident in societies, the most historical of all social organization. Yet all organizations develop institutions. My introductory class depends on six exams per quarter, my family depends on eating together once a week and going on vacation together in the summer, my friends and I go on a fishing trip once every season, my university has an opening-week convocation, and the university across the cemetery used to require freshmen to wear beanies until their football team scored a touchdown. These are all institutions that are part of various social organizations. They are real, and if we are part of these organizations, we must reckon with the established institutions.

> The institutions are *there*, external to him [or her], persistent in their reality. . . . They have coercive power over him [or her], both in themselves, by the sheer force of their facticity, and through the control mechanisms that are usually attached to the most important of them. . . .
>
> (Berger and Luckmann, 1966, 58)

THE MEANING OF INSTITUTIONS: A SUMMARY

Institutions are types of action patterns in society that people regard as important for solving ongoing social problems. They are the most important grooves that exist in society, the various ways we have historically decided to do things. They are accepted as part of the natural order of things; they are patterns that influence individuals in society. They exist as objective reality, impacting the lives of all of us. They are difficult to go against; their relative permanence makes them difficult to change. Yet, they do change over time, and they must change when they no longer deal adequately with the problems of society. Rapid change makes it difficult to identify what is and is not an institution. In the twenty-first century, it is difficult to identify whether the housewife role still dominates, the career woman, the single woman, the liberated woman, or if there is no typical institution at all related to the role of women in our society ("increasing choice of role" or "deinstitutionalized role").

A good way to understand the meaning of an institution is to imagine it existing on one side of a continuum (see Figure 7-1). We should think of a certain type of action, organization, or interaction as *more* or *less* an institution. Some will be very much an institution; some will not be an institution at all; most will fall somewhere between these two extremes. On one side of the continuum is the full-blown institution; on the other is a developing or a dying social pattern, not really an institution.

Perhaps heterosexuality is a pattern of action that comes close to meeting the criteria fully. It is important to the way this society tends to function; it is a solution to ongoing problems in society (mate selection, having sex, courtship, family); it is widely accepted as right, important, and even natural; and it has a long-established history of acceptance that influences every actor. The negative emotional reaction toward homosexuality and same-sex marriage seems to highlight the fact that lots of people regard heterosexuality as an institution to be protected. As more people in

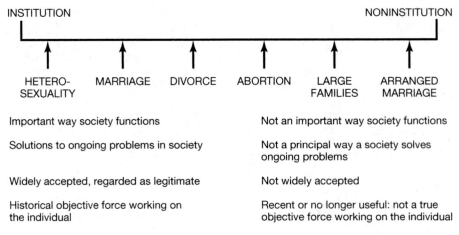

FIGURE 7-1   A Continuum of an Institution

society question the idea that only heterosexuality is legitimate, the institutional status of heterosexualilty will become tenuous.

The corporation and the secular state are also good examples of American institutions. Television has increasingly become a major institution during the past 60 years. It has become the way we get our news, entertainment, knowledge about the latest goods and fashion, and even formal adult education. The computer has become central to the way we live, and the family farm is no longer the institution it once was in our society. There are important battles going on over what institutions will dominate our family life; although the housewife role was once a prevalent institution, it no longer dominates the society. One of the most important divisive conflicts in our time is over the issue of abortion: Will abortion be established as an institution in our society?

Visitors to the United States are probably more sensitive than we are concerning what are and are not institutions here. They will immediately see patterns that are different from their own society. For example, we rely much more heavily on the automobile than almost any other people do; it is an institution that we take for granted, and one that any visitor will immediately notice. Separation of church and state might appear strange to an outsider who comes from a society with a state religion. Sometimes an institution, such as the fast-food industry or ATM cards, will develop in the United States and spread to other societies.

Sometimes there is conflict between institutions and our cultural beliefs. For a long time, our belief system has emphasized the central importance of small business, when in fact our society has created the largest corporate enterprises the world has ever known. "The independent small businessman is firmly rooted in the American imagination. His misfortune is that he is much less firmly rooted in the American economy" (Starr, 1982, 420). The myth of the small entrepreneur has remained a vital part of American culture—in people's hopes, in the study of economics, and in sociology. Starr traces the history of American medicine and shows how this profession has successfully fought the corporate trend for many years and how it has been the "heroic exception that sustained the waning tradition of independent professionalism" (Starr, 1982, 420). This is now ending—medicine has finally become part of corporate America. As the independent professional has become integrated into a corporate health care business, the culture that has been so long a part of the medical community has also begun to change.

> Everywhere one sees the growth of a kind of marketing mentality in health care. And, indeed, business school graduates are displacing graduates of public health schools, hospital administrators, and even doctors in the top echelons of medical care organizations. The organizational culture of medicine used to be dominated by the ideals of professionalism and voluntarism, which softened the underlying acquisitive activity. The restraint exercised by those ideals now grows weaker. The "health center" of one era is the "profit center" of the next.
>
> (1982, 448)

It is not the state that has taken over the profession of medicine; we do not have socialized health care. American medicine rapidly has become corporate.

INSTITUTIONS ARE IMPORTANT

Institutions are like social structure and culture. They are social patterns we learn, generally accept, and use to guide our decisions. They are the right ways we do things in this society. They are the grooves that tell us how to raise our children, spend our leisure time, participate in government, and deal with death. From the standpoint of the individual, institutions are controls.

From the standpoint of society, institutions exist to ensure that problems are successfully dealt with. Institutions are the ways society ensures cooperation and order. They are the means by which people are socialized to accept society's social patterns. They protect us, help give our lives meaning, settle disputes, and provide the basic necessities for those who live here.

We might better understand the importance of institutions by listing some of the reasons they are important to us.

First of all, *institutions deal with the problems that make it possible for people to live together in society.* Without institutions, nothing could be done cooperatively. If institutions are ineffective, things get done badly. If they are effective, things are done well, basic needs are met, and people are generally satisfied.

Second, *institutions, because they are grooves we see operating all around us, ensure enough uniformity in action among individuals so that cooperation is made possible.* They take away choice because they are the grooves that direct individuals' actions. Although society thrives to some extent on human differences, institutions cause us to travel in the same directions, at least to some extent. We know what people generally do in this society, and most of us do it. Peter Berger describes institutions as "imperatives," ordering what we do, narrowing choices. Marriage, for example, tells the individual that, in this society, this is the course of action that awaits him or her. It somehow does not seem so bad to most of us because institutions become the grooves we follow without our even knowing what is happening most of the time.

Finally, *many of the institutions are designed specifically to socialize, reward, and punish the individual to help ensure conformity to the social patterns of society.* As we saw in Chapter 3, socialization is the process by which the individual adopts the ways of a given society. These ways are internalized. It is through various institutions set up in society over a long period of time that socialization is accomplished. Religious and political institutions are developed to socialize us. The media—from advertisements to soap operas to sitcoms to MTV—socialize us. Our families, of course, are the most important institution for us in our early years, but the public schools pick up later and assume the job of introducing us to the rules of the larger society.

Of course, religious, economic, educational, and familial institutions reward us if we conform; courts, jails, and prisons are established to punish us if we do not. Every society has its own ways to deal with individuals to create "good citizens."

The bottom line is that human beings live their lives in society. To control individuals, institutions must function effectively. People cannot do whatever they feel like or choose to do; complete freedom is impossible if society is to exist. People cannot act without some direction instituted by society. Social institutions are central to that direction.

INSTITUTIONALIZATION AND DEINSTITUTIONALIZATION

Modernization means rapid change in society, and institutions embedded in the past are increasingly pressured to alter their ways or move over for new ways of doing things. For many of us, society's long-established institutions are not the grooves they once were; alternatives are increasingly springing up, and the media publicize them. The way we elect our leaders, the way we educate our young, the way we deal with crime and health care are continuously under scrutiny and are rarely simply accepted. In some areas such as kinship, we are experiencing "deinstitutionalization" to the point that there are choices to be made by each individual at every turn, rather than one established path for all people to follow.

The terms *institutionalization* and *deinstitutionalization* are useful for describing the developing patterns in society. As a pattern becomes widely accepted, is seen as morally right, becomes embedded and set, and is considered important for the society and individuals, we say it is "becoming institutionalized" or that it is "becoming an institution." When it ceases to be important or dominant or the only alternative, either another pattern replaces it or that area of life becomes deinstitutionalized, without any dominant single way of doing something. For example, the less marriage becomes the only way for people to live their adult lives in society, the more we can state that family and sex are areas of life that are becoming less institutionalized and that the individual has many options in these areas. Deinstitutionalization may be good. It increases choice, it offers more alternative ways, and it does not command obedience and sameness among the population. It also causes many of us problems: less certainty about what to do with our lives, less agreement and cooperation among people, and less certainty about what is and is not right and proper. Deinstitutionalization, like all else in social organization, is a complex matter with both benefits and costs.

THE REJECTION OF SOCIAL INSTITUTIONS

Not all communities, formal organizations, groups, and dyads accept society's institutions, and many that develop their own alternative patterns come into conflict with the larger society. These may be political radicals, minorities, young people, or individuals seeking a culture different from what American society offers, such as artists, students, the religiously committed, and some who want to maintain their ethnic group heritage. Sometimes, groups who seek alternative patterns are ignored, but more often those who support the institution see them as a challenge, and these groups are discouraged or even outlawed. Protecting institutions is almost always seen as a serious endeavor. Those who organize to legitimate homosexuality will usually have to overcome government, religion, schools, and the media.

Another example of alternative societal institutions by communities might be in very oppressed neighborhoods, where the institutions might be alternatives such as crime, violence, and gangs. In certain right-wing militia groups, legitimate actions necessary for goals often include secrecy, racial oppression, anti-federal government, tax evasion, and threatening and using violence. To some groups, violence against police in communities is acceptable, but to those in the larger society, such acts are clearly illegitimate. Also, several groups and neighborhoods continue to use Spanish as a language; historically, most Americans would claim that this is an attack on our traditional institution, the use of English.

Some alternative patterns of behavior are therefore regarded as harmless, while others are defined as serious threats to the dominant institutions. Who decides what behavior is harmless and what must be discouraged or dealt with as serious challenges to the social order? Those who have high positions also have the power to define what is an institution, what is an acceptable alternative, and what is a threat. Sometimes, "the people" may speak through elections or by other indirect means, and they may decide, for example, that homosexuals should still be treated by authorities as illegitimate; sometimes, an election can defeat a politician who attempts to institutionalize abortion; in the long run, however, institutions are determined by those who have power in society through either their positions or through the groups or formal organizations that have resources such as money or efficient organization to achieve their will.

SUMMARY

People interact and become organized. They develop social patterns. Social structure and culture are social patterns that inevitably arise. Over time, social institutions also arise. Social structure positions us and gives us role, identity, perspective, power, privilege, and prestige in relation to others. Culture tells us what we should believe; it gives us our truths, values, goals, and rules. Social institutions direct what we do in society: They are the grooves we are exposed to, the ways we are told our society works. Social institutions are the widely accepted, legitimate, historical, important ways that people like us are supposed to follow.

Two final points need to be stressed for a more complete understanding of institutions:

1. The conflict perspective in sociology reminds us that culture and institutions not only work to keep society together, they also work to maintain the social structure. Indeed, the culture and institutions that develop are, to a great extent, the products of those who are powerful in the social structure. To a great extent it was male power in society that encouraged the housewife role, female passivity, male dominance of the corporation, and the double standard that is still used to judge sexual behavior. It is mostly white Anglos who wish to keep English as an institution, and it is insurance companies that maintain private health insurance as an institution. Institutions, like culture, should be understood in part as products of those who have over time successfully used their power to develop and protect certain legitimate ways of doing things.
2. Institutions are really limits over individual choice. In general, they are grooves for all of us to follow. All societies need institutions. However, what then is a democratic society supposed to be? Probably, the answer is free choice as an important value in society's culture, and thus a view of institutions as alternatives we have developed historically rather than sacred alternatives, and therefore open for critical evaluation.

QUESTIONS TO CONSIDER

1. One of the ways to understand the nature of institutions is to begin by listing some of the ongoing problems any society must deal with to continue. What are these? Describe the various American institutions that try to deal with these problems.
2. What are the most important institutions in American life? You might try to divide them into political, economic, educational, kinship, criminal justice, and entertainment institutions.
3. Are there any institutions that have changed dramatically in your own lifetime? Why is it so difficult for people to accept change in their institutions?

REFERENCES

Baldwin, James. 1963. *The Fire Next Time*. New York: Dial Press.
Berger, Peter L., and Thomas Luckmann. 1966. *The Social Construction of Reality*. Garden City, NY: Doubleday.
Starr, Paul. 1982. *The Social Transformation of American Medicine*. New York: Basic Books.

RECOMMENDED READING

The following works are introductions to institutions in general or works aimed at describing or criticizing specific institutions.

Aberle, D. F., A. K. Cohen, A. K. Davis, M. J. Levy, Jr., and F. X. Sutton. 1950. "The Functional Prerequisites of a Society." In *Ethics*, 60:100–111.
Altbach, Philip G., Robert O. Berdahl, and Patricia J. Gumport. 1999. *American Higher Education in the Twenty-first Century*. Baltimore: Johns Hopkins University Press.
Anderson, Elijah. 1999. *Code of the Street: Decency, Violence, and the Moral Life of the Inner City*. New York: W.W. Norton & Company.
Ballantine, Jeanne H. 1989. *The Sociology of Education*. 2nd edn. Upper Saddle River, NJ: Prentice Hall.
Barton, Bernadette. 2006. *Stripped: Inside the Lives of Exotic Dancers*. New York: New York University Press.
Blumberg, Paul. 1981. *Inequality in an Age of Decline*. New York: Oxford University Press.
Borchard, Kurt. 2005. *The Word on the Street: Homeless Men in Las Vegas*. Reno, NV: University of Nevada Press.
Bowles, Samuel, and Herbert Gintis. 1976. *Schooling and Capitalist America*. New York: Basic Books.
Collins, Randall. 1979. *The Credential Society: An Historical Sociology of Education and Stratification*. New York: Academic Press.
Cookson, P. W., and C. H. Persell. 1985. *Preparing for Power: America's Elite Boarding Schools*. New York: Basic Books.
Coser, Lewis, and Rose Coser. 1974. *Greedy Institutions*. New York: Free Press.
Danziger, Sheldon, and Ann Chih Lin (ed.). 2000. *Coping with Poverty: The Social Contexts of Neighborhood, Work, and Family in the African-American Community*. Ann Arbor: University of Michigan Press.
DeParle, Jason. 2004. *American Dream: Three Women, Ten Kids, and a Nation's Drive to End Welfare*. New York: Penguin Books.
Edin, Kathryn, and Maria Kefalas. 2005. *Promises I Can Keep: Why Poor Women Put Motherhood Before Marriage*. Berkeley, CA: University of California Press.
Ehrenreich, Barbara. 2006. *Bait and Switch: The (Futile) Pursuit of the American Dream*. New York: Metropolitan Books.

Eitzen, D. Stanley. 2001. *Sport in Contemporary Society: An Anthology.* 6th edn. New York: Worth Publishers.

Eshleman, J. Ross. 1999. *The Family: An Introduction.* 9th edn. Needham Heights, MA: Allyn & Bacon.

Ewen, Stuart. 1976. *Captains of Consciousness.* New York: McGraw-Hill.

Feagin, Joe R. 1975. *Subordinating the Poor: Welfare and American Beliefs.* Upper Saddle River, NJ: Prentice Hall.

Fine, Gary Alan. 1987. *With the Boys: Little League Baseball and Preadolescent Culture.* Chicago: University of Chicago Press.

Galbraith, John Kenneth. 1979. *The New Industrial State.* 3rd edn. New York: New American Library.

Gans, Herbert J. 1995. *The War Against the Poor.* New York: Basic Books.

Goffman, Erving. 1961. *Asylums: Essays on the Social Situation of Mental Patients and Other Inmates.* New York: Doubleday (Anchor).

Hancock, Angie-Marie. 2004. *The Politics of Disgust: The Public Identity if the Welfare Queen.* New York: New York University Press.

Kanter, Rosabeth. 1977. *Men and Women of the Corporation.* New York: Basic Books.

Kosmin, Barry A., and Seymour P. Latchman. 1993. *One Nation Under God: Religion in Contemporary American Society.* New York: Harmony Books.

Kozol, Jonathan. 1991. *Savage Inequalities.* New York: Crown Publishers.

Lichtenstein, Nelson. 2006. *Wal-Mart: The Face of Twenty-First Century Capitalism.* New Press.

Lorber, Judith. 2005. *Breaking the Bowls: Degendering and Feminist Change.* New York: Norton.

Manning, Christel J. 1999. *God Gave Us the Right: Conservative Catholic, Evangelical Protestant, and Orthodox Jewish Women Grapple with Feminism.* New Brunswick, NJ: Rutgers University Press.

Marchevsky, Alejandra, and Jeanne Theoharis. *Not Working: Latina Immigrants, Low-Wage Jobs, and the Failure of Welfare Reform.* New York: New York University Press.

Mills, C. Wright. 1956. *The Power Elite.* New York: Oxford University Press.

Murphy, John W., and Dennis L. Peck. 1993. *Open Institutions: The Hope for Democracy.* Westport, CT: Praeger.

Piven, Frances Fox, and Richard A. Cloward. 1993. *Regulating of the Poor: The Functions of Public Welfare.* 2nd edn. New York: Vintage Books.

Postman, Neil. 1992. *Technopoly: The Surrender of Culture to Technology.* New York: Knopf.

Ritzer, George. 1993. *The McDonaldization of Society.* Newbury Park, CA: Pine Forge Press.

Rose, Peter I. (ed.). 1979. *Socialization and the Life Cycle.* New York: St. Martin's Press.

Scanzoni, Letha Dawson, and John Scanzoni. 1988. *Men, Women, and Change.* 3rd edn. New York: McGraw-Hill.

Sewell, W. H., R. M. Hauser, and D. L. Featherman. 1976. *Schooling and Achievement in American Society.* New York: Academic Press.

Shils, Edward S., and Morris Janowitz. 1948. "Cohesion and Disintegration in the Wehrmacht in World War II." In *Public Opinion Quarterly,* 12:280–294.

Silberman, Charles E. 1980. *Criminal Violence, Criminal Justice.* New York: Vintage.

Skolnick, Arlene, and Jerome Skolnick. 1986. *Family in Transition.* 5th edn. Boston: Little, Brown.

Stacey, Judith. 1996. *In the Name of the Family: Rethinking Family Values in the Postmodern Age.* Boston: Beacon Press.

Steinberg, Stephen. 1995. *Turning Back: The Retreat from Racial Justice in American Thought and Policy.* Boston: Beacon Press.

Straus, Murray A., Richard J. Gelles, and Suzanne K. Steinmetz. 1988. *Behind Closed Doors: Violence in the American Family.* New York: Doubleday.

Sumner, William Graham. 1906. *Folkways.* 1940 edn. Boston: Ginn & Company.

Venkatesh, Sudhir Alladi. 2006. *Off the Books: The Underground Economy of the Urban Poor.* Cambridge Mass.: Harvard University Press.

Weitzman, Lenore J. 1985. *The Divorce Revolution: The Unexpected Social and Economic Consequences for Women and Children in America.* New York: Free Press.

Wilson, Bryan. 1982. *Religion in Sociological Perspective.* New York: Oxford University Press.

Wilson, William J. 1987. *The Truly Disadvantaged: The Inner City, the Underclass, and Public Policy.* Chicago: University of Chicago Press.

Paul Citroen, Dutch (1929–1935). Metropolis, 1923. Collage of prints, photographs, and postcards, 30" × 23". *Prentenkabinet der Rijksuniversiteit Leiden, Netherlands.*

✦ 8 ✦

Organizations, Societies, and Globalization

So far in this discussion, we have focused on three patterns of social organization: social structure, culture, and institutions. *Social structure* means that people come to do things in relation to each other based on their positions. Culture means that people come to agree on matters of what is true, what things are worth working for, and which behavioral patterns are proper and right. An *institution* means an action pattern in society that has developed to deal with society's ongoing problems, a groove we accept as right and true.

Social patterns are not nearly as separate as has been presented thus far. We have divided them into structure, culture, and institutions to understand them better. It is sometimes difficult to identify whether a given pattern is part of structure, culture, or the institutional system. There is considerable overlap, and part of the reason for this is that social patterns influence and usually support one another. Social structure impacts institutions and culture because those at the top of the structure have the most to gain by developing, teaching, and protecting the prevailing institutions and culture. Culture normally justifies the institutions and structure, and institutions generally work to support the structure and culture.

Together, social structure, culture, and institutions are important to what individuals do. They play a part in almost everything. Individuals should be understood as located in structure, doing things in relation to that location, and guiding their actions and thinking along the lines of the cultural truths, values, goals, norms, and institutions.

SOCIAL ORGANIZATIONS INFLUENCE EACH OTHER

An organization never develops in a vacuum; it must be understood in relation to all other organizations, and this makes analysis difficult. In a real sense, we can identify each organization within a larger organizational structure, in a "position" with more or less power, privilege, and prestige than the others, becoming part of a relationship with the others, and taking on a role, an identity, and even a perspective.

An easy way to understand this is to look at American corporations. On close examination, we find a structure among corporations, with certain financial giants such as Morgan Trust playing the dominant role; others such as IBM, 3M, CBS, General Motors, and Merck fill less dominant but very powerful positions; still others such as Apple, JCPenney's, and LLBean fill less powerful positions in the corporate world. We can identify structure among automobile companies, oil companies, and computer and steel companies. There is even a complex structure among automobile, oil, and steel companies together. Sociologists have documented the extensive control by some financial organizations over other large corporations, the overlapping boards of directors of organizations that reveal underlying ties, and the role of merger and conglomeration in the business world.

Educational organizations have positions in relation to each other, as well. Some, such as Harvard, have more power, privilege, prestige, and have a definite role, identity, and perspective within the academic world. Of course, a university like Harvard will also have a position in the world of business, turning out people with degrees to fill positions in corporations, perhaps influencing those corporations, but also being heavily influenced by the corporations to turn out the "right kind of people." The ties with government are also evident.

There is structure among athletic teams, churches, gangs, and departments in colleges. There is a world structure consisting of societies, with each society coming to fill a position in the world system.

Structure, then, should be understood broadly. Not only does it include relations among individuals, it also includes relations among social organizations.

We can also see culture and institutions emerging among social organizations as individuals from each interact and come to share beliefs, values, norms, goals, and ways of handling ongoing problems. As people move from organization to organization, similarity is encouraged, a culture is developed and reinforced, and common institutions emerge. A common culture emerges among colleges, fashion designers, manufacturers, and communities as interaction takes place between leaders and members of these various organizations.

Societies, too, become increasingly similar through interaction. Simple agricultural societies, for example, become industrialized and urbanized as they are drawn into the world community.

Every organization must be understood, then, in the context of its social environment—other organizations occupying positions and sharing culture and institutions in interaction. Figure 8-1 illustrates this mutual influence. The problem of the sociologist is to understand the nature of these relationships. Within the automobile industry, there is interaction and an emerging social structure, with Toyota, Honda, and General Motors dominating. Ford and Chrysler compete in order to try to keep their position, which has become less dominant. All buy and sell European automobile giants. Each company has a position in the industry, with power, prestige, and privilege. Over time, all within the industry are influenced to share a worldwide market. Chinese and Korean corporations increasingly position themselves in the structure of automobile corporations. They compete, trying to win a bigger share of the worldwide market. They watch what other corporations do, and they adjust their strategies. Together, they share a culture of consumerism and present to the general public a view of speed, safety, labor unions, taxes, style, American capitalism, competition, and credit. Together, they try to influence Congress, courts, and the other corporations outside of the automobile business, such as steel and oil. In their hiring practices, they

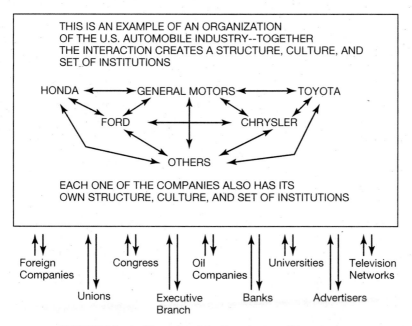

FIGURE 8-1 An Illustration of the Organization of Organizations

communicate to the universities for the kinds of people needed to fill the industry; in their advertising campaigns, they influence what television, radio, magazines, and newspapers deliver. Of course, they are never all powerful. Television, banking practices, and decisions made by oil companies will have great impact on the automobile industry, also. To understand any single organization, one must always understand interaction, structure, culture, and institutions among other organizations.

SOCIETY IN THE WORLD ORDER

We increasingly live in a world system in which travel, instant communication, trade, colonialization, wars, and emigration create a worldwide social structure, culture, and emerging institutions. Societies are not able to isolate themselves, they are influenced by others and they influence others. The multinational corporation facilitates this process. Labor, management, owners, and buyers in a corporation are no longer confined to a single society. The laborers in China, the owners in New York, the managers in both Hong Kong and New York, and the customers in Africa all make up the modern corporate world.

Karl Marx: A Future Worldwide Capitalist Order

In the nineteenth century, Karl Marx described a theory of society that has had a great deal of influence in the twentieth century. He believed that the key to understanding society is economics, the rise of capitalism was the most important development in nineteenth-century societies, the twentieth century will experience a worldwide revolution, and the future will belong not to nations or societies, but a worldwide society he called communism. To Marx communism meant peace, freedom, and equality, dominated by the workers of the world.

There is a lot to criticize Marx for—many of his predictions, his view of history, and the attempts by builders of communism ended up very differently than he desired. However, he saw something very important in the future. Capitalism will create a world order, a world where societies and nations will be dominated by larger and more powerful businesses. Giant businesses with very wealthy owners will truly dominate the world. He argued that the purpose of capitalism is ultimately to create profit to the owners of businesses. Profit depends on low cost and high sales. Low cost will mean the capitalist will be driven to find the very cheapest labor and will be driven to open more and more markets. Marx realized that in the future this meant a world capitalist economy. Once wages are high in one society, capitalists will go to other societies; once production of goods increases, more consumers will be found in other societies. In the end, instead of societies there will be large businesses with one worldwide structure, culture, and institutions. Those who own the businesses shall control the world, and nations and societies will no longer be important. Marx believed that this system could not last, and it ultimately be overthrown by the workers of the world.

Not too many sociologists or other academics believe that Marx was correct. World revolution is not very probable; there is little to believe that a worldwide system would eventually create freedom, equality, and a wonderful human being. Moreover, nations and societies continue to exist in the world. However, his view of the world's economic order is certainly coming to fruition. Cheap labor, worldwide trade, and new markets have become what we now call economic globalization, with an increasingly global society, developing its own structure, culture, and institutions.

Immanuel Wallerstein: Core Societies, Semi-Peripheral Societies, and Peripheral Societies

In 1974 Immanuel Wallerstein wrote a fascinating book concerning a worldwide social order. In later works he updated some of his research, but his basic outline is very valuable for understanding the relationship between societies in the world.

Wallerstein wrote that there is a worldwide social structure, with some societies having much more power, privilege, and prestige than others. By 1900, the world became both highly interdependent and dominated by Europe and the United States. The rest of much of the world was a source of inexpensive labor, raw materials, and agriculture. All societies changed as a result, but the poorer societies were changed to suit the needs of the more powerful societies. The powerful societies Wallerstein calls the "core societies," the "center" of world power in 1900; the poorer societies he calls "peripheral."

Since 1900 the structure of the world has changed, but there are still core societies and peripheral ones. The former Soviet Union became a core society with its control over Eastern Europe after World War II. Japan's rise to economic power also made it a core society as it industrialized. Great Britain became less of a core society after World War II, and the United States continued to be a core society, although its place as a core had to eventually compete with other nation-states such as China, India, and the European Union. Some countries, such as Brazil and China, are neither core nor peripheral societies (Wallerstein calls them semi-peripheral). The demise of the Soviet Union, and its loss of core status, resulted in a number semi-peripheral nations. Many societies, once outright colonies of the West, have learned from the West and, after gaining political independence, have tried to become economically independent—with mixed success. For some societies, the dependence on the West has been impossible to break (parts of Latin America, much of Africa, Middle East, and some societies in South Asia, for example).

The future of societies depends more and more on the important relations between societies. Globablization of trade constantly shifts the balance of power between societies. The power of the United States as a core society may well decline as competitors from China, India, and the European Union continue to take their place among core nation-states.

While Marx saw a world order where nations no longer existed and wealthy capitalists would rule, Wallerstein sees another type of world order where nations—core nations—will continue their domination of other nations—peripheral and semi-peripheral nations. Both Marx and Wallerstein focus on a world order, dependent on an economic power structure.

GLOBALIZATION IN THE TWENTY-FIRST CENTURY: ECONOMIC, POLITICAL, AND CULTURAL

The Meaning of Globalization

"The world is flat!" so proclaimed Thomas L. Friedman in his national bestseller *The World is Flat: A Brief History of the Twenty-First Century.* The world has become global not because of national or corporate unity but because of technology that has revolutionized communication, industrialization, marketing, information, and efficient business practices. This revolution makes opportunity "flat," that is, much more equal for individuals and businesses to be creative and successful.

This "flattening" of the world is a result of what he calls "Globalization 3.0," where, unlike previous globalizations, ostensibly 1.0 and 2.0, that saw countries and corporations, respectively, driving global connectivity, it "is the newfound power for individuals to collaborate and compete globally" that is now the main characteristic of twenty-first century globalization (Friedman, 2005, 10).

Friedman outlines several "flatteners" that have made modern globalization so pervasive. It began with the fall of the Berlin Wall on November 9, 1989, which precipitated the collapse of Soviet communism, effectively ending the Cold War and opening a once closed sector of the world to global capitalism and modern individualism. The emergence of Netscape, the first popular browser to surf the World Wide Web that could be used with any computer platform, was the second flattener. What he calls Work Flow Software, which could now connect all divisions within a corporation, from the sales and marketing departments to the inventory and billing sections, made corporate communication instantaneous and more efficient.

Other flatteners facilitated communication and trade among individuals and corporations. Open-source software encouraged scientists all over the world to collaborate in order to solve complex problems. Outsourcing allowed for technical expertise among societies. Off-shoring encouraged companies to relocate their manufacturing in other societies with cheap labor. Technological developments in supplying, shipping, and warehousing brought highly efficient worldwide trade. Any individual using a computer can access the largest knowledge base available all over the world instantaneously through the search engine. Finally, iPhones, laptops connected to the Internet, cellular phones, PDAs, and the like support instant communication all over the world.

Friedman gives us many of the technological reasons that individuals, businesses, and individuals are able to interact and form a global society. He applauds the flattening—the equalizing of opportunities—for more people to succeed in the world's economy than ever before.

However, globalization in the twenty-first century has become much more than economic. One of the most succinct and cogent definitions of globalization was provided by the British sociologist Anthony Giddens in his book *The Consequences of Modernity*. In it he notes that "Globalization can thus be defined as the intensification of worldwide social relations which link distant localities in such as way that local happenings are shaped by events occurring many miles away and vice versa" (1991, 64). Globalization connects: It brings people together. Economic, political, and cultural globablization has become the norm.

In a sense, globalization is nothing new. However, over the past 30 years, many technological revolutions have arisen and the trend toward globalization has accelerated as a result. Globalization can be seen in virtually all arenas of life: from international leisure and business travel, and the expansion of the Internet and World Wide Web that allows for instantaneous communication among people the world over, to the array of food choices that are now part of every local supermarket.

While globalization comes in different forms, the end result is the same: increasing global connectivity. The world of today is increasingly connected in three ways (see Lechner and Boli, 2000): economically, culturally, and politically. Globalization operates in these three levels, although it is the economic activity that is the principal force underlying global connectivity today.

Economic Globalization

Because globalization is driven by economic forces, the market place is the preeminent source of global connectivity today. The connection of global financial markets (the buying and selling of stocks, bonds, and mutual funds across national borders) and the corporation's pursuit of new sources of cheap labor and consumers to manufacture and to buy its products are the hallmarks of economic globalization. What's more, international bodies such as the World Trade Organization, the World Bank, and the International Monetary Fund, as well as a host of international agreements such as the North American Free Trade Agreement (NAFTA) and the General Agreement on Trade and Tariffs (GATT) are there for the sole purpose of facilitating free economic trade under the worldwide system of capitalism.

Economic globalization is behind corporate decisions to move manufacturing plants and facilities to countries with considerably cheaper labor costs, leading to massive deindustrialization in the industrial sectors in many countries like the United States. Cheaper labor costs, less stringent environmental regulations, and lower corporate taxes are all factors that make corporate off-shoring very attractive (see Brecher and Costello, 1994). But economic globalization, while it may mean the loss of working-class industrial jobs (and increasingly, white collar ones as well) in the United States and other post-industrialized nations, does make the signs of American corporate culture ubiquitous: The Golden Arches, IBM, and Microsoft are a few examples. Moreover, it is economic globalization that fuels the unprecedented amount of cultural exchanges that are occurring today.

Cultural Globalization

Globalization is also cultural. Any Japanese teenage would recognize the following symbols of American cultural globalization: Mickey Mouse & Disney World, McDonalds and KFC, and Nike's swoosh and flying Michael Jordon symbols. America's hegemony is political, economic, and cultural, so it goes without saying that the symbols of its dominance should be most recognizable the world over. But what is most interesting is how increasingly American children are now able to recognize the symbols of Japanese popular culture. Anime such as Naruto, Pokemon, and Dragon Ball Z have become household shows on children's television in the United States. This is cultural globalization, and it stems directly from the ease at which cultural exchanges occur today.

American children, and corporations for that matter, are as likely to be influenced by Japanese popular and technological cultures, and manufacturing innovations ("Japanization") as Japanese ones are likely to be influenced by American hip-hop subcultures and Hollywood media ("Americanization"). And hip-hop music is a wonderful exemplar of the globalization of an American subcultural pattern: That today you can find distinct hip-hip music from almost every culture on the plant (from French to Russian hip-hop) speaks volumes to exactly how pervasive cultural globalization has become. With exchanges of technology and popular culture, values, ideas, and norms are exchanged, and a world wide culture arises. But this diffusion is not without its critics, as we shall soon read.

Political Globalization

Political globalization is the third aspect of globalization. The creation of the United Nations during the post–World War II environment set the stage for political globalization in the late-modern world. The United Nations, and its 192 member nation-states, is the preeminent organization responsible for the maintenance of human rights and the observance of international law throughout the world. Political globalization includes, foremost, the diffusion of an ethic of human rights and security, and the United Nations, as a worldwide political body, is charged with the duty of defending this mandate, which in addition to upholding the Universal Declaration of Human Rights also oversees conventions eliminating genocide and torture, and international protocols on the rights of women and children.

However, political globalization extends beyond the workings of the United Nations. The efforts of Non-Governmental Organizations (NGOs) are also very crucial to the discussion of human rights within a framework of political globalization. NGOs such as Human Rights Watch (www.hrw.org) and Amnesty International (www.amnesty.org) are essential contributors to the discourse on human rights abuses around the world.

The success of political globalization is seen in the diffusing of human rights and democratic ideals to countries that have traditionally put the rights of the nation-state above those of people. The influence and success of political global-ization can be seen in the "Beijing Declaration," the resolutions on the rights of women and girls that came out of the United Nations' Fourth World Conference on Women in 1995. The signatories to this declaration agreed to "take all neces-sary measures to eliminate all forms of discrimination against women and the girl child and remove all obstacles to gender equality and the advancement and empowerment of women," in addition to other specific gender-based decrees (U.N. Beijing Declaration, 1995).

Political globalization is an indelible part of the late-modern landscape, and tra-ditional cultures are manifestly affected by its efforts to promote human rights and security across sovereign national borders.

The Criticisms of Globalization

Globalization, in all of its manifestations, has been criticized incessantly for its impact on society, especially the way in which it is affecting cultural and institu-tional patterns around the world. The traditional criticism of globalization was that it was very imperialistic, in that it tended to impose Western (read American) politi-cal values and cultural ideals on weaker nation-states and smaller cultures. These critics lament that local societies around the world are acquiescing to American (consumer) values, and in the process, the annihilation of indigenous cultural prac-tices, traditions, values, and tastes—in favor of global ones—is inevitable. The dis-appearance of local lifestyles and regional cultures in support of global ones can be seen in the increasing proliferation of American eating establishments in Europe and the non-Western world for example.

The strongest critic of this type of globalization is the sociologist George Ritzer. In his book *The Globalization of Nothing*, Ritzer (2004, 20) makes a rather convincing argument that globalization ultimately involves the exchange of a something (that is "unique, local, specific to the times, humanized, and enchanted") for a nothing (that is "generic, lacks local ties, time-less, dehumanized, and disenchanted"). These "nothings" are precisely responsible for the erosion of local and regional cultures. So for example, McDonalds and other processed fast foods (nothing) are displacing the slow, home-cooked meal (something); the mega-mall and Wal-Mart (nothing) are altering the local "downtown" shopping village (something). Moreover, "nothing" seems to be our biggest export: China and India now have Wal-Marts courtesy of American economic globalization.

CONCLUSION AND SUMMARY

Globalization in the twenty-first century changes almost everything. For many people, globablization is met by fear and criticism. Multinational corporations are becoming more and more powerful, and some control economic assets that are larger than the gross domestic products of entire nation-states. Cultural diversity among societies becomes undermined as emigration, economic ties, and easy communication make people more and more alike. The global political system may allow majorities to gang up on individual societies, and the future of societies may be determined by traditional enemies. Political globalization does not necessarily bring a peaceful and just world.

On the other hand, it is important to recognize that forms of globalization, especially economic and political ones, continue to aid in expanding the range of choices for groups that have been historically excluded from markets and politics in many parts of the world: women, children, the under-caste, ethic minorities, and the poor. The new emphasis on the political rights of women and children around the world is made possible because of the globalization of democracy and human rights and security.

Social organizations never exist within a social vacuum. They are rarely on their own in the types of social patterns they develop. The individual is influenced not by his or her face-to-face interaction; instead, larger and larger social forces influence the development of increasingly smaller organizations.

Individual actors interact, form structures, culture, and institutions in that interaction, and are in turn affected by those social patterns. The organization that develops with its resulting social patterns are influenced by the larger groups, formal organizations, community, and society within which they exist. The individual and his or her dyads and groups should be understood within a set of concentric circles, each one having something to say about what occurs.

Interaction among people from different organizations develops social patterns among those organizations. A structure develops that positions those organizations in relation to one another. A culture is created that ties those organizations together. Over time, institutions emerge. An individual organization must always be understood in terms of its position within these larger structures. This includes a world system in which people from many societies interact, form a structure, and, to some extent, develop a common culture and common institutions.

QUESTIONS TO CONSIDER

1. Can you identify the most important organizations in American life? Try to determine how they are able to achieve their will in society.
2. Your sociology class exists within larger and larger social organizations. Can you trace these links and try to establish how the larger organizations have some impact on your class?
3. To what extent is the world becoming a single society? To what extent are worldwide corporations becoming societies? To what extent might one claim that a worldwide working class or an upper class is becoming a society in itself?

4. Who has the power in the world? What would be Marx's position? Wallerstein? Friedman?
5. Do you agree that globabalization is a good thing, as Friedman generally argues?
6. What are some of the important criticisms of globablization?

REFERENCES

Brecher, Jeremy, and Costello, Tim. 1994. *Global Village or Global Pillage: Economic Reconstruction from the Bottom.* Boston, MA: South End Press.
Friedman, Thomas L. 2005. *The World is Flat: A Brief History of the Twenty-First Century.* New York, NY: Farrar, Straus and Giroux.
Giddens, Anthony. 1991. *The Consequences of Modernity.* Cambridge, UK: Polity Press.
Lechner, Frank J., and Boli, John. 2000. *The Globalization Reader.* Oxford, UK: Blackwell Publishers.
Ritzer, George. 2004. *The Globalization of Nothing.* Thousand Oaks, CA: Pine Forge Press.
United Nations. 1995. *Beijing Declaration, United Nations Fourth World Conference on Women.* www.un.org/womenwatch/daw/beijing/platform/declar.htm Accessed October 4, 2007.

RECOMMENDED READING

The following books examine the complex interrelationships among social organizations in society.

Berger, Peter L. 1963. *Invitation to Sociology.* Garden City, NY: Doubleday.
Blau, Peter M., and Marshall W. Meyer. 1987. *Bureaucracy in Modern Society.* 3rd edn. New York: Random House.
Dohan, Daniel. 2003. *The Price of Poverty: Money, Work, and Culture in the Mexican American Barrio.* Berkeley, CA: University of California Press.
Dye, Thomas R. 1986. *Who's Running America?* 4th edn. Upper Saddle River, NJ: Prentice Hall.
Foner, Nancy. 2005. *In a New Land: A Comparative View of Immigration.* New York: New York University Press.
Galbraith, John Kenneth. 1979. *The New Industrial State.* 3rd edn. New York: New American Library.
Haenfler, Ross. 2006. *Straight Edge: Hardcore Punk, Clean-Living Youth, and Social Change.* New Brunswick, NJ: Rutgers University Press.
Keller, Suzanne. 1963. *Beyond the Ruling Class: Strategic Elites in Modern Society.* New York: Random House.
Kornhauser, William. 1961. *The Politics of Mass Society.* New York: Free Press.
Korten, David C. 1995. *When Corporations Rule the World.* San Francisco, CA: Kumarian Press.
Korten, David C. 1999. *The Post-Corporate World: Life After Capitalism.* San Francisco, CA: Berrett-Koehler Publishers, Inc.
Lichtenstein, Nelson. 2006. *Wal-Mart: The Face of Twenty-First Century Capitalism.* New York: New Press.
Mann, Michael. 2004. *The Dark Side of Democracy: Explaining Ethnic Cleansing.* New York: Cambridge University Press.
Marx, Karl. 1845–1886. *Selected Writings.* 1956 edn. Ed. T. B. Bottomore. New York: McGraw-Hill.
Marx, Karl, and Friedrich Engels. 1848. *The Communist Manifesto.* 1955 edn. New York: Appleton-Century-Crofts.
Merry, Sally E. 2005. *Human Rights and Gender Violence: Translating International Law into Local Justice.* Chicago, IL: University of Chicago Press.
Mills, C. Wright. 1956. *The Power Elite.* New York: Oxford University Press.
Mintz, Beth, and Michael Schwartz. 1985. *The Power Structure of American Business.* Chicago: University of Chicago Press.
Olsen, Marvin E. 1978. *The Process of Social Organization.* 2nd edn. New York: Holt, Rinehart & Winston.
Perrow, Charles. 1986. *Complex Organizations.* 3rd edn. New York: Random House.
Wallerstein, Immanuel. 1974. *The Modern World-System.* New York: Academic Press.

Alberto Giacometti. *Diego*, 1953. Oil on Canvas, 39½" × 31¾" (100.5 × 80.5 cm).
Solomon R. Guggenheim Museum. New York, 55. 1431.

✦ 9 ✦

Social Order, Social Control, and Social Deviance

Human beings are social beings. They live together in social organization. They live in dyads, groups, formal organizations, communities, and societies. All organized life arises from social interaction over time. It is made up of social patterns, including social structure, culture, and institutions.

It must be clear by now that all organized life exerts control over the individuals that make it up. Social patterns control the individual—and, therefore, it is social patterns that make organized life possible. People are placed into social structure, and their actions are controlled through everything attached to their position: a role that tells them how to act, an identity that tells them who they are, a perspective that tells them how to view reality, and a rank dependent on the amount of power, privilege, and prestige associated with their position. People learn a culture in organization. They come to agree with one another about what is true, worthwhile, and right. People also exist within a set of institutions that show them how to act, socialize them, punish them, and reward them.

Sociology is a perspective that underlines the great power of organization over the individual's life. Much of what we do, think, and are can be tied to the social patterns that exist within the organizations of which we are a part. For many students, this is a disturbing realization. However, we must look at this from the viewpoint of organization. Without some control over the individual, social organization simply would not exist. Society, a business organization, a university, an athletic team, or simply a group of children wanting to play "kick the can" could not function if there were no controls operating on the individual.

Now we will consider the "problem" of social order. How is it that a number of individuals are able to come together into organization, sacrifice to some extent their individual wants and needs to that organization, and agree to temporarily control themselves so that the organization is able to continue? Without control, social order is impossible; without social order, we would not be socialized, nor could we act together in some cooperative endeavor. In fact, even freedom—whatever there is—can exist only within some underlying order within which it is encouraged to exist.

Social order—a concept often used but rarely defined—is a quality of all working organizations. The opposite of social order is easy to grasp: disorder, chaos, the absence of rules, disorganization. If there is no order, actors will act without taking one another into account or they will act without any concern for the cooperative effort. Action will be impulsive—uncontrolled—or it will be self-controlled without regard for the organization. Cooperation is made impossible.

Social order means that actions between individuals are predictable, orderly, patterned, and based on rules. Each actor is governed by the whole community to some extent. If order exists, actors do not act in just any way they feel or choose to act. Action is governed by mutual expectations, and contract governs the relationship. There is agreement that we will act a certain way (if you marry me, I will be faithful; if I rent an apartment from you, then I will pay you rent every month). Social order is cooperative social interaction.

Social order is made possible by "social control"—all the various ways a social organization attempts to control the individual actor. Roucek defines social control as "all the pressures by which society and its component groups influence the behavior of the individual members toward conformity with group norms" (1978, 11).

Social control and social order are necessary for the continuation of social organization. They are often good things, but we should not simply assume that they are always good. A society that oppresses people should not be supported simply because control and order are necessary. An organization that is racist or sexist in its orientation toward others is not to be supported if that organization violates our values. In fact, much of the change in every society comes from a refusal of people to be controlled by social patterns they regard as unjust, with resulting disorder and new directions.

The central question for every organization is, how much control and order? Too little can lead to chaos and a war of all against all. Too much means that little individuality and freedom will be tolerated, and peaceful change will be unlikely.

SOCIAL ORDER IS ESTABLISHED THROUGH STRUCTURE AND CULTURE

For most other animals, order is established through instinct and through instinctive battles between individuals for control.

What makes order possible in human organization? How is organization able to exist from day to day? Some organizations exist for a very long time, and some have even existed for centuries. How are individual actors able to cooperate and control their actions in such a way that organization continues?

The answer, of course, is the social patterns that arise in social interaction. Social patterns guide the actor; the actor acts in predictable and expected ways. Social patterns bring people together, make them interdependent, cause them to understand one another, and even make them feel as one. Almost all sociologists have described the role of social patterns as the foundation for social order in one way or another—although they do not always call them social patterns.

Emile Durkheim (1893), for example, shows us how both culture and structure bind people. Culture is especially important in simpler societies. Here, a common moral and value system is what binds people together. Durkheim called this "mechanical solidarity." People tend to be the same in such societies. Common beliefs, values, and norms are the glue. Crimes in such societies are regarded not as transgressions against other individuals so much as crimes against the whole of society and its common culture. Punishment and public executions serve to reaffirm this culture and give people the assurance that its truths, values, and morals are right. The worship of a common god and other sacred objects (objects that are symbolic of society) is also important because, according to Durkheim, this too serves to hold people together and assures them that their culture is valid. Durkheim called society's culture its "collective conscience" or "collective consciousness." The conscience (morality) and consciousness (awareness, understanding) of each individual are produced by the collective.

According to Durkheim, all societies have a common culture, and this pattern always holds societies together. Developed societies—particularly modern industrial societies—create complex social structures, where people occupy different positions in society. Such differences between people replace the sameness that characterizes simpler societies. Industrial societies develop a complex "division of labor," where occupations are increasingly different from one another. We work at various jobs. We specialize. Some of us become corporate executives, and some teach the families of corporate executives; some grow food, some transport it, and some prepare it for others. Such a society needs a common culture to some extent—after all, even if we are all different, we must agree on some things or we would not be able to trust one another. However, it is a solidarity based on social structure that becomes increasingly important. Durkheim calls this "organic solidarity" because society increasingly takes the form of an organism with many different parts, each part making a contribution to the whole. Structure unites society by making us all *interdependent*, where human differences ultimately contribute to the welfare of everyone. When a common culture becomes less and less central to social solidarity, and when people become increasingly different from one another, there develops more tolerance of individuality and less severe punishment for those who are defined outside the law. Modernization, in this sense, brings with it a more humane approach to establishing and maintaining social order.

By contrasting mechanical solidarity with organic solidarity, Durkheim shows us how both culture and structure are important ingredients for holding society together, thus creating a sound basis for social order.

Marx also shows us the role of both structure and culture. His analysis, though, is different from Durkheim's. He does not use the term *social order* but is more comfortable with the concept of *social control*. To Marx, *social control* refers to the various ways the powerful in society attempt to repress the individual, to control and manipulate the individual for the good of the few. To Marx, society is a system of class inequality, allowing the few who own the means of production to coerce and manipulate the many to accept society as it is. Power in the social structure brings control over jobs, government, army, police, courts, and the media, and this, in turn, brings control over the individual. Therefore, Marx begins with social structure in his understanding of order: Order is produced through the power of a few people high in the social structure. They establish order through force, control of jobs, and manipulation.

Marx also deals with culture in his analysis of order. The dominant ideas, values, and morals in society are produced by the powerful. They are meant to control the individual to help ensure "willing" conformity. Culture helps justify and protect the inequality in society, and it serves the powerful who produce it.

Thus, to Marx, social order is created from above. Position brings power; power brings the instruments used to create order so that privilege continues. Power also brings control over culture, including a people's ideas, values, and rules.

Here, then, are two very different social thinkers, both of whom recognize the importance of both social structure and culture for social order. To Durkheim, structure means greater interdependence; to Marx, structure makes it possible for a few to control and oppress the many. Durkheim tells us that culture makes us alike in ideas, values, and norms—we form a consensus, and this creates order among us. Marx sees culture as an important way in which the ruling class controls people and keeps itself in power.

There is more than what Marx and Durkheim describe. Social structure distributes people into positions that are ranked in society; it controls every individual, even the upper classes and those who have political power. People come to know how to think and act because they are placed, socialized appropriately, and controlled by those above them in the social structure. Moreover, culture creates order in part by making it easier for people to communicate with and understand one another, and ultimately facilitates cooperation in organized life.

SOCIAL ORDER DEPENDS ON WORKING INSTITUTIONS

Social institutions are also social patterns, and they too are important for control and social order. Durkheim described institutions as social facts, real entities that control the individual from "out there" but also become internalized through socialization. Durkheim especially saw religious and educational institutions as shapers of human beings who are capable of controlling themselves. Marx saw all institutions as having the same function as culture: to protect the rich and powerful. Institutions are the tools of the ruling class; the individual is socialized and directed by them.

Earlier, we described institutions as patterns established to deal with the ongoing problems of society. They are necessary for satisfying the basic needs of the people who live together in society. If institutions work well, then basic needs are met and people are satisfied. If they do not work well, then problems become more serious and disorder can result. The United States has an array of basic health care institutions: private doctors, hospitals, insurance, HMOs, Medicare, private nursing homes. Do these institutions work? Do they deliver effective health care to the population? If the answers are "yes," then they contribute to social order. If they do not, then something is seriously wrong in society, and to that extent social order is threatened.

Like all societies, the United States has political institutions meant to control, direct, socialize, and lead individuals and organizations in society so that the goals of society can be cooperatively achieved. Indeed, it is the political institutions that usually create the goals, sometimes reflecting the goals of most or many people, sometimes reflecting the goals of a few—their own or those of another elite (for example, the ruling class). Political institutions are responsible for identifying and dealing with institutions that do not work well. So, for example, health care institutions must be altered, directed, replaced, or strengthened by political institutions—if the political institutions actually work well.

It is safe to say that the end of the former Soviet Union came in part because the old institutions simply did not work. The economic and political institutions created a huge bureaucracy that served only its own needs. The various republics were not tied together into one society, and socializing all the people to accept sacrifice for the good of the future generations was no longer effective. The military took too much from the people, and the emphasis on coercive control was oppressive and counterproductive. Order inevitably broke down when institutions no longer solved the ongoing problems of Soviet society.

As Americans, we should not be too smug. Most of us accept capitalism as an institution that works. We are prosperous, and part of this prosperity is because of capitalism. Yet, like all institutions, capitalism does not work perfectly. Many people are left out of the prosperity, and there are consequences for social order. We have yet to adequately answer how to deal with the great gaps of wealth and power that exist, and we are probably fearful of critically evaluating something so dear to us. What happens to society when institutions develop serious problems among large numbers of the population? What happens to society when people are unwilling to question and alter their institutions? What happens when educational, familial, political, criminal justice, and health care institutions do not work, and problems become more serious? Ultimately, the consequences go back to the problem of order: Can order be achieved when institutions no longer work well but are accepted uncritically and ignored as the source of serious social problems?

SOCIAL ORDER DEPENDS ON SOCIALIZATION

One of the most important functions of institutions is to socialize people in organization so that individuals "willingly" conform. Durkheim wrote that in a sense individuals must agree to leave their conscience at the door of organization to accept the social patterns as their own.

"Willingness" arises from socialization, the fourth foundation for social order. It is through the process of socialization that social organization creates our wants, gives us its culture, and places us in our positions. *Socialization* refers to the process by which the individual is taught to know the society and to learn its culture, structure, and institutions, as well as his or her place there. Through socialization, we learn to accept social organization because we are taught that it benefits us, or it *is* us, or we must accept it to survive. To become socialized is to "become" society, to make it part of us, to internalize it. Each social organization we enter and each we form sets up procedures to make new members learn the patterns and ensure that things work smoothly.

Consider what human beings are at birth, able to do little except depend on others. Human helplessness assumes a social nature. Immediately, adults begin to teach their infants who they are, where they fit into the family and society, and what rules and values to act on. These lessons affect the children and direct them until, gradually, they become what they have been taught. Every society establishes institutions—for example, family, public schools, Sunday school, television, and the Boy Scouts—to socialize the young. We exist as a society in large part because socialization is successful:

> Every year our nation is invaded by several million "things" (one searches for the right word) that are immense, incalculable threats to the social order. They threaten total chaos. They are barbaric. They do not love democracy and suspect communism. They have no belief for the Judeo-Christian tradition. They have no modesty. They do not speak our language, nor know our history, nor value our customs. They lack any motive or knowledge which leads them to share, to give and take, to compromise, to accommodate, to cooperate. They are impulsive and demanding. They do not respect authority, show respect to their elders, or express deference. Though they do not swear, steal, chew tobacco, fornicate, desecrate the flag, or use four-letter words, they are unaware certainly that they should not do so. They have no manners, no respect for others, no respect for tradition. They have not learned to keep up appearances, to knock before entering, to be silent in church, or to worry about bad breath and underarm stains.
>
> These invaders are human infants. . . . Something must be done. We need them—because without them the society dies out for lack of people—but we need them on our terms, not theirs. The process of getting them on our terms is called *socialization*.
>
> (Campbell, 1975, 1)

The kinship institutions are very important for the socialization of a child. The family, the first group within which there is regular interaction, is made up of the first people the child uses as models, and it is the first source of rewards and punishments. The family is important for the emotional well-being of the child and is central to the development of self and conscience. Because its teachings come first, the family influences all later learning. The adults confront the child with a world where alternatives do not seem to exist:

> It is only much later that he discovers that there are alternatives to this particular world, that his parents' world is relative in space and time, and that quite different patterns are possible. Only then does the individual become aware of the relativity of social patterns and of social worlds.
>
> (Berger and Berger, 1972, 55–56)

The public school is an institution designed to socialize the young and create "good citizens." It attempts to teach ideas and actions that society (and those who have powerful positions in society) has determined are important. We are supposed to learn what America means, what its history is, and why we should believe in its culture. Although many Americans believe that schools are the chief means for escaping low position in society, for the most part schools actually function to help people learn their place, to learn what it means to be a woman or a man, black or white, rich or poor. Schools shape the individual's expectations of self and usually succeed in teaching people not to "expect too much." Malcolm X, an important African-American leader in the 1960s, described his experience in eighth grade, where Mr. Ostrowski, his English teacher, tried to influence Malcolm's expectations of himself:

He told me, "Malcolm, you ought to be thinking about a career. Have you been giving it thought?"

The truth is, I hadn't. I never have figured out why I told him, "Well, yes, sir, I've been thinking I'd like to be a lawyer." Lansing certainly had no Negro lawyers—or doctors either—in those days, to hold up an image I might have aspired to. All I knew for certain was that a lawyer didn't wash dishes, as I was doing.

Mr. Ostrowski looked surprised, I remember, and leaned back in his chair and clasped his hands behind his head. He kind of half-smiled and said, "Malcolm, one of life's first needs is for us to be realistic. Don't misunderstand me, now. We all here like you, you know that. But you've got to be realistic about being a nigger. A lawyer—that's no realistic goal for a nigger. You need to think about something you can be. You're good with your hands—making things. Everybody admires your carpentry shop work. Why don't you plan on carpentry? People like you as a person—you'd get all kinds of work."

The more I thought afterwards about what he said, the more uneasy it made me. It just kept treading around in my mind.

What made it really begin to disturb me was Mr. Ostrowski's advice to others in my class—all of them white. . . . They all reported that Mr. Ostrowski had encouraged what they had wanted. Yet nearly none of them had earned marks equal to mine.

(Malcolm X and Haley, 1964, 36–37)

It took Malcolm X many years to understand his life and how it was shaped by many others. He turned against his early socialization because of people he interacted with later. Many of us do not ever look back objectively at our socialization. We never do come to realize that much of it was an attempt by various representatives of society to get us to accept the social patterns that exist. Our taken-for-granted worlds appear to us as reality rather than as resulting from socialization.

No sociologist emphasizes the central role of schools more than Durkheim. Those organisms born into the world ignorant must be shaped and made into good citizens and must go from being purely selfish to being cooperative and committed to the whole. To Durkheim, socialization or "moral education" takes society and its rules from existing "out there" and incorporates them into the individual's very being. This process internalizes the police force external to the individual, and the individual comes to direct self in accordance with society's demands. In all societies, this is the task of the family and religion. In industrial society, this task is shared with the specialized educational institutions such as the public schools.

LOYALTY TO THE ORGANIZATION IS THE FIFTH FOUNDATION FOR SOCIAL ORDER

Socialization teaches us *loyalty*—being faithful to the group, organization, community, or society, and adhering to its beliefs. If the social organization can inspire people to feel part of something bigger than themselves, they will identify the organization with their own personal future, their own dreams, their own life's meanings. Societies develop loyalty in their members by waving their flags, marching their armies, displaying their heroes, and giving their speeches. Fraternities do it through initiation ceremonies, the frat house, secrecy, and traditions. A ring, a marriage ceremony, and a shared place of residence aid the development of loyalty to the marriage dyad.

These symbols of loyalty distinguish insiders from outsiders, the "in" groups from the "out" groups, "us" from "them." They encourage members to feel part of something good and to feel that they share this good with only certain selected others. An emotional bond is established, and this aids the smooth functioning of the organization.

Loyalty to the social organization may arise from two sources. Sometimes loyalty is a result of a sense of *we*, an emotional commitment to the organization that identifies the organization with one's own identity. This characterizes many smaller societies, communities, groups, and dyads. Cooley (1902) described such organizations as "primary"—those face-to-face relationships in which a sense of *we* prevails and where personal emotional attachments exist. In such organization, the individual identifies self with the whole, and personal goals are really organizational goals. An emotional commitment exists among all those in the organization.

It is difficult to establish a sense of *we* in a large organization. Nations celebrate independence day, presidents give speeches that begin with "my fellow Americans," and schools teach us about the great heroes and stirring events of our history. Wars sometimes bring us together as a nation, at least temporarily, as do national crises such as assassinations of societal leaders, natural disasters, and terrorist actions against citizens and national symbols. Formal organizations may sponsor social events to encourage emotional attachment, or they may publish weekly staff newspapers announcing the promotions, achievements, recent hirings, and general office gossip. Christmas parties and bowling teams also help bring us together and establish emotional ties to the organization.

In modern society, loyalty is often established through a second source: The organization must give us something in return. Even the family and friendship groups depend on *conditional loyalty*, more a rational commitment than an emotional one. Instead of a sense of *we*, a sense of *I* is most important. It is what society does for *me* that matters, it is whether my family meets *my* needs, whether this company looks out for my interests, whether this club gives *me* pleasure that determines my loyalty. Loyalty depends; it is conditional, it fluctuates, it is fickle. Much of our socialization into modern society is aimed at convincing us that, as individuals, we will get something in return for our loyalty.

Loyalty to social organization is aided by our social nature. Humans need other people in their early years for survival, and most of us need others throughout our lives for our sense of worth. Almost all of us seek friends and have a need to be part of a group, a formal organization, a community, or a society. To be alone is something most of us fear. Others fulfill our emotional needs, and we develop our identities in group life. We want to give loyalty to the social organizations that are important for fulfilling our emotional needs; we are willing to sacrifice some of our individuality. Indeed, for most of us, loyalty does not seem to be a sacrifice at all. Some of us hunger for being part of something larger than ourselves so much that we are willing to give up all individuality—we may, for example, join a religious or political movement that demands total loyalty.

Organizations also encourage loyalties by establishing boundaries between those in the organization and those outside. The structure, culture, and social institutions help distinguish members from nonmembers. Social interaction tends to cut ties with outsiders by encouraging relationships within the organization. Over time, we get used to the patterns of our own organization; we tend to take them for granted and regard them as better than the patterns that others follow—often as the only desirable patterns to follow.

Organizations often manufacture physical and symbolic boundaries to encourage a sense of loyalty. A college campus is a set of buildings set apart from the rest of the community; a house acts as a physical boundary, as do a nation's borders, a factory, a membership card, a written contract. Physical boundaries help establish who "we" are and who "they" are. They encourage interaction among members and discourage interaction with outsiders. Symbolic boundaries such as uniforms, rings, football teams, theme songs, national anthems, and hairstyles may establish boundaries, too. Stereotyping others, calling them "uncivilized," "heathen," "communists," "terrorists," or "uncool" are ways some of us try to establish boundaries. Segregating others, creating ghettoes, and passing discriminatory laws also do this.

Although loyalty may often make us too obedient, too conforming, too unjust to outsiders, too biased in our search for truth, too suspicious of differences, it still is important for the continuation of organization, because order can be established more peaceably and voluntarily. Through emotional commitment, conditional commitment, or the establishment of boundaries, organizations usually become more stable, more ordered, and more cooperative.

To sum up, social order is established in the following five ways:

1. Social structure places us, makes us interdependent, and encourages control of the many by the few.
2. Culture makes people similar to one another in the truths, values, goals, and rules they follow.
3. Social institutions deal with the ongoing problems of society.
4. Institutions socialize us so that society gets inside us and we become "willing" partners in society.
5. Institutions encourage us to feel part of organization. Loyalty is encouraged by developing a sense of we, by convincing members that the organization is beneficial, and by establishing boundaries between those within and those outside the organization.

There is a sixth and final way, however, that social order is established, and we have not yet considered it. This is what sociologists call the use of social controls (or *social sanctions*).

SOCIAL CONTROLS CONTRIBUTE TO SOCIAL ORDER

Socialization is never perfect: For many, loyalty is never felt; for some, the patterns are not willingly followed. This is true in every organization: in society, in the university, in families, and in businesses, to name a few. If socialization worked perfectly, there would be little individuality, no criminals, no revolutionaries, no dissatisfied members, and no one unhappy with the social structure. Thankfully, humans are not only conforming members of organization, they are also rebels, questioners, suspicious, creative, and individualistic.

To encourage reluctant members, social organizations develop a system of rewards and punishments so that people will have another reason to conform. These are called *social sanctions*, or *social controls*. They aid conformity but do not guarantee it. In fact, if only negative sanctions (punishments) are relied on, it is at great cost because resources must be allocated to watch people and punish them; anger and resentment are the likely results. If an organization relies only on positive sanctions, people tend to conform only to be paid, and conformity remains highly conditional (I will conform only if I am paid); a more positive voluntary commitment tends to be lost.

We are all familiar with negative sanctions—the pressures applied to bring people back in line if they stray. We can all stretch our status positions to some extent; we can also be individuals within culture, but only to a certain extent. Beyond a certain point, people frown at us, they reject us, they yell at us, they embarrass us, they imprison us, they threaten to throw us out, they point a finger or a fist or a gun at us. We may conform to social organization out of fear that negative sanctions will be applied if we do not. The ultimate sanction is being thrown out of the social organization (imprisonment, expulsion, deportation, or execution). It is the bottom line.

Positive sanctions reward us if we do conform. A smile, a raise in salary, an "A" grade in class, a compliment, a promotion, a purple heart, a birthday present all work to encourage acceptance of position, structure, culture, and institutions. Even thinking about future rewards encourages conformity.

Indeed, socialization is so effective in society that social sanctions become internalized. We exert our own social controls on ourselves, we become our own police officers, so to speak. We feel guilty and punish ourselves, or we feel good and pat ourselves on the back. External sanctions become internal ones; society out there gets inside all of us. Socialization causes us not only to take on our positions and to accept our cultures and institutions, but also leads us to police our own behavior.

Human beings are pushed around, in a sense. We are told what to do; we are rewarded, and we are punished. In any social situation, sanctions are promised, threatened, and used. We must please many people, and we should face the fact that many of our claims of "free choice" are probably wishful thinking:

> The individual who, thinking consecutively of all the people he is in a position to have to please, from the Collector of Internal Revenue to his mother-in-law, gets the idea that all of society sits right on top of him had better not dismiss that idea as a momentary neurotic derangement.
>
> (Berger, 1963, 78)

SOCIAL DEVIANCE

It is impossible to ensure total conformity to organization, nor is that ever desirable. Society needs thinkers, not robots; problem solvers, not sleepwalkers; creative, self-directing persons, not simply conformists. Everyone breaks the established rules occasionally, and some break the rules much of the time. As children, we learn to test adults: We bend the rules of authorities, they act back, we test again. In real life, everything is dynamic and involves conflict.

The problem is always *"How much* individuality is acceptable?"* How much bending of the rules can be tolerated? Americans value individuality; yet we all have our limits, and certainly authorities do. Every social organization draws lines and brings negative social controls to bear on those outside those lines. High schoolers recognize well that there are certain acceptable ways to dress and act around peers; outsiders are nerds, uncool, weird. We declare certain people to be mentally ill; we punish others as criminals. Wherever there are social patterns, there are those who are unacceptable, who are condemned as "immoral," "sick," "unnatural," or "antisocial."

Deviance is the term used by sociologists to refer to that action defined by society and its defenders to be outside the range of the acceptable. Deviance is actually created by society, by *reaction* to certain actions, rather than by the actor who does the acting. It is society's rules and lines that create the boundaries between what is and what is not deviant; it is the perception of "too much individuality" that makes people upset enough to define something or someone as deviant. Erich Goode defines deviance as follows:

> . . . by deviance I mean one thing and one thing only: behavior that some people in a society find offensive and which excites — or would excite if it were discovered — in these people disapproval, punishment, condemnation, or hostility. . . . It is based on a judgment made by somebody. It isn't simply behavior, but behavior that is evaluated in a certain way.
>
> (1978, 24–25)

Goode makes his point through the example of homosexuality. Is homosexuality deviant? Many people call it an illness, something that is "unnatural," something that is deviant *in itself*, not just because we say it is. But Goode is consistent with his definition. It is deviant *only* because of our reactions to it and our belief that it is a violation of something important that we believe in (1978, 376–377).

Labeling something deviant is really trying to exercise social control over people. Such labels stigmatize the individual and attempt to discourage such acts. Labeling also socializes people: To stray from the acceptable means that you too might be stigmatized.

Not all individuality can be condemned. Not everyone who strays can be punished. All societies are selective. Those who are condemned tend to be those who, through their acts, *threaten* us. Revolutionary acts threaten powerful groups, illegal acts threaten those who perceive the law to be important to their welfare, "weird" religious cults threaten those who view God and life in a more traditional way, and "kinky" sex threatens those of us who regard more traditional acts to be the healthy and moral way. Where we condemn acts as deviant (not just different), there is something important at stake for us.

Deviance is universal; however, each society has a different view of what is deviant, and it changes from generation to generation. Even when it might appear that almost all societies agree on some general category of action as deviant (for example, murder or incest), careful examination will show that they differ in their definitions of what specific acts are to be included in the category.

Deviant acts are sometimes written into the law. Where laws are passed and punishment for violation is relatively severe (rather than, for example, simply a fine), we have instances of deviance having become a "crime." Some deviant acts — for example, those we see arising from mental illness — are considered deviant in this society, not criminal. For a long time, divorce was also considered deviant, but not criminal.

Society is made up of many organizations that have different views of deviance. To pro-choice groups, pro-life groups are wrong, antiwoman, fanatical, and irrational. To pro-life groups, pro-choice groups are antilife, immoral, antifamily, and murdering. Whose definition prevails? If we realize that society is made up of a number of groups in conflict, each group asserting itself with the resources available to it, it is easy to see that power makes a big difference in society's definition of deviance. Money, leadership, and organization matter; friends in Congress matter; control over schools and media matters. Clearly, the upper class has more say than others in what crimes are most serious (and these often prove to be the crimes most frequently committed by the lower classes). Mothers Against Drunk Driving (MADD) in a very short time has influenced political leaders, judges, and the public to regard drunk driving as a deviant act to be harshly condemned. Leadership, organization, and intelligent use of the media were important sources of power that paid off for this group.

Before the landmark 2003 Supreme Court decision in Lawrence & Garner versus the State of Texas, which legalized consensual homosexual sex between adults, many jurisdictions defined homosexuality as criminal behavior. Moreover, before 1973, the American Psychiatric Association listed homosexuality among its many mental disorders in its Diagnostic Statistical Manual (DSM). These legal and medical definitions of homosexuality as criminally deviant and psychologically abnormal, respectively, were successfully challenged by the gay and lesbian community through social activism. Their movements were successful in challenging the legal and medical communities' definition of homosexuality, and gay and lesbian activists are increasing their activism around the issue of gay marriage today.

Almost any act, then, can be defined as deviant and subsequently persecuted. Remember that, to the Puritans, dancing and drama were considered deviant; to some people, working on the Sabbath is deviant; to others, cheating on exams is; and, to still others, studying for school all the time is. Power differences create priorities in society, which then become reflected in the law and court systems, and in our punishments.

The condemnation of certain acts as deviant and of certain people as deviants is a way that authorities attempt to establish social order. Condemnation is itself a negative social control. It attempts to maintain structure and culture, it socializes the population about what is acceptable, and sometimes it even helps bring the community together. In condemning others, people can become more convinced that their rules are right, their truths correct, and their social organization superior to others.

Clearly, however, widespread deviance brings conflict, sometimes disorder, and almost always social change. Widespread violent crime brings fear and heightens distrust of the rules, of the authorities, and of other people. It threatens our taken-for-granted social patterns. Large social movements—for example, the civil rights movement, the feminist movement, the anti-Vietnam War movement—question the very nature of society, stretch and sometimes break the rules, challenge the authorities, and are almost always labeled deviant as they engage in organized action. Conflict and disorder almost always bring social change, sometimes slight, sometimes dramatic.

SUMMARY

Deviance well emphasizes the fact that society and people are far more complex and dynamic than the earlier chapters of this book indicated. People are not simply located, socialized, controlled, and passive actors. They decide to shape their roles, to say "no" to their socializers, and to go in directions never intended by authorities.

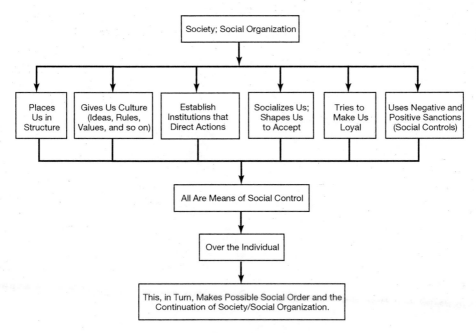

FIGURE 9-1 "Social Organization, Social Control, the Individual, and Social Order"

Yet, what a mistake it is to ignore the concepts of social order and social control. Each social organization—from dyad to society—establishes means by which it attempts to control its members and establish social order. The patterns of structure, culture, and institutions help guarantee order, as do socialization procedures, the encouragement of loyalty, and social controls (See Figure 9-1). The condemnation of certain acts and people as deviant is probably the best example of how organization uses negative social controls. Deviance should be thought to be acts of people regarded as threatening to something important in the social organization. Condemnation benefits social order; widespread deviance may challenge it and is often an important source of social change.

QUESTIONS TO CONSIDER

1. What is the meaning of social order?
2. Describe a group that you once were part of and that is no more. Why did it disappear?
3. Suppose that you were to set up an organization—for example, a club, a church, a school, or a small community. What would you do to try to ensure that social order would successfully be established?
4. Is it true that deviance is universal, yet the things that societies define as deviance is not?

5. Apply this chapter to your own university. In what ways do social structure, culture, socialization, loyalty, social controls, and deviance contribute to social order there?

REFERENCES

Berger, Peter L. 1963. *Invitation to Sociology.* Garden City, NY: Doubleday.
Berger, Peter L., and Brigette Berger. 1972. *Sociology: A Biographical Approach.* 2nd edn. New York: Basic Books.
Campbell, Ernest Q. 1975. *Socialization, Culture, and Personality.* Dubuque, Iowa: W.C. Brown.
Cooley, Charles Horton. 1902. *Human Nature and the Social Order.* 1964 edn. New York: Schocken Books.
Durkheim, Emile. 1893. *The Division of Labor in Society.* 1964 edn. Trans. George Simpson. New York: Free Press.
Goode, Erich. 1978. *Deviant Behavior: An Interactionist Approach.* Englewood Cliffs: NJ: Prentice Hall.
Malcolm X., and Alex Haley. 1964. *The Autobiography of Malcolm X.* New York: Grove Press.
Roucek, Joseph. 1978. "The Concept of Social Control in American Sociology." In *Social Control for the 1980s.* Ed. J. Roucek. Westport, CT: Greenwood Press, pp. 3–19.

RECOMMENDED READING

The following works focus on the question of social order, social control, and social deviance. In one way or another they investigate the question of this chapter: What holds society together?

Aberle, D. F., A. K. Cohen, A. K. Davis, M. J. Levy, Jr., and F. X. Sutton. 1950. "The Functional Prerequisites of a Society." In *Ethics*, 60:100–111.
Adler, Patricia A., and Peter Adler. 1997. *Constructions of Deviance: Social Power, Context, and Interaction.* 2nd edn. Belmont, CA: Wadsworth.
Anderson, Elijah. 1999. *Code of the Street: Decency, Violence, and the Moral Life of the Inner City.* New York: W.W. Norton & Company.
Ballantine, Jeanne H. 2000. *The Sociology of Education.* 5th edn. Upper Saddle River, NJ: Prentice Hall.
Barton, Bernadette. 2006. *Stripped: Inside the Lives of Exotic Dancers.* New York: New York University Press.
Becker, Howard S. 1973. *Outsiders.* Enlarged edn. New York: Free Press.
Becker, Howard S. 1976. *Boys in White: Student Culture in Medical School.* Rev. ed. Chicago: University of Chicago Press.
Bellah, Robert N., Richard Madsen, William M. Sullivan, Ann Swidler, and Steven M. Tipton. 1985. *Habits of the Heart: Individualism and Commitment in American Life.* New York: Harper & Row.
Berger, Peter (ed.). 1998. *The Limits of Social Cohesion.* Boulder, CO: Westview Press.
Breed, Warren. 1955. "Social Control in the Newsroom: A Functional Analysis." In *Social Forces*, 33:326–335.
Chambliss, William J. 1973. "The Saints and the Roughnecks." In *Society*, 11:24–31.
Cooley, Charles Horton. 1909. *Social Organization.* 1962 edn. New York: Schocken Books.
Coser, Lewis. 1956. *The Functions of Social Conflict.* New York: Free Press.
Currie, Elliot. 2004. *The Road to Whatever: Middle-Class Culture and the Crisis of Adolescents.* New York: Metropolitan Books.
Dahrendorf, Ralf. 1958. "Toward a Theory of Social Conflict." In *Journal of Conflict Resolution*, 2:170–183.
Durkheim, Emile. 1915. *The Elementary Forms of Religious Life.* 1954 edn. Trans. Joseph Swain. New York: Free Press.
Ehrenreich, Barbara. 2006. *Bait and Switch: The (Futile) Pursuit of the American Dream.* New York: Metropolitan Books.
Elkin, Frederick, and Gerald Handel. 1989. *The Child in Society: The Process of Socialization.* 5th edn. New York: Random House.
Erikson, Kai T. 1966. *Wayward Puritans: A Study in the Sociology of Deviance.* New York: John Wiley.

Erikson, Kai T. 1976. *Everything in Its Path.* New York: Simon & Schuster.

Erikson, Kai T. 1986. "On Work and Alienation." In *American Sociological Review,* 51:1–8.

Ewen, Stuart. 1976. *Captains of Consciousness.* New York: McGraw-Hill.

Gamson, William A. 1968. *Power and Discontent.* Homewood, IL: Dorsey Press.

Goffman, Erving. 1963. *Stigma: Notes on the Management of Spoiled Identity.* Upper Saddle River, NJ: Prentice Hall.

Goode, Erich (ed.). 1996. *Social Deviance.* Boston: Allyn & Bacon.

Goode, Erich. 2000. *Deviant Behavior: An Interactionist Approach.* 6th edn. Upper Saddle River, NJ: Prentice Hall.

Hull, Kathleen E. 2006. *Same-Sex Marriage: The Cultural Politics of Love and Law.* Cambridge, UK: Cambridge University Press.

Irwin, John. 1985. *Jail: Managing the Underclass in American Society.* Berkeley: University of California Press.

Kephart, William M. 1993. *Extraordinary Groups: An Examination of Unconventional Lifestyles.* 5th edn. New York: St. Martin's Press.

Lemert, Edwin M. 1967. *Human Deviance, Social Problems, and Social Control.* Upper Saddle River, NJ: Prentice Hall.

Luker, Kristin. *Dubious Conceptions: The Politics of Teenage Pregnancy.* Cambridge, MA: Harvard University Press.

Mann, Michael. 2004. *The Dark Side of Democracy: Explaining Ethnic Cleansing.* New York: Cambridge University Press.

Merry, Sally E. 2005. *Human Rights and Gender Violence: Translating International Law into Local Justice.* Chicago, IL: University of Chicago Press.

Messner, Steven E., and Richard Rosenfeld. 1994. *Crime and the American Dream.* Belmont, CA: Wadsworth.

Nisbet, Robert. 1953. *The Quest for Community.* New York: Oxford University Press.

Peters, Thomas J., and Robert H. Waterman, Jr. 1982. *In Search of Excellence.* New York: Warner Books.

Pfohl, Stephen. 1994. *Images of Deviance and Social Control: A Sociological History.* New York: McGraw-Hill, Inc.

Pfuhl, Erwin (Erdwin) H., and Stuart Henry. 1993. *The Deviance Process.* 3rd edn. New York: Aldine DeGruyter.

Quinney, Richard. 2000. *Bearing Witness to Crime and Social Justice.* Albany: State University of New York Press.

Rose, Peter I (ed.). 1979. *Socialization and the Life Cycle.* New York: St. Martin's Press.

Shibutani, Tamotsu. 1955. "Reference Groups as Perspectives." In *American Journal of Sociology,* 60:562–569.

Shibutani, Tamotsu. 1970. "On the Personification of Adversaries." In *Human Nature and Collective Behavior.* Ed. Tamotsu Shibutani. Upper Saddle River, NJ: Prentice Hall.

Shils, Edward S., and Morris Janowitz. 1948. "Cohesion and Disintegration in the Wehrmacht in World War II." In *Public Opinion Quarterly,* 12:280–294.

Simmel, Georg. 1908. "Conflict." In *Conflict and the Web of Group Affiliations.* 1955 edn. Trans. Kurt H. Wolff. New York: Free Press.

Strauss, Anselm L. 1978. *Negotiations: Contexts, Processes and Social Order.* San Francisco: Jossey-Bass.

Sumner, William Graham. 1906. *Folkways.* 1940 edn. Boston: Ginn & Company.

Thrasher, Frederic. 1927. *The Gang.* Chicago: University of Chicago Press.

Tichenor, Veronica J. 2005. *Earning More and Getting Less: Why Successful Wives Can't Buy Equality.* New Jersey: Rutgers University Press.

Tocqueville, Alexis de. 1840. *Democracy in America.* 1969 edn. New York: Doubleday.

Toennies, Ferdinand. 1887. *Community and Society.* 1957 edn. Trans. and ed. Charles A. Loomis. East Lansing, MI: Michigan State University Press.

Wrong, Dennis H. 1994. *The Problem of Order: What Unites and Divides Society.* New York: Free Press.

Wuthnow, Robert. 1987. *Meaning and Moral Order: Explorations in Cultural Analysis.* Berkeley, CA: University of California Press.

Yinger, Milton J. 1982. *Countercultures: The Promise and Peril of a World Turned Upside Down.* New York: Free Press.

Jose Clemente Orozco, "Zapatistas," 1931. Oil on canvas, 45" × 55" (114.3 × 139.7 cm). The Museum of Modern Art, New York. Given Anonymously. Photograph © 2002. The Museum of Modern Art, New York. © Clemente V. Orozco. Reproduction authorized by the Instituto Nacional de Bellas Artes.

✦ 10 ✦

Social Power

Bertrand Russell, a famous twentieth-century philosopher, put the matter better than anyone: "The fundamental concept in social science is Power, in the same sense in which Energy is the fundamental concept in Physics" (1938, 10).

Social power in many ways unites this whole book and is at the very heart of the sociological perspective. One cannot grasp how sociologists view reality without considering this concept.

THE MEANING OF SOCIAL POWER

Social power, like *social order*, is one of those terms we all use but rarely define. In fact, the more we try to define it, the more the concept seems to elude us. Weber wrote that power has something to do with "achieving one's will," and that is a good place to begin. People who have power achieve their will in relation to others. When they want something, they get it; they win in the relationship. Weber believed that social power accompanies social action—therefore, power is an element of a willful act; it accompanies an intentional attempt to achieve one's will or to get one's way.

Three Definitions of Power

Actually, there are three ways to use the word *power* that make sense. Power is the *ability to achieve one's will*. It is potential. I have power to the extent that in the future *I will be able* to achieve my will in relation to others. Corporate executives have power: If they want, they can achieve their will in government, in communities, and in relation to employees. The United States has power in the world: If its leaders want, they can achieve their will in relation to Israel, China, Egypt, or the United Nations. Some social scientists call this ability *potential power*, the probability of achieving one's will *in the future*.

The second way the word *power* makes sense is to describe one's *actual power*. I have power to the extent that *I have already been successful* in achieving my will in relation to others. Corporate executives have power (actual power): In the past, they have been successful in achieving their will in relation to government, to communities, and to employees. The United States has power in the world: It has successfully achieved its will in relation to Israel, China, Egypt, and the United Nations.

The third way *power* is used is in the context of *trying to achieve one's will*. This we might call *exerted power*. Thus, corporate executives exert power when they try to get their way with government, communities, or employees. The United States exerts power in relation to Israel, China, Egypt, and the United Nations.

Power, then, is a complex concept because it is used in many ways, three of which we have described here. To say that "someone has power" may mean either power ability or actual power; to say that someone "uses power" means that the actor exerts power.

Resources and Social Power

To further clarify the meaning of power, we might introduce here the concept of resources. To "achieving will," add the idea of "resources" to power. Resources include *anything an actor possesses* that aids him or her to achieve will in a relationship. Money is a resource, as are good organization, large numbers of people, an army, the police, the courts. "Power ability" depends on resources: *the greater one's resources, the greater one's ability to get one's way.* "Actual power" also depends on resources; it refers to *how successful one has been in applying his or her resources* in actual situations. "Exerting power" is *using one's resources in a relationship* to achieve one's will. Power involves actors having or using *resources* to *achieve their will* in relation to others.

Social power is involved in every instance of interaction. Whenever people interact, they attempt to achieve their will in relation to the others. This can mean selling them something, influencing their views of the world, or controlling their actions. Whether or not they succeed depends on their resources, and it also depends on the resources of those with whom they are interacting. "I have more power than Elaine" means that I can get my way if I want or that I have gotten my way in the past in interactions with Elaine, or it can mean both.

Influence, Control, and Powerlessness

Finally, we should briefly look at what it means to "get one's way" or to "achieve one's will." Normally, relationships are very complex, and no one gets his or her way completely. The outcome of exerting power is normally "influence," moving the others in the direction one desires. Sometimes it is "control," getting one's way without much resistance on the part of the others. We might put this on a continuum for clarification, as illustrated in Figure 10-1. In any relationship I may be able to control the other, influence the other (greatly or slightly), or have no influence on the other. Influence is soft; control is much more dramatic and extreme. The more control one has in a relationship, the more one is able to achieve his or her will.

The opposite of power is *powerlessness*. To be powerless means to be helpless in relation to others, to be determined by the will of others. Powerlessness means that one lacks control over one's own life, is unable effectively to resist the exertion of power by others, and lacks the ability to influence the direction of social

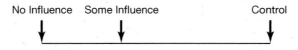

FIGURE 10-1 Possible Outcomes of Exerting Power

organization, including society. Powerlessness brings dependence on others and exploitation (selfish use) by others, if they choose.

Whenever people interact, they bring resources to that interaction. They each try to influence the direction of the interaction. There is always conflict because each will have at least a slightly different goal. The greater their resources, the greater their potential power in the interaction. The more successful they are in the interaction, the more control—or actual power—they have in the relationship. If they lack resources, they are powerless; if they are powerless, they are dependent on the other; if they are dependent, they can be exploited by the other; certainly they are controlled.

This is a model of power we can apply to all types of social situations. It is a good beginning to understanding social power. Power is the opposite of dependence and powerlessness. It has to do with resources and achieving will in a relationship. Potential power means one will or will not be able to influence/control others in the future. Actual power means that one has effectively or ineffectively succeeded in using resources in relation to others to achieve will in the past. Exerting power is the attempt by actors to use resources to influence or control others in a relationship.

Now we will apply this model to an understanding of social organization.

AUTHORITY

Amos Hawley wrote, "Every social act is an exercise of power, every social relationship is a power equation, and every social group or system is an organization of power" (1963, 422). Although for many of us, power is something that sounds bad, it is an inherent part of all social life.

Earlier in this book, we described the nature of social structure. Social structure is a network of social positions, each one of which has attached to it a certain amount of power. That means *positions are resources*. They give the actors, who fill them, the ability to achieve their will. High position in organization brings influence or control over others in organization. When there is disagreement, those in high positions normally win. Of course, there are always other resources that can be brought to situations—guns, money, intelligence, attractiveness, knowledge, physical strength, for example—but positions are of great importance wherever there is organization.

Max Weber's insights on authority are very important here. Weber pointed out that power can arise from many different bases or resources. Our power may be based on fear, money, or promises, for example. Nothing is as permanent and stable, however, as *authority*: position in organization regarded by others as *legitimate*. When rulers overthrow others, what do they immediately seek? Legitimacy. What do kings treasure? Legitimacy. What do revolutionary heroes work for? Legitimacy. In fact, parents, teachers, managers, and boards of directors carefully guard their legitimacy. Legitimacy is very important. It means, in essence, that someone (because of position in organization) has the *right to command others*, and others have *an obligation to obey.* In general, if one accepts his or her place in organization, one grants legitimacy to those above, and one claims legitimacy in relation to those below. Authority is power based on the resource we might call *legitimate position.*

When people interact and come to be placed into status positions, others in the organization get used to that structure, and all know what to do. As structure is formed, those positions become unequal—and again, this comes to be accepted over time. Eventually, the tradition becomes a great ally, and those in organization, because they accept tradition, will accept the inequality. Weber called such authority *traditional* and pointed out, for example, that in highly traditional organization (such as tribal societies), tradition determines who fills what position (usually determined by blood), and people simply accept what tradition commands. Therefore, those in high position in traditional organization have three important resources: legitimacy, tradition, and the organization itself. To disobey authority is to disobey position, tradition, and to be disloyal to organization.

In the twentieth century, traditional authority overwhelmingly changed to *legal-rational authority.* This means that structure is written in the law. Positions are described in a constitution; whoever fills those positions is given a right to command, and others are supposed to feel an obligation to follow. Now those in high position have four important resources: position, legitimacy, constitution/law, and the organization itself. Again, to disobey authority is to disobey legitimate position, the law, and to be disloyal. Nations are founded on this, and almost every organization we enter today has elements of legal-rational authority, which makes power in organization stable over time, and allows business to be carried out without much difficulty.

Sometimes, Weber pointed out, there arises an extraordinary individual within society who gathers around him or her large numbers of people who regard that individual with great awe. This is *charismatic authority.* The individual, because his or her personal qualities are regarded as special, is granted legitimacy. People obey not because of tradition or law, but because of their attraction to the individual, who is usually regarded to be chosen by a special sacred source, by history, by fate, or by the supernatural. Napoleon, Jesus, Gandhi, Martin Luther King, Jr., and Lenin are examples. Such people are revolutionary, and occasionally they overthrow the established authority in society. Of course, their task is then to establish a new social structure with new positions regarded as legitimate. Their task is to make their own charismatic authority (which is personal) into traditional or legal-rational authority.

Weber's analysis is very insightful. It reminds us how important position in organization is as a power resource. We can apply his points to virtually every social relationship. We eventually develop a structure that we come to accept. Acceptance of the structure is the acceptance of its inequality of positions; it is, over time, the acceptance of authority or power arising from positions regarded as legitimate.

There is more to position than legitimacy, however. Let us look further.

THE INEVITABILITY OF INEQUALITY IN ORGANIZATION

Most of us say we believe in democracy. We say that we believe that the people should somehow rule themselves. However, the concepts of "social structure" and "authority" seem to contradict the possibility of democracy, to some extent, because both concepts emphasize obedience and inequality of power.

No one makes this point better than Robert Michels (1876–1936), who developed an important sociological theory that has come to be called the *iron law of oligarchy* (1915). Oligarchy means the "rule of a few," and Michels's law translates into the idea that wherever organization exists, there will be a few people who dominate. This is not because we are evil or weak or stupid; it is, instead, Michels argues, because organization itself releases strong tendencies for this to occur.

It all begins with leaders. Wherever leaders are chosen to coordinate the activities of any group, formal organization, community, or society, then the tendency toward oligarchy begins. Michels did not emphasize legitimacy as Weber did. Instead, he pointed out that position itself is a tremendously important resource in many different ways. With it come access to information, control over what others below are told, greater knowledge of the working of organization, and an alliance with others in high positions. Over time, those in high positions come to believe that the organization is "theirs," that they know what is good for it, so they increasingly act to protect themselves, and much of what they do is designed to keep themselves in power. Those below give up control of the organization: They cannot easily know what is going on among the leaders, so they increasingly find themselves having to trust others above them, they spend little time organizing themselves into an opposition, and they even come to believe that questioning leaders—those "who are in a position to know"—is not wise. It becomes increasingly difficult to challenge decisions that have already been made by those in high position.

Both Michels and Weber underline the importance of positions as resources as the basis for bringing power to certain actors in social organization. Weber focuses on the strength of legitimacy; Michels focuses on the strength of the leadership position itself. Both emphasize the tendency for subordinates to find themselves in positions that require obedience.

CLASS POSITION AND POWER

Social power was a very important concept to Karl Marx, too. Marx believed that real power came from ownership: ownership of the means of production in society. If one owned the means of production (factories, large businesses, large farms, banks), then one possessed a great resource. One had great power in relation to others. He called such people "the ruling class."

Whereas Weber and Michels emphasized the importance of positions in organization as sources of power, Marx emphasized class, or *economic position*. If one was part of the ruling class, then one had control over other people's jobs, and this gave great control over other people's lives. The ruling class in society, because of the great importance of its economic power, is also able to control government, the law and courts, education, the military, and all other important aspects of society. The ruling class is also able to control the dominant ideas, values, and norms in society. That is because its members have the resources necessary to perpetuate their ideas, values, and norms. Control over property gives one greater control over culture, too.

Weber, too, saw the importance of class in determining power in society. Weber's definition of class was broader than Marx's. A *class* to Weber was simply one's economic rank in society based on a whole number of criteria: income, wealth, ownership of wealth-producing property, and so on. Economic rank—class—meant the ability of an individual to achieve his or her will in the economic arena. Thus, *class* to Weber was "economic power." And Weber, like Marx, saw that economic power could often influence power in government and in other human relationships. Thus, in addition to his emphasis on authority in organization, Weber also emphasized economic power as a power resource.

Both Marx and Weber are emphasizing what most of us have come to accept in our commonsense notion of reality. "Money is power": Wealth, in the form of control over the means of production (in the case of Marx), or in many forms (as in the case of Weber), brings the individual or group the ability to win in relation to others. It means that one is better able to direct society to meet his or her own interests; it means that society is built to conform to one's own interests rather than those of others. It means that in interaction with others, one is more likely to get his or her way; it also means that it is difficult for others to control their lives (that is, have independence).

Poverty is at the other end of the spectrum. Marx described the worker in a very dependent position. Nothing is more important than economic survival. If one is dependent on someone else for this, then the other has control over his or her life. If I work for someone else, if my job depends on him or her, then my life is not my own. This is the heart of Marx's thinking about power and powerlessness. Workers are exploited: They work for other people who get rich from their labor. They are paid little so that the employers can grow rich. This is the heart of a class society. The wealthy control the lives of the many.

To both Marx and Weber, poverty is powerlessness. It is a position of dependence on others for survival, for work, for food and shelter. Spending time surviving allows little time for influencing society. Poverty brings no power resources: One has no money and no position in society. Generally, poor people lack organization and leaders trying to bring about change because the business of poverty is survival.

To a great extent, then, it makes good sense to think of class as *power*. Class position brings people resources or lack of them. As long as a society is a class society, there will be an *inequality of power*. Describing society simply as a democracy is to overlook this important fact.

ORGANIZATION AS POWER

Robert Michels believed that the masses in organization were really incapable of organizing themselves and significantly controlling organization. Disorganization, ignorance, poor communication, leaders who exploit the masses or coopted by the elites, make masses incapable of organizing themselves in order to exert power successfully. Both Marx and Weber argued that organization is a very important power resource.

Indeed, for Marx, this was the workers' only real resource against the power of the ruling class. Someday, Marx believed, workers would come together, communicate, and share a consciousness of class position—a realization that society is organized by and for a few people in the ruling class and that the rest are simply controlled and exploited. Eventually, this will bring organization, conflict, and revolution.

Weber, too, saw the central importance of organization. Indeed, Weber believed that organization is a third source of power in society (in addition to authority and class). Everywhere people organize themselves. Some organizations are made up of and represent upper-class people: business associations, private clubs, and political pressure groups. There are also middle-class and working-class organizations: unions, professional associations, and so on. Society also supports organizations of people who share interests other than class interests: African-American, Jewish, Hispanic, Catholic, and Protestant organizations; women's organizations; fraternal organizations. Doctors, lawyers, teachers, and plumbers form organizations, as do those who oppose or defend the right to own guns or have an abortion. All these organizations mean power in society. Alone, the individual can do little; together, people can pool their resources and affect society. Of course, all such groups are not equal. Effectiveness depends on leadership, commitment, careful organization, money, numbers, and knowledge.

THREE THEORIES OF POWER

We have tried to show that social power arises from various sources, not just one.

1. Power arises from *authority*. Authority means that one fills a position in organization that others regard as legitimate. One has a recognized right to command. Such authority may arise from tradition, from the law, or from a belief by people that one has extraordinary personal qualities.
2. Power arises from *positions of leadership* in organization. Positions of leadership bring extraordinary opportunities to control people in organization and to direct the organization.
3. Power arises from *wealth*. It arises from class position in society. Poverty brings powerlessness.
4. Power arises from *organization* itself. People who are well organized have greater ability to achieve their will than those who are not organized.

Modern theories of social power are built on these ideas. There are three basic theories, and each one sees a different system of power in American society. Each points to a different source of power:

1. **Pluralism.** Power is distributed throughout society among many competing organizations.
2. **The power elite.** Power is in the hands of a few people who fill certain key positions in society.
3. **The corporate elite.** Power is in the hands of a few who control the modern corporation.

Pluralism

Of the three theories, *pluralism* is the only theory that describes power diffused throughout most of society. It is a theory consistent with what many people believe about power in the United States. It is a theory that does not focus on inequality of class and inequality of position; instead, it focuses on organizations of people as the most important source of power in American life.

Pluralism is actually a theory of democracy. How can millions of people rule themselves? How can we get everyone involved? How can we check our rulers? How can we check those who have wealth and position? How can we fight the inequality that exists in society so that everyone participates? The answer the pluralist gives is always that *power arises from organizations of people.*

In the nineteenth century, Alexis de Tocqueville described Americans as joiners. We join together to get our way. We join together to make sure that our interests are being met. We join together to get rid of political leaders we dislike, and we join together to make sure that laws we believe in are passed. It is through organization— political parties, religious organizations, pressure groups, occupational and business associations—that people are able to participate effectively in government. Such participation means that a few leaders will not rule (as Michels feared), that the upper class will not control us (as Marx thought), and that authority will not command without question (as Weber predicted). To the pluralist, power rests in the people through their organizations.

To the pluralist, democracy means conflict within rules. It is disagreement over ideas and interests. It is competition for power. Because there are so many groups and because we each belong to several groups, in the end, all of us are represented, and the interests of everyone are eventually met, at least to some extent. When some people are not represented, they get together and form another organization.

There is no illusion here that democracy is the power of the individual. Few social scientists accept this notion. Instead, power is said to belong to groups struggling to get their interests met. There is no belief here that those who fill positions in government have the real power; real power lies in the competing organizations, which represent the people and influence those in political positions.

This first model of power may be correct to some extent. Clearly, organizations of people play a role in influencing the government. However, most sociologists are critical of this theory precisely because it overlooks too much the concepts emphasized throughout this book (and throughout the sociological perspective): social structure, social class, and social power. Most argue that some version of an elite theory of power better explains American society and most other societies.

The Power Elite

The Power Elite (1956), by C. Wright Mills, an important American sociologist, was a landmark book because it took issue with pluralism and documented the dominance of a power elite in the United States.

Mills is very sociological in his approach. The United States is dominated by a few people who fill positions in three sectors: the economy, the military, and the government. Specifically, the United States is run by a few corporate executives, the top officers in the military, and the few who control the executive branch of government. These constitute three elites in society. Mills excludes the legislative and judicial branches of government from his power elite.

On the one hand, these elites compete for power. In the post-Civil War period, the economic elite dominated the United States. With the Depression in the 1930s, the political elite rose to the top; after World War II, the military elite took over.

On the other hand, the three elites are one. Mills tries very hard to show us that these elites intermarry, come from the same families, go to the same schools, interact, and know each other well. He shows that corporate boards are filled with retired generals, political leaders come from corporate boards, and generals come from rich families.

Mills describes the masses in a similar way as Michels: disorganized, apathetic, without knowledge, and trusting.

Mills has many critics, but his influence has been great. Most believe that he exaggerated the power of the military, but many sociologists see a wisdom in his general view: an attempt to take power seriously, to uncover the important positions in society, and to show who fills them and with what result. There is also an element of Marx here: The power elite rules primarily in its own interests, and it influences everything we do and all we believe in and value.

The Corporate Elite

There are those who have built on Mills. For example, G. William Domhoff (1967) has identified the power elite in seven sectors in society, dominated by an upper social class of families with great wealth. There are those who try to fight the ideas of Mills, who study power along pluralist lines. There are also those, such as Suzanne Keller, who accept the idea that modern society is dominated by an elite, but believe that the elite is really several elites, competing for dominance, each checking one another, each representing different interests in society, almost acting like a pluralism among the elites.

However, probably the most important groups influenced by Mills are those who have concentrated their attention on certain positions in society: the top positions in the modern corporation. Money is not the most important resource. Neither is political or military position, or even class position. Organizations do not rule society either. The most important resources in modern society are a few positions in the corporation belonging to the executives and the boards of directors. To fill these positions is to have a resource that allows for great influence in society and in the world.

The modern corporation controls huge amounts of wealth. It employs large numbers of people, produces the goods in society, and controls much of the money. Corporations pay for the advertising and thus influence our wants, our ideas, and our values. They influence the kind of work we all do, and they influence the nature of our education. Their activities influence which area of the country is prosperous and which is poor, and thus they even influence where we all live. They influence every aspect of American life.

The success of corporations depends on what the government and military do. Their success depends on a foreign policy that guarantees friendly foreign governments, a military policy that encourages the production of military goods, and a tax policy that encourages corporate growth. Many corporations are multinational, and thus their success depends on a world order that guarantees markets for their products and a stable source of labor and raw materials. It is therefore essential that political and military leaders are influenced as much as possible.

Increasingly, our society is characterized by larger and larger businesses. This dramatically increases the power of the corporation and those who control the top positions there. There are thousands of U.S. mergers by thousands each year, and some of them include many of the giant corporations, including many of the financial corporations. D. Stanley Eitzen and Maxine Baca Zinn concisely summarize an acceleration of this trend toward larger and larger corporations.

There are thousands of mergers each year, as giant corporations become even larger. . . . The ten largest mergers in U.S. history have occurred in the past fifteen years (e.g. Time, Inc., joining with Warner Communications, Disney merging with Capital Cities/ABC, the combining of Wells Fargo and First Interstate Banks, Philip Morris taking over Miller Brewing, and Texaco buying out Getty Oil).

(1997, 29)

We might add to this the recent mergers of Warner and America Online as well as Wells Fargo and Norwest. And the trend is obviously worldwide with the increasing dominance of multinational corporations:

In essence, the largest corporations control the world economy. Their decisions to build or not to build, to relocate a plant, or to start a new product or scrap an old one have tremendous impacts on the lives of ordinary citizens in the countries they operate from and invest in.

(Eitzen and Zinn, 1997, 32)

Who controls the corporation, and who is it that influences our lives? The answer, according to many researchers who have spent a great deal of time and effort investigating the matter, is a very few individuals who are united in a number of ways with one another, and who have close relationships with political leaders in society. Corporate leaders—executives and boards of directors—do not simply fill positions in one corporation. They are often involved in several. In a study of 123 corporations done by the U.S. Senate Committee on Governmental Affairs, it was found that in 1978, the 13 largest of these corporations had overlapping memberships with 70 percent of the other corporations. A truly corporate elite—united in interests, in outlook, and in power—has emerged:

The unplanned consequence, however, is the formation of a communications network that defines an inner circle of the business community in each country that can rise above the competitive atomization of the many corporations that constitute its base and concern itself with the broader issues affecting the entire large-firm community.

(Useem, 1984, 57)

To those who research the corporate elite, American society is increasingly controlled by a small economic elite, an elite that fills the top positions in a few corporations and influences more and more the lives of all of us in society and indeed in societies all over the world. Power is highly concentrated, according to this theory of power, and real democracy is a fiction.

SUMMARY

The introduction of the concept of "power" into our analysis of interaction and social organization is critical for understanding human beings. Power is a central part of social structure and social class. Those who have power shape the culture and institutions that make up society. Those who have power have the most to gain by social order, and it is they, more than anyone, who develop the instruments of social control. The study of all interactions and all social organizations must, in the end, take into account power: potential power, actual power, and the exertion of power. We are not all equals. Some are able to influence, and some are influenced; some control, and some are controlled. Power rests on resources, so to understand power, it is critical to examine the distribution of resources in society.

It may appear to many of us that we are a democratic society. We have a Bill of Rights, we vote, we have a "free" press, and some would say that we have a free capitalistic system. These sound nice, they appear to be true to many of us, but if we focus on the question of "power in society," democracy seems more difficult to achieve, and we become less confident that it has been achieved in the United States.

Each theory of power summarized in this chapter reminds us of the importance of equality to democracy, the relationship of equality to freedom, and the difficult task it is to create any society resembling a democracy. We are a society of corporations, each with great amounts of power, together dominated by an elite, united to some extent. We are also, of course, a class society, and in our everyday lives, the upper class is more powerful than the rest of us, and the poor have almost no power in relation to the rest of us. As a society we may, as the pluralists argue, work for our own interests through various groups and successfully compete on some issues, but the relative power of such groups cannot be overlooked. So many factors, including authority and the tendencies for organizations to form oligarchies, make democracy so difficult to work for. Perhaps we need to think again in degrees—perfect democracy is an impossible dream, but becoming a more democratic society may be something worth working for.

To ignore the concept of "social power" when we examine human relationships and human society is to ignore the most important qualities that govern human life.

QUESTIONS TO CONSIDER

1. What is the meaning of social power? In describing this, describe the meaning of potential power, actual power, exertion of power, resources, influence, control, and powerlessness.
2. What dyads or groups are you part of? Identify the resources that various people have in that organization. Identify who is the most powerful.
3. Positions bring power to those who fill them. Take an example of a position: president of the United States, president of your university, instructor in your classroom. Can you describe—using both Weber and Michels—the many ways that positions can be used as a resource to achieve will in that social organization?
4. Who has the most power in American society? Identify their resources. What proof do you have that these people actually have achieved their will in relation to others?
5. What is pluralism? To what extent does pluralism describe the nature of American society? What factors work against pluralism?

REFERENCES

Domhoff, G. William. 1967. *Who Rules America?* Englewood Cliffs, NJ: Prentice Hall.
Eitzen, D. Stanley, and Maxine Baca Zinn. 1997. *Social Problems.* 7th edn. Needham Heights, MA: Allyn & Bacon.

Hawley, Amos H. 1963. "Community Power and Urban Renewal Success." *American Journal of Sociology* 68:422–431.

Michels, Robert. 1915. *Political Parties*. 1962 edn. Trans. Eden Paul and Cedar Paul. New York: Free Press.

Mills, C. Wright. 1956. *The Power Elite*. New York: Oxford University Press.

Russell, Bertrand. 1938. *Power*. New York: W.W. Norton.

Useem, Michael. 1984. *The Inner Circle*. New York: Oxford University Press.

RECOMMENDED READING

The following works examine the nature of power as well as the organization of power in the United States.

Adler, Patricia A., and Peter Adler. 1997. *Constructions of Deviance: Social Power, Context, and Interaction*. Belmont, CA: Wadsworth.

Arendt, Hannah. 1958. *The Origins of Totalitarianism*. Cleveland, OH: Meridian Books.

Baltzell, E. Digby. 1964. *The Protestant Establishment: Aristocracy and Caste in America*. New York: Vintage.

Barnes, Sandra L. 2005. *The Cost of Being Poor: A Comparative Study of Life in Poor Urban Neighborhoods in Gary Indiana*. New York: State University of New York Press.

Blau, Peter M. 1964. *Exchange and Power in Social Life*. New York: John Wiley.

Blau, Peter M., and Marshall W. Meyer. 1987. *Bureaucracy in Modern Society*. 3rd edn. New York: Random House.

Boggs, Carl. 2000. *The End of Politics: Corporate Power and the Decline of the Public Sphere*. New York: The Guilford Press.

Brown, Michael, Martin Carnoy, Elliot Currie, Troy Duster, David Oppenheimer B., Majorie M. Shultz, and David Wellman. 2003. *Whitewashing Race: The Myth of a Color-Blind Society*. Berkeley, CA: University of California Press.

Carmichael, Stokely, and Charles V. Hamilton. 1967. *Black Power*. New York: Random House.

Chirot, Daniel. 1994. *Modern Tyrants: The Power and Prevalence of Evil in Our Age*. New York: Free Press.

Dahrendorf, Ralf. 1959. *Class and Class Conflict in Industrial Society*. Stanford, CA: Stanford University Press.

Domhoff, G. William. 1983. *Who Rules America Now? A View for the 80s*. Upper Saddle River, NJ: Prentice Hall.

Domhoff, G. William. 1998. *Who Rules America? Power and Politics in the Year 2000*. Upper Saddle River, NJ: Prentice Hall.

Domhoff, G. William, and Richard Zweigerahaft. 1998. *Diversity in the Power Elite: Have Women and Minorities Reached the Top?* New Haven: Yale University Press.

Dye, Thomas R. 1986. *Who's Running America?* 4th edn. Upper Saddle River, NJ: Prentice Hall.

Emerson, Richard. 1962. "Power-Dependence Relations." In *American Sociological Review*, 27:31–41.

Ewen, Stuart. 1976. *Captains of Consciousness*. New York: McGraw-Hill.

Galbraith, John Kenneth. 1979. *The New Industrial State*. 3rd edn. New York: New American Library.

Gamson, William A. 1968. *Power and Discontent*. Homewood, IL: Dorsey Press.

Gans, Herbert J. 1995. *The War Against the Poor: The Underclass and Antipoverty Policy*. New York: Basic Books.

Goldberg, Michelle. 2006. *Kingdom Coming: The Rise of Christian Nationalism*. New York: W.W. Norton.

Hancock, Angie-Marie. 2004. *The Politics of Disgust: The Public Identity if the Welfare Queen*. New York: New York University Press.

Harris, Scott R. 2006. *The Meaning of Marital Equality*. New York: University of New York Press.

Healey, Joseph F. 1997. *Race, Ethnicity, and Gender in the United States: Inequality, Group Conflict, and Power*. Thousand Oaks, CA: Pine Forge.

Hull, Kathleen E. 2006. *Same-Sex Marriage: The Cultural Politics of Love and Law*. Cambridge, UK: Cambridge University Press.

Hunter, Floyd. 1953. *Community Power Structure*. Chapel Hill, NC: University of North Carolina Press.

Johnson, Heather B. 2006. *The American Dream and the Power of Wealth: Choosing Schools and Inheriting Inequality in the Land of Opportunity*. New York: Routledge.

Keister, Lisa A. 2005. *Getting Rich: America's New Rich and How They Got That Way.* New York: Cambridge University Press.

Keller, Suzanne. 1963. *Beyond the Ruling Class: Strategic Elites in Modern Society.* New York: Random House.

Kerbo, Harold R., and John A. McKinstry. 1995. *Who Rules Japan? The Inner Circles of Economic and Political Power.* Westport, CT: Praeger.

Lenski, Gerhard E. 1966. *Power and Privilege: A Theory of Social Stratification.* New York: McGraw-Hill.

Lichtenstein, Nelson. 2006. *Wal-Mart: The Face of Twenty-First Century Capitalism.* New Press.

Lipset, Seymour Martin, Martin Trow, and James Coleman. 1956. *Union Democracy: The Inside Politics of the International Typographical Union.* New York: Free Press.

Lukes, Steven. 2005. *Power: A Radical View.* 2nd edn. United Kingdom: Palgrave MacMillan.

Mann, Michael. 2004. *The Dark Side of Democracy: Explaining Ethnic Cleansing.* New York: Cambridge University Press.

Marcuse, Herbert. 1964. *One-Dimensional Man.* Boston: Beacon Press.

Marger, Martin N. 1987. *Elites and Masses.* 2nd edn. New York: Van Nostrand Reinhold.

Marx, Karl. 1845–1886. *Selected Writings.* 1956 edn. Ed. T. B. Bottomore. New York: McGraw-Hill.

Marx, Karl. 1867. *Capital.* Vol. 1. 1967 edn. New York: International Publishers.

Marx, Karl, and Friedrich Engels. 1848. *The Communist Manifesto.* 1955 edn. New York: Appleton-Century-Crofts.

Merry, Sally E. 2005. *Human Rights and Gender Violence: Translating International Law into Local Justice.* Chicago, IL: University of Chicago Press.

Milgram, Stanley. 1963. "Behavioral Study of Obedience." In *Journal of Abnormal and Social Psychology,* 67:371–378.

Mintz, Beth, and Michael Schwartz. 1985. *The Power Structure of American Business.* Chicago: University of Chicago Press.

Murphy, John W., and Dennis L. Peck. 1993. *Open Institutions: The Hope for Democracy.* Westport, CT: Praeger.

Olsen, Marvin E. (ed.) 1970. *Power in Societies.* New York: Palgrave MacMillan.

Olsen, Marvin E. 1978. *The Process of Social Organization.* 2nd edn. New York: Holt, Rinehart & Winston.

Phillips, Kevin. 1990. *The Politics of Rich and Poor.* New York: Random House.

Tichenor, Veronica J. 2005. *Earning More and Getting Less: Why Successful Wives Can't Buy Equality.* New Jersey: Rutgers University Press.

Tocqueville, Alexis de. 1840. *Democracy in America.* 1969 edn. New York: Doubleday.

U.S. Bureau of the Census. 1984. *Statistical Abstract of the United States.* Washington, DC: U.S. Government Printing Office.

Weber, Max. 1924. *The Theory of Social and Economic Organization.* 1964 edn. Ed. A. M. Henderson and Talcott Parsons. New York: Free Press.

Wilson, William J. 1973. *Power, Racism, and Privilege.* New York: Palgrave MacMillan.

Wrong, Dennis. 1980. *Power, Its Forms, Bases and Uses.* New York: Harper & Row.

Will Barnet (b. 1911) EARLY SPRING, 1976. Oil on canvas,
43⅛" × 82⅛". *Will Barnet/Licensed by VAGA, New York, NY.*

✦ 11 ✦

Symbols, Self, and Mind:
Our Active Nature

Chapter 10 described the place of social power in social relationships. Much of it questions the reality of freedom and democracy in human affairs. Indeed, if we look back at earlier chapters, we can see a continuous tendency to describe the human being as an actor controlled in society, molded by institutions, positioned in social structure, and socialized to accept the culture of society. Sociologists tend to be what is sometimes called "deterministic."

If a perspective is deterministic, this means that the cause of human behavior is thought to be outside free choice. So, for example, if we believe that God causes all that happens, or if we think that everything is fated, that everything is caused by the position of the stars, we also tend to be deterministic in how we see the human being.

Determinism is definitely part of what much of sociology is. It just seems to "come with territory" because the real purpose of sociology (as well as all other sciences) is to understand what *causes* something—what causes human action. The question does not lend itself to an investigation of freedom and individuality.

Yet sociologists will almost always become defensive when people charge that their perspective does not account for at least some freedom. It is true that almost every sociologist believes that the human being is to some extent an individual and to some extent free. However, much of our work documents social patterns, socialization, and social control, leading students to wonder how individuality and freedom are possible in a sociological perspective.

The work of George Herbert Mead (1863–1931) begins to crack sociological determinism to some extent. Mead, who was a social theorist at the University of Chicago, was really a philosopher and psychologist, but his work had a major impact on sociology students at Chicago, and through them, he has found a very important place in the discipline of sociology. Mead wrote about the links between the individual and society, and always emphasized the interdependence of the two. Society makes the human being, yet the human being, in turn, makes society. We are social beings, Mead argued, but our most important individual qualities (all of which arise from society)—symbols, self, and mind—also allow us to exercise some control over our lives.

INDIVIDUALITY AND FREEDOM

Perhaps the most important questions thinking people ask concern the relationship between the individual and society: Are we simply the product of our social life? Do we make free choices? Do we have any impact on the direction of society? Is there any real individuality?

Many of us go through college and the rest of our lives without seriously considering such questions. "Of course, I am an individual." "Of course, I am free." Such assertions are part of our taken-for-granted reality; they are embedded in the culture of the United States. Indeed, we say we enjoy living in this society because we are free and we are allowed to be individuals. The problem is far more complex than this, however — as the first 10 chapters of this book make clear: How free are we, and how much individuality can we really claim, given the importance of social structure, culture, socialization, social controls, and social power?

If we scrape the surface of our own philosophies of life, we will see that ideas about freedom are central to our views on a number of matters. Most of us assume freedom when we argue that individuals will be judged by God in the *choices* made in life: good or evil, faith or nonfaith, truth or falsehood. Our attitudes toward poverty, crime, and punishment are based on our ideas concerning the individual's ability to exercise choice. When other people act, we may hold them responsible for what they do, or we may say that "they have no choice." It is always interesting to notice how many of us will fall into the trap of blaming the individual who does things we disapprove of and then talk about a good home, luck, opportunities associated with social class, or religious training as being responsible if the individual does something we like.

A philosophy of freedom is central to our political ideas. The 1960s were a cry to extend freedom to African Americans, and the 1970s to women. Presidents Kennedy and Johnson tried to fight poverty and extend freedom to the poor. We were told that the Vietnam War was fought for freedom; we were also told that it must be stopped in the name of freedom. Presidents Reagan and Bush ran for office in the name of economic freedom, and much of Reagan's foreign policy was defended as the last great hope for political freedom in the world. Freedom from Iraqi aggression was reason for our first war against Iraq; the second war eventually became a war for Iraqi freedom. Freedom was also a major theme in NATO and UN actions during the Clinton administration, remains central to the Israeli–Palestinian conflict, and seems always to be an issue in Congress in every important bill debated. Groups cry out for freedoms of choice, speech, worship, and the press. To many in the United States, communism has been the enemy of freedom; to others, there is little freedom in a world where corporations dominate. The failure of communism is seen by most Americans as the triumph of freedom. All sides in war usually claim that they fight for freedom; it is very difficult to determine who in truth does so. Perhaps the problem is so complex that many sides fight for freedom, but for different people.

Individualism is also central to U.S. culture. The pioneer, the farmer, the immigrant who makes it big, and the poor man who becomes president are our heroes. The appeal of rock music is in part the worship of the individual, and the respect we have for powerful people in history leads back to this value. That is why, perhaps, social science is not always welcome to the political and economic leaders of our society. After all, social science critically evaluates what most of us accept — the reality of individuality and freedom.

Not all societies value freedom and individualism. In some, commitment to kin is far more important. In some, commitment to tradition, God, or society itself overshadows freedom or individuality. In some, nationalism, material success, or immediate pleasure sacrifices any commitment to freedom.

It is important to separate freedom from individuality. *Freedom* means that *the actor actively makes choices and directs himself or herself in situations. The actor is in control of his or her own life.* This may mean the actor is an individual; it may also mean the actor is like other individuals. The actor, for example, may actively choose to conform or to be like others.

Individuality means that *the actor is unique. The actor is different from others around him or her.* This may arise from freedom: The actor may actively refuse to think or act in a certain way simply because others do so, or the actor may rationally choose a certain direction. Individuality can also spring from something other than freedom, however. For example, it may result from internal forces over which the actor lacks control; or it may result from other individuals or groups that shape the actor to be different from those outside the immediate interaction. I may be an individual who flies off the handle all the time, making me different from others around me, but that does not mean I am free. Or I may be shaped and controlled by a religious group that is unique, making me very different from everyone else in my neighborhood. Being different does not necessarily make me free.

Freedom has to do with *cause.* Science tends to see cause in nature; religion sometimes sees cause in the supernatural. Sociology tends to see cause in society. But if freedom does exist, it exists when the individual is somehow his or her own cause, exercising control over self and situation. No such freedom can ever be complete — it is always limited — but it is important to recognize that *to the extent that the actor has control over his or her life, we can say that he or she is free.* To the extent that other forces (internal or external) control the actor, we say that he or she is not free.

Individuality has to do with *differences.* All humans are individuals to some extent. Indeed, all snowflakes and all stars are individuals. Even in totalitarian societies, we can identify characteristics that make each individual at least slightly different. When a person stands out, he or she is said to be very different from others, and we usually call that person an individual. To the extent that a person is truly different from those around him or her, it makes sense to call that person an individual.

HOW CAN WE EXPLAIN INDIVIDUALITY?

In part, individuality is like all other human qualities: It arises in interaction with others. We are all different — and some of us are very different — partly because we each have a *unique set of interactions, positions, cultures, and socialization experiences. We are all subject to a different set of social controls. Each actor faces a different set of influences; each is the convergence of a different set of social forces.* Even people in the same family will be different: Each sibling is in a different position in the same family structure and is influenced by a different set of siblings ("You are my brother; I am your brother — we each have different brothers"). People in the same family will still have gender differences and differences in generation, and all will have different friends, teachers, and adults with whom they interact. Societies — or families — cannot create identical actors precisely because each actor has a different set of social organizations and a different history of interaction. And interaction can never be fully controlled or predetermined.

We are all different in part because of biological differences. Boys and girls are physically different, and some would go further and identify some intellectual and emotional differences. As individuals, we have different temperaments, potentials, and appearance. Each of these helps make us unique. Others around us will react to such qualities, and in their reactions compound or direct these differences.

We are also individuals because all of us have at least some control over our own choices. We are probably all free to some extent, able to choose "no" over "yes" sometimes, and "maybe" at other times. It is important to see that not only does society control and shape us, but that we, in turn, take away some control from society and shape our own lives. Whatever is told us is shaped into our own unique ideas. Whatever we are told to do is, to some extent, considered and uniquely altered or even rejected. In this way, freedom is linked to individuality. Freedom allows us to make ourselves in ways that others do not expect or desire; freedom allows us to question and make our own choices into what we believe and do, creating at least some individuality in all of us.

We are individuals, then, partly because (1) each of us has a different interaction history and is subject to a different set of social forces; (2) each of us is biologically different, and the reactions of others to these differences also enter into what we all become; and (3) each of us because we have some freedom are able to create our own uniqueness to some extent. Of course, some of us are much more individuals than are others, but this can usually be linked to these three sets of causes.

But how can we account for freedom? Are we born with this quality? Is it part of our "nature"? Is it, like individuality, traceable to our social life?

THE ORIGIN OF HUMAN FREEDOM

George Herbert Mead and sociologists who share his views believe that *freedom, like everything else about us, comes from our social life.* Humans are social to their very core, and we are not only imprisoned by this fact but also set free by it. It is responsible for our ability to break out, to control our self, to act back on society, and to direct our self away from what the socializers and controllers want. To understand this, we must understand that other people, by socializing us to become what they want, actually *provide us with tools to decide independently what we want.* More specifically, it is through socialization that the individual takes on three important qualities—*symbols, self, and mind*—and these, in turn, become qualities that become the basis for human freedom.

To understand this process better, let us now turn to each one of these concepts.

HUMAN BEINGS ARE SYMBOL USERS

Human beings, totally helpless at birth, without instinct to guide them, must rely on other people—on socialization—to show them the way to deal with situations. This is accomplished by the child imitating the adult, through rewards and punishments given by the adult, but most of all through the words used by the adult to identify the world, the person, the rules, the patterns, and so on. Even an action—any kind of punishment, for example—usually includes a set of words that identifies the type of behavior isolated as wrong ("Don't pick those flowers" or "Don't ever pick any flowers" or "Don't ever pick flowers that have not bloomed" or "Don't ever pick flowers that belong to someone else" or "Don't ever pick flowers without asking me first"). A category of reality is labeled; we are taught how we are supposed to act in relation to that category of reality. With the use of words we are able to act appropriately in many situations we encounter; we do not simply respond to flowers, but we come to understand the many subtle ways we are supposed to act toward them.

Unlike other animals that can be trained to respond to words, the child learns how to *use* words. Our socializers are symbol users; we then take on these symbols and they become ours to use. This transforms us into beings who can *think, choose, control self,* and ultimately *break off from the controls of the socializers. Socialization, because it depends so much on symbols, ends up leading to actions unplanned by the socializers.*

The Meaning of Symbols

Words are symbols. Indeed, the only function of words is to be symbolic. That is why they are created in the first place. However, *objects* can be made into symbols too (for example, a flower or ring, which may mean friendship or love or marriage). Many of our *acts* are also symbols. When I shake my fist, I am telling you I feel angry; when I throw my arms around you, I am telling you something about my feelings about seeing you. Raising your hand in class is an attempt to tell me you want to say something; stomping out of the room in the middle of the lecture tells me you are angry; putting your coat on tells me you are ready to leave.

Symbols are words, acts, and objects used intentionally—on purpose—to communicate and represent something. Communication can be among people or within the individual (talking to self). We share something with others; we converse with ourselves.

When we say that symbols also represent something we are saying, that they are "meaningful" acts, they make sense to the person using them, and thus they are used on purpose. The actor who gives them off understands that X represents—stands for—Y, something very different. *Wine* represents a supernatural being, the word *elephant* represents a type of animal characterized by a long trunk, and a *kiss* represents an expression of love. To say that a symbol is used to represent something is to say that the one who gives it off understands his or her own acts of communication. Not only does the symbol user communicate, but the message given is understood by the communicator. This quality of symbols—what George Herbert Mead called "meaningful"—makes communication possibilities infinitely greater, complex ideas possible, and thinking (talking to oneself) a central characteristic of the symbol user.

Symbolic conversation is not simply responding to the stimuli of one another, but intentionally communicating and representing something we want others to know about us.

Not all communication involves symbols. Almost all animals communicate without symbols. The calls, sounds, or movements of one act as a stimulus to the other, which responds automatically. For Mead, however, the special quality of symbolic communication is the fact that the one who communicates both understands his or her own communication and intentionally communicates. This makes it possible to apply the symbols we learn to thousands of situations, conversations, letters we write, poetry we create, and problems we have to solve.

Of course, using symbols does not always work smoothly. Sometimes I use symbols to communicate but no one listens. Or sometimes I do not mean to communicate but others will interpret my acts as symbolic. Or I can mean one thing by my symbols but others think I mean something else. Symbols are almost never perfectly shared, and there is often the possibility for misunderstanding. For a "perfect" symbol to exist, it would have to be perceived and understood by others in exactly the same way it was intended by the user. This is not possible.

Of course, part of human communication is not really symbolic. We communicate without realizing it; we give off body language that others respond to or interpret. To say that humans are symbol users much of the time is not to deny all these other ways we communicate, but to isolate one very important human quality and examine its usefulness.

How is meaning established? How do we come to understand what something represents? The answer is obvious: Symbols are created among people as they interact. Symbols are social, not instinctive. They are assigned meaning through agreement; meaning is not fixed in nature but actually established and changed. We can make any word, act, or object into a symbol. A rock is not usually thought to be a symbol, but you and I can determine that a certain rock in a certain place will represent danger. I can show off my horse, and my horse becomes a symbol of my wealth, my skill, or my values. Words are established to specifically be symbols. A gesture such as giving you the peace sign is a symbol, and crossing my arms can also be a symbol if I am trying to show impatience. Symbols are shared among people, and whatever people decide should be a symbol becomes one. The actor understands what people use a representation for and uses it whenever he or she finds it useful.

The Importance of Symbols

There are two ways symbols play a central role in our lives:

1. *Human social organization depends on symbols.* Most other animal societies are based either on instinct or imitation; they do not have the complexity and flexibility that symbolic behavior permits. Human society demands lifelong socialization, and human socialization uses symbols. All that is cultural — values, goals, norms, and truths — is symbolic. All accumulation of knowledge that is passed from one generation to the next depends on socialization through symbols. Further, social organization demands that human beings symbolically communicate with each other as they cooperate, as problems are encountered and worked out. Ongoing symbolic communication is central to group problem solving.
2. *The human individual depends on symbols.* Symbols are what we use to communicate with ourselves; that is, most of our thinking consists of symbol use. It is through word symbols that we analyze situations, define them, apply our past experience, and predict the consequences of our action. Symbol use means we are problem solvers in our world; we plan our action rather than just respond to stimuli. Symbols also allow us to catalog experiences, to store it all in a tremendously complicated memory bank, to organize a mass of meaningful details that becomes available to us for application in particular situations. While we act, we are not limited to the present physical situation. We can think of the past and future, and

we can consider things we never encountered directly, like Russia or heaven or outer space. Finally, symbols open up to consideration of an abstract world, a world that is only symbolic, a world that does not exist in our physical environment. We can consider things like freedom, love, God—and most of the concepts of a perspective such as sociology. And we can create new, fictional worlds by actively manipulating symbols into different combinations.

Symbols and Freedom

So symbols are the basis for human thinking, and thinking in turn is basic to what we do in situations. We do not just respond to the world presented to us by others; we manipulate that world in our heads with the use of symbols, and we act accordingly. We do not just fill status positions. We also think about them, we define our roles in them, make decisions on how to act, and even change the position as we go along. Sometimes we may conform without much thinking, but almost always there is some analysis on our part, some decision making. Teachers fill status positions and conform to expectations of students, but they also critically evaluate those expectations. Sometimes teachers worry about what student expectations appear to be, and they think about how to make their teaching better and even how to try to influence student expectations. Students, too, do more than simply fill status positions. They evaluate, plan, try shortcuts, play around with the situations they encounter, and when trouble arises, they think of ways to deal with it.

The interesting thing about word symbols is that the individual is able to manipulate them creatively, to arrive at unique solutions to problems, to develop new ideas, term papers, books, and artistic products. Indeed, there is some creativity in everything we do. The situations we encounter every day are not identical to earlier situations, so we must adjust ourselves ever so slightly, apply what we know, and work out our action. Each person we meet and every problem we confront demands that we think out our actions ourselves rather than depend entirely on what we have learned from others. It is through the internal manipulation of symbols that humans become creative, active, choosing individuals. And this fact introduces the possibility for freedom into the action of human beings.

Rather than requiring mechanical robots or instinctive ants, human social organization demands *thinking* actors. Part of the "problem" with thinking actors is that they are difficult to control completely, so actors within all social organization end up questioning, criticizing, challenging, and shaping the direction of their own lives in social organization. Symbols, then, as well as capabilities they make possible in the human being, make us all into potentially free actors, at least to some extent.

WE POSSESS SELF AND MIND

Along with symbols, self and mind are also important qualities that make possible a more active, free being.

What is a self? Is it our true essence? Is it the same as our personality? Is it a little person within us waiting to be encouraged to grow and unfold?

For most sociologists, the *self* simply means *the person as object*, an object that the actor can look back at and act back on. We all act toward our environment, toward other people and objects, but we can also act back toward our self. We can talk to our self. We can look at our self and judge ourselves as good or bad, nice or not nice, beautiful or ugly, wise or stupid. We can look at our self in relation to others and assess how people are acting toward us; we can assess the effects of their acts on us, and our acts on them. We can also call our self a name—to give ourselves an identity (man, American, boss). We direct our self; that is, we exercise self-control. We tell ourselves how to act. This constant conversation with our self is a big part of the reason we end up acting as we do.

What is the significance of selfhood? Let us try to be a little more systematic.

1. *The conversation we all carry on with the self is called thinking.* Thinking is the actor pointing things out to himself or herself, figuring out situations, problem solving, analyzing what others are doing, assessing what he or she is doing in relation to others, and so on. Thinking—talking to self with symbols—allows us to make decisions in situations, to control what we do in situations.

2. *Selfhood means we are able to talk to self about self.* We see ourselves in situations; we are *self-aware*. We become our own object in the environment that others are acting toward. We realize that we are affected by others and that we have an effect on others. We can *assess* how we do. We can judge our self, liking or disliking what we do and what we are. Over time, we develop a *self-concept*. And we call ourselves names—that is, we establish *identities*, and we tell others who we think we are. To be able to look back on our self opens up all kinds of actions that make us active beings rather than responding organisms.

3. *To possess a self also means that we can exercise self-direction in situations.* Instead of simply being pushed around by our environment—conditioned or manipulated by it—we are instead able to turn back on our self, think and see ourselves in the situation, and *tell ourselves how to act* in the situation. We are in control to some extent, holding back action, planning action, trying out plans, and evaluating and reevaluating our efforts. Sometimes, we do this very consciously and deliberately; most of the time, we do this very quickly and are barely conscious of what we are doing.

Selfhood thus makes each of us a being in conversation with self, conscious of self, and in control of self. It means we are able to temper the influence of others on what we do. It does not mean that others are not important; it means only that, in addition to the influence of others, the actor is able to interpret, add to, plan, assess, and, to some extent, control the situation.

But Mead makes the important point that the self, like symbols, is created by others in interaction with the individual. We come to see ourselves only by first seeing ourselves through the acts and words of others. Others are the looking glass through which we become aware that we exist.

The self develops in stages. First, we see others acting toward us, and we imitate their acts toward ourselves ("preparatory stage"). When we begin to take on language, we are able to understand the perspectives of "significant others," such as parents; we take on these perspectives as our own, and we talk to self as they do ("Nice boy." "You are intelligent." "You are Frank's brother." "Don't ask for a cookie until after dinner."). Mead calls this stage the "play stage" because the child uses the perspective of one person at a time to talk to self. Eventually, we are able to assume the perspective of many people simultaneously and thus develop a "generalized other," made up of all those who are important to us. We converse with self and control self from that perspective. We have then become a member of society because we are now able to assume the perspective and rules of society.

This stage Mead calls the "game stage" because we are now able to understand the rules of a cooperative whole.

We are dependent on others for the development of our self; yet, as self develops, we are able to take some control from others, we begin to hold private conversations, and we make choices in situations. The actor who has a mature self is able to take or leave what others say and do, interpret what is going on, and determine his or her own directions. We borrow the perspectives of others, but alter them to fit our needs to some extent; we use them as guides. We are able to tell ourselves to conform or to refuse conformity, to play a role as others expect or to test others, and to act creatively or to leave the social organization. *The self, although grounded in society, allows for some individuality, some creative interpretation, and some self-direction and choice.*

Mead links mind to self and symbols. *Mind* is easily confused with *self* and *symbols*. It arises in the human being at the same moment self and symbols arise. It is the third human quality that allows for some freedom.

Mind is thinking, all the conversation the actor carries on with self. Mind is the talking the actor does to himself or herself. This activity involves all the ways the actor points things out to self. Earlier in this chapter, when we described the various ways the actor acts toward self, we were describing *mind*.

Mind is not brain, nor is it all brain activity. It is, instead, a certain kind of brain activity, that activity we call thinking or talking to oneself. Mind action goes on all the time. We talk to ourselves from the moment we wake up until the moment we fall asleep at night. Thinking—mind action—becomes most obvious to us when we confront a new situation or when our action is interrupted and a problem must be overcome. Then our thinking becomes more conscious and deliberate; we must plan ahead. However, almost every situation demands some thinking as we act— quick, ongoing talking to self.

Mind is the third building block of freedom. There is no self-control or symbol use without mind; there is no active control of our environment without mind. To talk to self—to think, to *have mind*—means that we do not simply respond but that we actively play out our situation in our heads and can figure out what action we will take. What we think cannot be totally free, but without some thinking, freedom is impossible.

Symbols, self, and mind are easily confused because they are so intimately connected. Simply remember that *symbols* are things the individual uses to communicate (including communicating with self), *self* is the object the individual communicates to (with symbols), and *mind* is all the action—with symbols— that we engage in toward the self.

SUMMARY

Mead's greatest insight is the idea that symbols, self, and mind—all interdependent and basic to our active nature—arise from society. We are not born with these qualities; instead, we are born with the potential to develop these qualities through social interaction with other humans. This captures very well how social humans are. Even our ability to act back, to say no, to control our self, and to shape organization that shapes us is a social creation. What forms us forms even our potential for some freedom.

It is very difficult to determine whether freedom exists. If it does, then it is important to define it carefully, as this chapter has attempted to do. There are other approaches to freedom, but this chapter has been a good beginning for understanding it and the possibility that some freedom is possible. Think of freedom as control over one's own life; think of nonfreedom as something other than the actor controlling his or her life. There are always factors we can identify that control our lives (this book has tried to identify many of these social factors). However, the question remains: Do we have any control, and if we do, where does this ability come from? This chapter, based on the ideas of George Herbert Mead, tries to break out of the usual determinism that sociology teaches and presents at least some possibility for freedom. Unlike most discussions of freedom, however, Mead's work does not simply *assume* freedom but tries to identify the human qualities that make freedom possible: symbols, self, and mind. And all these qualities, of course, are socially created (see Figure 11-1).

QUESTIONS TO CONSIDER

1. This chapter argues that humans are to some extent free because of symbols, self, and mind. Can you explain this? Do you agree?
2. What is freedom? What is individuality? To what extent do you think human beings are free, or individuals? What do you think is the origin of freedom and individuality?
3. Human beings are social to their very core. How does this chapter support this proposition? What do you think of this argument?

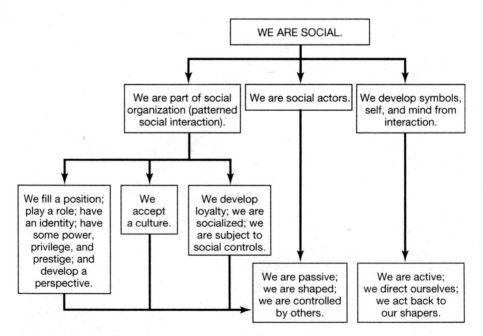

FIGURE 11-1   The Effects of Our Social Nature

RECOMMENDED READING

The following works focus on the issues of freedom, individuality, and the importance of symbols, self, and mind.

Becker, Ernest. 1962. *The Birth and Death of Meaning*. New York: Free Press.
Berger, Peter. 1963. *Invitation to Sociology*. Garden City, NY: Doubleday.
Berger, Peter L., and Thomas Luckmann. 1966. *The Social Construction of Reality*. Garden City, NY: Doubleday.
Blauner, Robert. 1964. *Alienation and Freedom: The Factory Worker and His Industry*. Chicago: University of Chicago Press.
Blumer, Herbert. 1962. "Society as Symbolic Interaction." In *Human Behavior and Social Processes*. Ed. Arnold Rose. Boston: Houghton Mifflin.
Blumer, Herbert. 1969. *Symbolic Interactionism: Perspective and Method*. Upper Saddle River, NJ: Prentice Hall.
Brim, Orville G., Jr. 1968. "Adult Socialization." In *Socialization and Society*. Ed. John A. Clausen. Boston: Little, Brown.
Brim, Orville G., Jr., and S. Wheeler (eds.). 1966. *Socialization After Childhood*. New York: John Wiley.
Charon, Joel M. 2004. *Symbolic Interactionism: An Introduction, an Interpretation, an Integration*. 8th edn. Upper Saddle River, NJ: Prentice Hall.
Cooley, Charles Horton. 1902. *Human Nature and the Social Order*. 1964 edn. New York: Schocken Books.
Elkin, Frederick, and Gerald Handel. 1989. *The Child in Society: The Process of Socialization*. 5th edn. New York: Random House.
Freud, Sigmund. 1930. *Civilization and Its Discontents*. 1953 edn. London: Hogarth Press.
Fromm, Erich. 1962. *Beyond the Chains of Illusion*. New York: Simon & Schuster.
Goffman, Erving. 1959. *The Presentation of Self in Everyday Life*. New York: Doubleday (Anchor).
Hertzler, Joyce O. 1965. *A Sociology of Language*. New York: Random House.
Hewitt, John P. 2000. *Self and Society*. 8th edn. Needham Heights, MA: Allyn & Bacon.
Jenkins, Richard. 1996. *Social Identity*. New York: Routledge.
Lindesmith, Alfred R., Anselm L. Strauss, and Norman K. Denzin. 1999. *Social Psychology*. 8th edn. Thousand Oaks, CA: Sage Publications.
Lukes, Steven. 1973. *Individualism*. New York: Harper & Row.
McCall, George J., and J. L. Simmons. 1978. *Identities and Interactions*. New York: Free Press.
Mead, George Herbert. 1925. "The Genesis of the Self and Social Control." In *International Journal of Ethics*, 35:251–277.
Mead, George Herbert. 1934. *Mind, Self and Society*. Chicago: University of Chicago Press.
Meltzer, Bernard N. 1972. *The Social Psychology of George Herbert Mead*. Kalamazoo, MI: Center for Sociological Research, Western Michigan University.
Prus, Robert. 1996. *Symbolic Ineraction and Ethnographic Research: Intersubjectivity and the Study of Human Experience*. New York: State University of New York Press.
Rose, Peter I. (ed.). 1979. *Socialization and the Life Cycle*. New York: St. Martin's Press.
Rosenberg, Morris. 1979. *Conceiving the Self*. New York: Basic Books.
Rousseau, Nathan. 2002. *Self, Symbols, and Society: Classic Readings in Social Psychology*. New York, NY: Rowman & Littlefield Publishers, Inc.
Shibutani, Tamotsu. 1961. *Society and Personality: An Interactionist Approach to Social Psychology*. Upper Saddle River, NJ: Prentice Hall.
Shibutani, Tamotsu. 1986. *Social Processes: An Introduction to Sociology*. Berkeley, CA: University of California Press.
Strauss, Anselm L. 1978. *Negotiations: Contexts, Processes and Social Order*. San Francisco: Jossey-Bass.
Warriner, Charles K. 1970. *The Emergence of Society*. Homewood, IL: Dorsey Press.
White, Leslie A. 1940. *The Science of Culture*. New York: Farrar, Straus & Giroux.
Whorf, Benjamin Lee. 1956. *Language, Thought, and Reality*. New York: John Wiley.

Lawrence, Jacob (1917–2000) © ARS, NY. The migration gained in momentum.
1940–1941. Panel 18 from The Migration Series. Tempera on gesso on composition
board, 18" × 12". Gift of Mrs. David M. Levy (28.1942.9). *Art Resource, New York.*

✦ 12 ✦

Social Change

INDIVIDUAL CHANGE AND SOCIAL CHANGE

Individuals change. They grow up. They change their directions, their ideas, their friends, and their values. As they change roles, they too change, and as they change groups or communities, they change again. Every organization we enter means change because we are faced with new kinds of controls, structure, culture, and social institutions.

All interaction means that we must alter what we do according to what others are doing. Their expectations matter to us, and we give them some consideration. As a result, our directions change, and we make new plans for our lives. In interaction, we negotiate with others over our roles. We experience role conflict, and we change. We think about our situations and our lives because we have symbols, mind, and self, and we decide to go in new ways.

The sociological view of the individual is that the individual continuously changes. Change basically occurs for two reasons: (1) The individual is a symbol-using, problem-solving, active being with self and mind, always thinking and making choices, which often take him or her in new directions; (2) the individual is a social being; as the social context changes, the individual will change. The individual may go into new organizations, the individual may assume new positions in organization, the organization itself may change, or society may change. Most of this book has focused on these ideas. We have tried to link the individual to a social context; we have tried to show that both individual consistency and change are linked to that social context.

However, until now, we have not focused on *social change*. Our emphasis has been on order and stability in organization. But social organization also changes. Change is easily as important a topic in organization as order and stability.

With all the factors defending order in organization, how is change possible? What causes social change? This is a difficult question, which sociologists have only begun to understand and most others explain only in oversimplified terms. "Things don't really change—there is nothing new under the sun," cries the skeptic.

"History repeats itself," says the pessimist. "Change is bad. Materialism and selfishness are weakening our moral fiber," preaches the minister. "The social order and social change is God's plan for us," teaches another. "Change is the responsibility of each individual," argues the moralist. "Economics, it's all economics—that's the source of all change," some try to prove, or "It is only through revolution that things change," cry the disgruntled.

Everyone seems to have a key to social change. Each of these people may have something important to say, but each thought is far too simple. Social change and its causes are not simple.

In fact, even defining what constitutes social change is not an easy matter. How much does something have to change to call it change? Has the relative position of African Americans and whites changed since the Civil War? Yes and no, depending on one's definition of change.

We might say that change means *something is significantly different today than it has been in the past.* We might say that social change means that a *social pattern (structure, culture, institution) is significantly different from what it has been in the past.* Social change is a lot easier to understand if we focus on social patterns—after all, if social patterns are so central to all organization, then they should be our focus when we examine social change.

The question to be considered then is, what causes social patterns to change? There are many factors, and sociologists differ as to which is the most important. In this chapter we will summarize six:

1. *Acts of individuals and groups* who work for change are sometimes important for bringing about change.
2. *Social conflict* between groups and between individuals is sometimes important for bringing change.
3. *Influences from outside the organization* are sometimes important for bringing about change within the organization. Such outside influences include both other organizations and the physical environment.
4. *Technology* often brings change; the application of knowledge to problem solving is instrumental for producing change. Industry, bureaucracy, and computers are three examples of technology having great impact on society.
5. *Changes in population* bring change to organization. As numbers increase or decrease, patterns change; as population migrates from one place to another, organization changes.
6. *Change in one social pattern* affects other social patterns. As structure changes, for example, both culture and social institutions will change. As one social institution changes, other social institutions will be affected, as will culture and social structure.

ACTS OF INDIVIDUALS AND GROUPS CHANGE ORGANIZATION

Social organization changes through the acts of social actors, communicating to, interpreting, and influencing one another. Each actor occasionally tries to have an impact on the social patterns, and some may be slightly successful. This is more true in dyads than it is in societies, and it is more true of small societies than of large ones. Because all human social organization is made up of active symbol-using beings with minds and selves, there are always actors who make attempts to test, to redefine the environment, to alter others, perhaps to deviate from or challenge social patterns.

Some actors have more impact than others. This is because of the amount of *power* one has in the social organization. In society, those people at the top of the various stratification and political systems are able to influence the direction of change much more dramatically than those at the bottom. Indeed, one aspect of all status positions, you may recall, is power, the ability to achieve one's will in relation to others in social organization. When Andrew, my son, was growing up, it was difficult for him to change things in our family (although he kept trying), because my wife and I have the power positions. The president of the university I worked for could have changed that organization more easily than I could have, and much more easily than any student could have. In society, the president of the United States can have considerable impact, and so can the head of General Motors or the chief justice of the Supreme Court or the head of the State Department. The power of the owners of the big corporations in American society has been extensively documented. Corporate leaders influence foreign policy, even playing a significant role in revolutions, as seems to have the case in the overthrow of Allende in Chile, for example. Oil company chiefs have an important influence on this society's energy policies by controlling resources and continuously reminding us how dependent we are on the product they produce and distribute to us.

But in spite of these examples of individual impact, the power of structure, culture, social institutions, and social controls, embedded in the past, makes it very difficult to make substantial changes in social organization (except perhaps in the dyad or small group). We all want to believe that the individual makes a difference in organization, but when faced with the patterns of social organization, each of us in reality has minimal power to direct and shape social organization the way we choose. We are all caught up at every level in social organizations whose patterns have great stability. These patterns work against change, especially dramatic change.

The paradox is that those in the positions to bring about the most change are least likely to desire change; having made it to the top, they have the greatest investment in the organization. Their goals, values, and identities will be tied to it. It is easy to complain about the conservatism of the powerful in a social organization, but we too are transformed by our new status positions as we rise in the hierarchy. Thus the nature of social structure itself works against the ability of individuals to have great impact. Those with the most power are usually least willing to change the social organization; those at the bottom have the most to gain with change but are the least able to effect change.

It is also important to emphasize that those with power have more than their positions on their side. Social controls protect the powerful, and socialization from family to school to media teach all in society the importance of accepting the patterns as they are. Those who attempt to protect society as it is will have law, policy, government, religion, and all other "legitimate" social organizations and institutions on their side. Social change directed by dissatisfied individuals is made difficult to carry out.

Some individuals, however, do have impact. Napoleon, Jesus, Lenin, Mao, Hitler, Mohammed, and Martin Luther King, Jr., come to mind. Max Weber (1922) called such individuals "charismatic authority." They are powerful because they attract a following who regards them as expressing an almost supernatural quality (as if chosen by history or God or gods). They are revolutionary: They arise *against* the traditional or legal order. They gain a following, and although they often fail to achieve their goals completely, they may have impact either through a revolution (as did Castro and Mao), or by influencing authorities (as in the case of Martin Luther King, Jr.). Mikhail Gorbachev is a fine example of an individual who dramatically and clearly had an impact not only on his own society (the former Soviet Union) but on the whole world. And his impact was unique: He was not a revolutionary who rose up outside the established patterns, but an individual who, after rising up within the Soviet political structure, decided to bring dramatic change to that structure, and in the process produced changes he never imagined initially, including his own fall from power. President George W. Bush was critically important in determining war in Iraq, altering the Middle East, the United States, and much of the world.

Still, it is easy to exaggerate the influence of the single person. Individual success always depends on more impersonal social forces, of which the individual is largely an instrument. Hitler came to power at a time of economic and social collapse; Napoleon's armies attacked a European order already in decay.

Individuals may have some impact on social organization, but organized groups are likely to have more impact. Most of us who are dissatisfied simply grumble and do little; sometimes we try to change something; occasionally we join with others. The National Association for the Advancement of Colored People (NAACP), Mothers Against Drunk Driving (MADD), and the National Organization for Women (NOW) are examples of formal organizations created to bring change in society, and they have been successful to some extent. Solidarity in Poland and various organizations of artists and intellectuals in the former Soviet Union and Eastern Europe have also been important forces for social change. Environmental groups, religious groups, and peace groups may make important change.

When large numbers of people work together in a *loosely organized effort to change society*, they constitute a *social movement*. Some examples are the gay rights movement, the women's movement, the civil rights movement, the anti-Vietnam War movement, and the animal rights movement. Such attempts to influence the direction of society are successful to the extent that many individuals can pool their resources and exert power. Charismatic leadership helps considerably, but so do determination, organization, large numbers, and material resources.

Groups, formal organizations, communities, and social movements change society, but it is difficult, and success is usually limited. Their impact is similar to the impact individuals have. Social structure, culture, and social institutions tend to be highly embedded and stable. The greatest impact will come from those who have the greatest power in society; most often, social movements and protest organizations have little power, and they are opposed by those who have social power and by groups organized to resist change. The change that does occur through organized efforts usually takes place within a context of more far-reaching and impersonal social forces, which encourage such change. Authorities who lose their legitimacy, institutions that no longer deliver, and culture that is no longer believed will be vulnerable to organized opposition. The recent changes in the Soviet empire did not occur in a vacuum. They were influenced by a breakdown in communist institutions, by forces of nationalism, and by an increasing inability to compete with the West militarily and economically.

Sometimes, social movements get widespread support and result in revolution, which means that a rapid and profound change in social patterns takes place.

Usually, what we call a revolution does not actually alter the old structure, culture, or social institutions significantly, and the people in positions of power are simply replaced by others. Most historians point out, for example, that the American Revolution was not really a revolution at all, but that the old structure and culture remained intact; indeed, some argue, the American Revolution might be best understood as a war fought to protect the established society. Occasionally, as in the French Revolution in 1789, the Russian Revolution of 1917, or the more recent Cuban or Chinese revolutions, there will be a major upheaval that has great impact. The old order is truly overthrown, and a new society emerges. But this is rare, usually exaggerated in terms of its scope, and in most cases, what is claimed to be a revolution proves to be a minor change in the long run. It is difficult to predict how dramatic the Iranian revolution was or the anticommunist revolutions in Europe have been. We are too near them in time. We must remember always that it is difficult to simply wipe out the old; it is tempting to return to the security offered by tradition.

The power of organization is great; it has arisen over time, it is protected by a number of forces, and people are socialized to be accepting actors. Individuals, organizations, and social movements may have impact, but there are other, often more important, factors to consider.

SOCIAL CONFLICT CHANGES ORGANIZATION

Conflict (open struggle between actors) brings change to social organization. In part, we must understand change as resulting from efforts by individuals, organizations, and social movements to bring change in society being opposed by the efforts of others who counter change. To work for change inevitably brings open conflict with those who have a stake in the social patterns. *This conflict itself causes change*: I act in my interests, you act in yours; you struggle against me, I struggle against you; usually the social world we exist in is never the same again.

Most sociologists emphasize the importance of conflict in social change. Durkheim emphasized the role that deviance plays: Actions bring the reactions of society, and individuals or groups are labeled deviant and dealt with. However, unless they are controlled completely, they continue to act, and, over time, their acts become legitimate, or, at the very least, they change society's definitions.

Conflict between actors may mean a discussion of differences, an argument, violence, a strike, mass imprisonment, or even attempted revolution. Society changes—through compromise, a major adjustment, or even by greater repression. If open conflict is feared by those in power positions, they may alter the social organization to a degree to prevent conflict; for example, a small amount of the valued things may be redistributed, such as income or economic opportunity.

Of course, for Karl Marx, social conflict is the most basic cause for social change. More than anyone, Marx appreciated the power of those who rule society and their tendency to use structure, culture, and institutions to hang on to that power. More than anyone, Marx appreciated the inability of one individual or group to influence a society in any significant way. It was only the conflict that inevitably arises between the people, on the one hand, and the ruling class, on the other hand, that society really changes. This conflict is class conflict, between those who rule and those who are exploited and excluded. The reactions by the wealthy and by authority to the increasingly angry acts of the labor class and the poor simply bring unity on each side, more serious conflict, and ultimately total revolutionary conflict—which brings a new society.

Ralf Dahrendorf (1959, 125) argues the more typical sociological position: "All that is creativity, innovation, and development in the life of the individual, his group, and his society is due, to no small extent, to the operation of conflicts." Organization can never satisfy the needs and interests of everyone equally; there is always struggle over what it offers to its members (struggle over rights, power, money, prestige, who pays taxes, who is deviant, and what ideas and values shall be adhered to). As long as human differences exist in organized life—and this will always be so—there will be social conflict; as long as there is social conflict, there will be social change.

EXTERNAL SOCIAL ORGANIZATIONS AND ENVIRONMENTS CHANGE SOCIAL ORGANIZATION

People travel to other societies. Sometimes they learn the new ways and settle there. Sometimes they bring armies and conquer other societies, forcing those other societies to become economically and politically dependent on the conquering society. Sometimes the continuous interaction that goes on between people from different societies through emigration or travel, learning, and sharing takes place. Societies change because other societies bring new ways.

When European nations conquered and explored most of the rest of the world in the eighteenth and nineteenth centuries, they brought with them their cultures and institutions. Often the traditional structures of the conquered society were forced to change, and these changes had permanent consequences. Even after colonial domination, these societies retained many of the ways of their former colonial masters. The old ways were no longer perceived as satisfactory. Traditional structures were no longer strong, culture did not seem as true, and old institutions were not workable in their world.

The drive to industrialize and modernize has had a tremendous impact on most societies in the twentieth century. For the most part, industrialization has been thrust on the world through Western expansion. Either because of the belief that industrialization and modernization are good things (because they are seen as a way to get rid of foreign domination), or because powerful interests in the society encourage them, most of the world, through contact with Western nations, has gone through tremendous structural, cultural, and institutional changes. Japan's history in the nineteenth and twentieth centuries is the most dramatic example of contact with outsiders, rapid industrialization, and dramatic social change. Yet Japan is also an example of a society that has been able to retain some core elements of its traditional culture and institutions. It is a blend of the old and new. It illustrates well that social change does not occur the same way in all societies. Modernization occurs in the context of old social patterns. Much of the conflict in the Middle East is a result of social change; tradition versus modernity has become a central concern for governments, groups, and individuals.

It is not just society that changes because of outside social influences. A community (Dallas, Texas) or a formal organization (General Motors Corporation) changes because other communities and formal organizations change and have an impact through interaction. As the U.S. economy changes and becomes increasingly international in scope, industry gets bigger, labor unions lose power, and individual businesses must change or be left behind. As one business changes, it causes competitors to change. Japanese automobile companies influence similar American companies to change, and, as a U.S. automobile company changes, it is watched carefully, and other companies adjust. As the companies change, the dealers and unions change, and all of these may affect Fran's Diner, which has tripled business as a result. A rebellion at the University of California at Berkeley may affect all universities. A new kind of high school program in Minneapolis can be copied by high schools all over the country.

Thus, we should understand that social organizations are related to one another in many complex ways, and as one changes, it can affect others. Societies influence one another, as do communities, formal organizations, and groups.

Remember, too, that social organizations always exist within larger social organizations. As the larger ones change, they will cause smaller organizations to change. Changes in the world affect individual societies. As societies change, so will all social organizations within society, from dyad relationships to families to businesses and communities. As society builds schools to educate children, the family's culture may be made less important: Its norms, values, truths, and goals are changed, threatened, or rejected entirely. In the United States, families are increasingly choosing to home school their children or have them attend private school in order to protect their children from the many changes taking place outside their community. One of these structural changes is to protect changes in gender roles: Opportunities to be educated in public universities, to be able to rise in the corporate world, to determine to follow professional roles traditionally reserved for men, will lead many children to alter the nature of families in society.

Not only does the outside social environment change social organization, the physical environment is also an important influence.

Structures, cultures, and institutions develop in response to the kinds of problems people face together. Some of these problems come from changes in the physical environment. Climatic changes may bring about a time of hardship in the farming community; small farmers go bankrupt, and the large corporate farm wins out because it has the resources to adjust to climatic changes. Climatic change may affect the occupational structure in society (fewer farmers), the political and class structure (less power in rural areas), and the prevailing societal institutions (the small family farm). The availability of large populations of wild animals has been central to hunting societies in Africa. What happens as these animals are destroyed by the pressures of increasing human population? The old ways will no longer be applicable to the changing physical environment. Earthquakes, tornadoes, floods, and famines lead to change in communities, as does the slower process of environmental pollution and global warming.

Note one final point: The social and physical environments have two paths of influence on social change. On one hand, they directly influence change: They favor some classes, some institutions, and some cultural values, ideas, and rules. They destroy others. Cities are destroyed by earthquakes or fire or plague; changes in climate destroy agriculture or alter the way people live. The industrialists from the West open up trade in a rural society, and they bring to power a rising middle class or they create a new industrialized urban poor.

On the other hand, environmental changes bring about change indirectly. They create social conflicts in society: Scarcity brings struggle over what is left to fight for, new classes rise up against the old, and those who follow tradition are fought against by those who believe in progress.

TECHNOLOGY CHANGES SOCIAL ORGANIZATION

Why do we act in the world the way we do? Max Weber pointed out that much of the way people do things can be divided into tradition and rationality. "We act the way we do because that is the way people like us have always acted" (tradition). "We act the way we do because it works for the problems we need to solve" (rationality). All societies are made up of both types of actions. After all, all societies must develop ways to feed their people, and tradition determines part of it, but figuring out how to deal with new situations must take over now and then.

Weber described modern society as increasingly rational. There is an increasing tendency to escape traditional action and replace it with rational action: the application of knowledge to solving problems. This is the meaning of technology, and although there has been technology in every human society, modern life is thoroughly technological, and wherever new technology is introduced, change in society occurs.

Technology is the application of knowledge to the solution of practical problems. Machines are the most obvious examples of technology, but advances in technology are also birth control devices, medicine, and developments in transportation and communication. Some sociologists consider technology to be the most important source of social change. The invention of the wheel, modern agricultural techniques, health care breakthroughs, the automobile, the telephone, and the computer significantly altered society, communities, formal organizations, groups, and dyads. Sociologists William Ogburn and Meyer Nimkoff (1955), in a study that has influenced a great deal of thinking and research on the family, traced the following developments to the impact of technology: growing emphasis on romance, earlier marriages, smaller families, fewer functions for the family to perform in society, more wives working outside the home, and more separation and divorce. A case study of a small town in 1951 documented how a seemingly minor technological change—switching from steam engines to diesel engines—literally wiped out a whole community whose existence was based on trains stopping there for water (Cottrell, 1951). It is fascinating to study how the automobile has affected everything in American life from travel to sexual behavior. One only has to witness the impact of television in the last 60 years and the almost-daily breakthroughs in computer technology to begin to appreciate the role of technology in American society. Clearly, the Internet has transformed almost all societies in a very brief few years, truly revolutionizing communication and access to information.

People do not normally create technology to change society. Instead, they do it to solve a problem at hand. They do it, for example, to conquer a disease or put up a sturdier building. However, these developments together have profound effects on the nature of society and on its social structure, culture, and institutions. The development of birth control devices, whatever their original purpose, has made a tremendous difference in a woman's ability to control her own life, and this, in turn, has had great effects on equality of men and women and the nature of the family. The mechanization of farming has dramatically changed the occupational structure of this society, has created a highly urbanized society, and has helped create American economic power in the world. Few people foresee very accurately the ultimate influence of their creations, and rarely do they create them simply to influence. However, whatever their purpose, the technology makes a great difference.

Bureaucracy is technology; it is social technology. Bureaucratic organization is a modern attempt to purposely create structures that can deal with the problems of a complex technological society. It is a calculated way of organizing people; it is an attempt to achieve goals efficiently and effectively. Like the machine, bureaucracy is an attempt to apply knowledge to a practical problem. "John, we have got to make our business work better. We can no longer rely on how we have always done things. They don't work. Let's streamline. Let's cut waste. Let's organize our business so that everyone knows exactly what to do. Let's not trust success to chance; let's try to assure it through careful thoughtful organization." This is the meaning of bureaucracy. The introduction of this view of organization to society has tremendous influence on the direction of society.

Max Weber (1922) wrote extensively on *bureaucracy*. A bureaucracy is an organization where the following principles are used:

1. Positions are clearly and formally defined. Individuals know what they are supposed to do.
2. There is a clearly laid-out power structure, organized in a hierarchy. People know who is responsible to whom.
3. Rules are written down, and written records are kept of all activities. This helps ensure organizational stability over time.
4. Activities are impersonal. Feeling and tradition are minimized. Efficiency is the most important yardstick for determining what is done.
5. Selection, evaluation, and promotion of people who fill positions are based on technical knowledge and performance, rather than on friendship, family, or tradition.

Weber fully understood that no bureaucracy works exactly this way. In a sense, if bureaucracy worked as intended, these would be its qualities. He contrasted bureaucracy with earlier forms of organization (such as traditional organization) and showed that these earlier forms cannot achieve efficiency nearly as well, nor was efficiency usually their goal. He understood that, although many bureaucracies fall short of these five characteristics, modern organization comes closer to these than traditional organization, and that the drive toward bureaucratization was an important source of change throughout modern society.

Technology should now be added to our understanding of why change takes place in organization. Machinery, mass production, specialization of labor, medicine, bureaucracy, and computers all change society as old ways are replaced. It is not only small specific acts that are changed, but social institutions, culture, and social structure. Family farms eventually give way to agribusiness; love of tradition eventually gives way to love of progress; rural decentralized sources of wealth and power give way to more urban and centralized sources. Government, economy, leisure time, health care, equal rights for women, and almost everything else in society change because of human efforts to use their heads to problem solve. And, by the way, technology not only affects change directly, but also, like the external environment, brings about social conflict. To Marx, for example, it was machines that would be largely responsible for increasing unemployment, meaningless work, and economic disasters; these would eventually lead to angrier workers, greater conflict, and total revolution.

CHANGES IN POPULATION CHANGE SOCIAL ORGANIZATION

Numbers matter. As the number of people in an organization grows, forces are set loose, encouraging change. Population growth in the United States changed the nature of political, economic, and educational institutions. Larger numbers made possible the Industrial Revolution and rise of urban America. People migrating in large numbers to cities created social problems, which necessitated change. African Americans migrating to southern and then northern cities made the civil rights movement possible in the twentieth century.

Look at your own friendship groups. When there are two people interacting, a certain pattern develops, but as more individuals enter into the group, the patterns change—we're not always sure how. For example, going to lunch with a friend makes possible the sharing of intimate concerns, but when a third is invited, intimacy is made more difficult.

A business that becomes a large corporation of several thousand employees has problems of coordination, morale, loyalty, and social controls that a business with only three or four employees does not have. Structure changes—for example, a more formal and complex (differentiated) structure is created. Culture changes—efficiency replaces friendship and intimacy as values.

Religious groups, when they are small, have a simple structure and a shared culture that exerts strong controls on the individual and encourages emotional ties. But as the religious groups become larger, not everyone knows everyone else by name, people must be formally elected to positions of leadership, emotional ties weaken, the structure and culture change, and the group becomes a formal organization.

Small towns become big towns, and big towns become cities or metropolitan centers. Urban life alters society's occupational structure, its class system, and dominant-minority group relations. Urban life alters the relationship between men and women, giving the latter greater opportunity to succeed in the economic and political order. Urban life brings a change in leisure activities, level of education, ideas, and values. Urbanization brings problems of transportation, law enforcement, education, health, and government that cannot be dealt with through the traditional ways that characterize small-town life. Problems bring solutions; solutions bring new structure, new institutions, and changing culture.

Formality, complexity, and centralization are tendencies that accompany increasing size (including the large church, the large business, the large urban center). It is difficult to rely on informal controls and face-to-face interaction to achieve organizational goals. Increasingly, people come to know the organization through written documents—laws, job descriptions, procedures. Complexity also accompanies size. This simply means that there are more status positions added, both in terms of rank levels (vertical) and in terms of division of labor (horizontal). Not only is there a manager, but now there is also an assistant manager and a part-time assistant manager for evening hours. Not only are there salespeople, but each specializes in a slightly different item. Finally, size also brings the tendency for centralization of decision making: Coordination of large numbers tends to bring the need for fewer and fewer people making more of the important decisions.

More than just size of population changes organization. Increasing the number of elderly or teenagers or births or deaths changes the values, ideas, norms, and institutions in society. Change in population distribution becomes an important source of power in society. Emigration and immigration are also extremely important causes of change. The immigrants to the United States from eastern and southern Europe changed the nation; the African Americans moving from the rural south to northern industrial cities altered society, and the Asian and Hispanic immigration is now changing us as a society. Immigration from North Africa and the Middle East is changing Europe. In the many wars in Africa, the Balkan nations, and the Middle East, societies change dramatically as refugees are forced to leave their homes.

Population changes—in numbers, distribution, and migration—are important causes of social change.

CHANGE IN SOCIAL PATTERNS CAUSES
CHANGE IN OTHER SOCIAL PATTERNS

Institutions are part of social organization. They are the legitimate procedures established to deal with the problems of society. Although institutions are changed by all the forces described earlier in this chapter, they are also independent sources of change. As the institution of marriage changes, for example, or the public school, or the modern corporation, or the American presidency, many other patterns in American life also change. We might think of the effects of institutions as follows:

1. *As one institution changes, so do other institutions*, because institutions are interrelated. As television becomes increasingly more important, public schools, political campaigning, and the socialization of children are altered considerably.
2. *As institutions change, so do other aspects of culture*, such as norms, values, goals, and truths. As professional sports become more central to society, competition and striving to be number one become more important values in society. Also, the belief that leisure should be directed at watching others perform becomes more accepted.
3. *As institutions change, so does social structure.* Changes in the institution of marriage alter the relationship between men and women in society; changes in our tax system (such as the end of the estate tax or the establishment of flat tax) will have an important influence on the extent of inequality in our class system. Health care institutions have changed greatly, and we are now trying to determine the directions in which they should go. One of our biggest problems as a society is structural: How should we develop institutions where everyone in society is able to afford decent health care? Those most affected are those who are disadvantaged in our present health care system: It is their standard of living that is at stake.
4. *As institutions change in society, smaller levels of social organization are affected*: communities, formal organizations, groups, and dyads. Bureaucratization in society influences individual formal organizations to become increasingly bureaucratic. Increasing legitimization of divorce in society causes individual familial relationships to change.

For many sociologists, the most important institutions are economic. Feudalism and capitalism are economic institutions, and as Western society moved from one to the other, maximizing profit replaced subsistence, planning replaced spontaneous effort, modern ways replaced traditional ways, and a drive toward increased consumption of goods influenced the development of a rising middle class and an urban labor force.

Changing culture also influences social change: It alters structure, institutions, and other aspects of the culture. A classic analysis of how culture is a source of change was made by Max Weber in *The Protestant Ethic and the Spirit of Capitalism* (1905). Here Weber argued that the development of a Protestant religious philosophy (a set of truths, values, norms, and goals) was instrumental to the development of a capitalist-oriented middle class in Europe (and thus altering the class structure). This middle class in turn transformed certain European societies to develop capitalist economic institutions. Weber showed that a certain kind of Protestantism (represented in the United States by the Puritans) taught a culture that valued hard work, the belief that success in this life was proof of election by God for salvation, and that an important norm that people should follow is to save and reinvest what they earn rather than to spend. This culture, Weber emphasized, encouraged the development of an economic order that included its own culture, institutions, and structure.

And changes in social structure will surely affect culture and institutions. Marx argued this most clearly. Because the culture and social institutions are produced by those who are most powerful in society, as the class structure changes, the culture and the institutions will also. Thus, Marx pointed out, as the capitalist class replaced the feudal lords as the dominant class in society, it was their values, their ideas, their norms, and their goals that became dominant in society. It was also their educational, political, economic, educational, media, leisure, and kinship institutions that prevailed. In a basic sense, all important aspects of society were established and controlled by and for those who controlled the "substructure" of society, the ruling class.

Look at how our changing social structures in the United States have impacted our rural–urban balance, our banking systems, our taxes, our leisure, our families. Our world, because our social structures have changed, has come to rely more and more on stock markets, multinational corporations, and equal opportunities for women in sports, education, health care, occupations, and family life.

SUMMARY

This chapter has emphasized the complexity of social change. Society changes for many reasons. Actors as individuals and groups cause change, as does social conflict. Other societies and the physical environment bring change. New technology creates change. Changes in population creates change in society, and changes in one social pattern usually bring about change in others.

It is very difficult to fathom change because of the interdependence of all these forces. It is much easier to blame a small group, or a single discovery, or a single isolated force (such as economics or war) for a particular change. In fact, change occurs for many reasons, sometimes one reason is particularly important, and at other times, another reason is more important. The strength of the sociological approach to change is to try to isolate these causes, to understand their interdependence, and to identify under what conditions a certain cause becomes important. The only inevitability, however, seems to be change itself.

The word "organization" seems to imply continuity and order, but this is misleading. Change and conflict are certainly as much a part of social organization as order and continuity. Organization is always changing, sometimes slightly, sometimes a lot. We all interact and create social patterns, and these patterns become powerful; yet interaction is also dynamic and creates forces for change. Organization is a complex and subtle balance between continuity and change, order and disorder, and cooperation and conflict. As Marvin Olsen states in his book on social organization (1978, 4), "All social life [is] a dynamic process of becoming rather than a static state of being."

There is no easy way to understand change. There are many causes of change. Each society's unique social patterns make it difficult to generalize about change between societies. Thus, most sociologists have long given up hoping to find universal laws of social change. Instead, we understand change by isolating tendencies, general directions, and trends.

QUESTIONS TO CONSIDER

1. Does the individual really make a difference in social organization? Can the individual change society?
2. What is the most important cause of social change?
3. Why is it so difficult to understand social change?
4. Are human beings biased against social change? Why or why not?

REFERENCES

Cottrell, W. F. 1951. "Death by Dieselization." In *American Sociological Review*, 16:358–365.

Dahrendorf, Ralf. 1959. *Class and Class Conflict in Industrial Society*. Stanford, CA: Stanford University Press.

Ogburn, William F., and Meyer Nimkoff. 1955. *Technology and the Changing Family*. Boston: Houghton Mifflin.

Olsen, Marvin E. 1978. *The Process of Social Organization*. 2nd edn. New York: Holt, Rinehart & Winston.

Weber, Max. 1905. *The Protestant Ethic and the Spirit of Capitalism*. 1958 edn. Trans. and ed. Talcott Parsons. New York: Scribner's.

Weber, Max. 1922. *Theory of Social and economic organization*. 1957 edn. Ed. A. M. Henderson and Talcott Parsons. New York: Free Press.

RECOMMENDED READING

The following works examine social change—its meaning and its causes.

Altbach, Philip G., Robert O. Berdahl, and Patricia J. Gumport. 1999. *American Higher Education in the Twenty-first Century*. Baltimore: Johns Hopkins University Press.

Aronowitz, Stanley, and William DiFazio. 1994. *The Jobless Future: Sci-Tech and the Dogma of Work*. Minneapolis, MN: University of Minnesota Press.

Beeghley, Leonard. 1996. *What Does Your Wife Do? Gender and the Transformation of Family Life*. Boulder, CO: Westview Press.

Bell, Daniel. 1973. *The Coming of Post-Industrial Society: A Venture in Social Forecasting.* New York: Basic Books.

Blumberg, Paul. 1981. *Inequality in an Age of Decline.* New York: Oxford University Press.

Buechler, Steven M. 2000. *Social Movements in Advanced Capitalism.* New York: Oxford University Press.

Chirot, Daniel. 1986. *Social Change in the Modern Era.* New York: Harcourt Brace Jovanovich.

Chirot, Daniel. 1994. *Modern Tyrants: The Power and Prevalence of Evil in Our Age.* New York: Free Press.

Coser, Lewis. 1956. *The Functions of Social Conflict.* New York: Free Press.

Dahrendorf, Ralf. 1958. "Toward a Theory of Social Conflict." In *Journal of Conflict Resolution,* 2:170–183.

Dahrendorf, Ralf. 1959. *Class and Class Conflict in Industrial Society.* Stanford, CA: Stanford University Press.

Durkheim, Emile. 1893. *The Division of Labor in Society.* 1964 edn. Trans. George Simpson. New York: Free Press.

Edin, Kathryn, and Maria Kefalas. 2005. *Promises I Can Keep: Why Poor Women Put Motherhood Before Marriage.* Berkeley, CA: University of California Press.

Ennis, Phillip H. 1992. *The Seventh Stream: The Emergence of Rock 'n' Roll in American Popular Music.* Middletown, CT: Wesleyan University Press.

Flacks, Richard. 1971. *Youth and Social Change.* Chicago: Markham Publishing.

Foner, Nancy. 2005. *In a New Land: A Comparative View of Immigration.* New York: New York University Press.

Freeman, Jo. 1999. *Waves of Protest: Social Movements Since the Sixties.* Lanham, MD: Rowman & Littlefield.

Galbraith, John Kenneth. 1979. *The New Industrial State.* 3rd edn. New York: New American Library.

Gamson, William A. 1968. *Power and Discontent.* Homewood, IL: Dorsey Press.

Gamson, William A. 1975. *The Strategy of Social Protest.* Homewood, IL: Dorsey Press.

Garner, Roberta Ash. 1977. *Social Change.* Skokie, IL: Rand McNally.

Gitlin, Todd. 1987. *The Sixties: Years of Hope, Days of Rage.* New York: Bantam.

Giugni, Marco, Doug McAdam, and Chris Tilly. 1999. *How Social Movements Matter.* Minneapolis: University of Minnesota Press.

Goldstone, Jack A. (ed.). 1986. *Revolutions: Theoretical, Comparative, and Historical Studies.* New York: Harcourt Brace Jovanovich.

Gouldner, Alvin. 1954. *Patterns of Industrial Bureaucracy.* New York: Free Press.

Gurr, Ted R. 1970. *Why Men Rebel.* Princeton, NJ: Princeton University Press.

Gusfield, Joseph. 1970. *Protest, Reform, and Revolt.* New York: John Wiley.

Haenfler, Ross. 2006. *Straight Edge: Hardcore Punk, Clean-Living Youth, and Social Change.* New Brunswick, NJ: Rutgers University Press.

Hancock, Angie-Marie. 2004. *The Politics of Disgust: The Public Identity if the Welfare Queen.* New York: New York University Press.

Inkeles, Alex, and D. H. Smith. 1974. *Becoming Modern.* Cambridge, MA: Harvard University Press.

Jones, Landon Y. 1980. *Great Expectations: America and the Baby Boom Generation.* New York: Coward, McCann & Geoghegan.

Larana, Enrique, Hank Johnston, and Joseph R. Gusfield. 1994. *New Social Movements: From Ideology to Identity.* Philadelphia: Temple University Press.

Lauer, Robert H. 1982. *Perspectives on Social Change.* 3rd edn. Boston: Allyn & Bacon.

Lengermann, Patricia Madoo, and Ruth A. Wallace. 1985. *Gender in America: Social Control and Social Change.* Upper Saddle River, NJ: Prentice Hall.

Loe, Meika. 2004. *The Rise of Viagra: How the Little Blue Pill Changed Sex in America.* New York: New York University Press.

Lorber, Judith. 2005. *Breaking the Bowls: Degendering and Feminist Change.* New York: W.W. Norton.

Mann, Michael. 2004. *The Dark Side of Democracy: Explaining Ethnic Cleansing.* New York: Cambridge University Press.

Manning, Christel J. 1999. *God Gave Us the Right: Conservative Catholic, Evangelical Protestant, and Orthodox Jewish Women Grapple with Feminism.* New Brunswick, NJ: Rutgers University Press.

Marx, Karl. 1845–1886. *Selected Writings.* 1956 edn. Ed. T. B. Bottomore. New York: McGraw-Hill.

Marx, Karl, and Friedrich Engels. 1848. *The Communist Manifesto.* 1955 edn. New York: Appleton-Century-Crofts.

Moore, Wilbert E. 1974. *Social Change.* 2nd edn. Upper Saddle River, NJ: Prentice Hall.

Murphy, John W., and Dennis L. Peck. 1993. *Open Institutions: The Hope for Democracy.* Westport, CT: Praeger.

Newman, Katherine S. 1988. *Falling from Grace: The Experience of Downward Mobility in the Middle Class.* New York: Free Press.

Newman, Katherine S. 1993. *Declining Fortunes: The Withering of the American Dream.* New York: Basic Books.

Ogburn, William F. 1950. *Social Change.* New York: Viking.

Piven, Frances Fox, and Richard A. Cloward. 1979. *Poor People's Movements: Why They Succeed, How They Fail.* New York: Vintage.

Porta, Donatella della, and Mario Diani. 1999. *Social Movements: An Introduction.* Blackwell Press.

Postman, Neil. 1992. *Technopoly: The Surrender of Culture to Technology.* New York: Knopf.

Skolnick, Arlene, and Jerome Skolnick. 2000. *Family in Transition.* 11th edn. Needham Heights, MA: Allyn & Bacon.

Smelser, Neil. 1963. *Theory of Collective Behavior.* New York: Free Press.

Stacey, Judith. 1996. *In the Name of the Family: Rethinking Family Values in the Postmodern Age.* Boston: Beacon Press.

Sztompka, Piotr. 1993. *The Sociology of Social Change.* Oxford: Blackwell Press.

Turnbull, Colin. 1972. *The Mountain People.* New York: Simon & Schuster.

Turner, Ralph H., and Lewis M. Killian. 1972. *Collective Behavior.* Upper Saddle River, NJ: Prentice Hall.

Wallerstein, Immanuel. 1974. *The Modern World-System.* New York: Academic Press.

Yinger, Milton J. 1982. *Countercultures: The Promise and Peril of a World Turned Upside Down.* New York: Free Press.

Zald, Mayer N., and John D. McCarthy (eds.). 1988. *The Dynamics of Social Movements.* Cambridge, MA: Winthrop.

Zellner, William W. 1995. *Countercultures: A Sociological Analysis.* New York: St. Martin's Press.

Kathe Kollwitz 1942. Seed for Sowing Shall Not Be Milled.
Courtesy Galerie St. Etienne, New York.

✦ 13 ✦

The Family in Society

THE IMPORTANCE OF THE FAMILY TO SOCIOLOGY

Auguste Comte, who is often identified as the first sociologist, was truly dedicated to the idea that society was an entity in and of itself. Society is not simply a bunch of individuals. In fact, he went on, individuals have never existed without society, and the basic unit of society has never been the individual at all. The basic unit of society is the group we call the *family* because it is the family that forms the individual and makes society possible. It is the family that makes us social beings ready to take on our positions, a culture, and social institutions. It is unimaginable, therefore, to even consider the possibility for human society or the human individual without considering the role of the family. For this reason alone, it makes good sense to focus on the role of the family if we wish to understand society.

The study of the family brings together many of the concepts we have examined through this book. The family is an excellent example of an institution, and more exactly, a *set* of institutions. Each family in society is a group—usually the most important group within which most of us live our entire lives—and it therefore has its own social patterns: a structure, a culture, and a set of institutions within it. Change in the larger society and in the whole world inevitably affects the social patterns of the family group. Social power and social conflict are important elements in family life; the family places people in the social stratification system; the family is responsible for much of our socialization. It is in the family that the child first encounters role, inequality, power, norms, values, language, identity, and all the other elements that comprise social life. Most of the chapters in this book come together nicely as we examine the family.

This chapter on the family especially highlights many of the ideas contained in Chapter 12, "Social Change." The study of the family is truly a study of social change. The rate of change in our family life accelerated in throughout the twentieth century. Modern society has brought individualism and choice in our lives, and this has affected what our families have become. Many of our problems as individuals and as society can be traced to the changes in the family, and many of the benefits we enjoy can also be traced to these same family changes. Our attitudes toward unmarried couples living together, premarital sex, women's and men's roles, having children, and socializing children have undergone considerable change. In both family structure and sexuality, we regard more and more varied behavior as normal and agree less and less about what constitutes deviant behavior.

> At mid-century, most families consisted of a married couple, neither of whom had been married to someone else previously, and their children. Beginning in the 1960s, however, family patterns were altered by great rises in divorce, childbearing outside of marriage; and, since about 1970, cohabitation. As a result, the first-marriage, two-parent family must now share its prominence with single-parent families and families formed by remarriages. The large numbers of immigrants from Latin America and Asia have brought their own cultural traditions, which often include a greater emphasis on ties to other kin beyond the parents-and-child household, such as grandparents, uncles, and aunts. Among African Americans, the percentage of two-parent households has declined greatly while the importance of ties to other kin has increased. Across all racial and ethical groups, married women have become much more likely to work outside the home.
>
> (Cherlin, 1997, 11)

To highlight how much change has taken place, according to the U.S. Bureau of the Census, in 1950, the housewife-mother/breadwinner-father/children arrangement characterized about 70 percent of all American families. In 1989, this described only 11 percent (U.S. Bureau of the Census, 1990).

MEANING OF THE FAMILY

All humans are born into a situation in which at least one adult has responsibility for their care. For most of us, our survival depends on that adult (or those adults) for many years. We begin life totally dependent; increasingly, we learn to survive on our own. As we learn, we come to understand how the adults socializing us have survived and how their parents before them survived. We learn their culture, we learn our place in relation to them, and they teach us our place in the community and society. Together, we and the adults who are primarily responsible for our socialization form our family.

Is the Family Universal?

Universally, some sort of family life seems necessary. There must be a primary group of some kind to protect, care for, and socialize the very young. Through the family, the individual learns what he or she must do to control behavior in order to live around others. Through the family, the individual also takes on symbols, self, and mind. And through the family, the individual finds comfort and security, love and support, so that he or she develops the confidence in self and ability to form close, cooperative relationships with others.

The form that this family takes is not universal, however, and that is why it is hard to define the family across time and space. What is and is not universal about the family (and thus part of a consistent definition) has teased the social scientist from the beginning. In our search, we seem to have arrived at a very sociological position: *Nothing is universal about the family except that such a primary group is necessary for the early socialization of children.*

Why Is Definition Difficult?

Most people have very strong opinions about what constitutes a family. No single definition can satisfy everyone. Our emotions get in the way of our definition because there is a strong tendency for us to define the family according to what we think the family *should* be rather than what it is. We tend to be ethnocentric in our definition, and it becomes difficult for us to include family patterns that are out of the ordinary in our definition. For example, many of us are so used to one male and one female who are married constituting the adults in the family that we have difficulty accepting homosexual marriage, nonmarried partners, or single parents as "normal" families. Many of us are afraid that if we widen our definition of the family to include such patterns, we are undermining something that is sacred, right, and true.

But the social scientist must try to overcome emotional bias in definition. If we look at the United States, we see many types of primary groups that socialize children; when we look at other societies throughout the world and throughout the past, we begin to be more convinced that there are a multitude of family types. We are faced with the difficult task of looking at this diversity and teasing out the common characteristics. Like all institutions in society, familial institutions are certain patterns that a society develops over time, and those institutions are not inevitable, nor are they necessarily the best for every society or every individual. We regard these patterns as right and true because they are part of our socialization.

The Family: A Primary Group in a Household

What definition of the family makes good sense? We begin to understand by remembering that *the family is a primary group in society.* A "primary group" consists of a small number of closely knit people who engage in ongoing, face-to-face interaction, who value the group as an end in itself, and who meet many of their emotional needs through that group. A primary group is a group toward which the individual has a strong commitment; in the case of the family, this is a long-term commitment. It is called *primary* because it is so important to the individual's life and because it is so important to society.

A *family is a primary group that almost always lives together in a household* (a shared residence). It may consist of parents and their children (called a *nuclear family*), or it may consist of one parent and children, or two individuals and no children. In many societies, the family that lives together in a household consists of more generations and may include aunts, uncles, nephews, and nieces. Often a family may even consist of the parents of the adults and even adult male siblings, their wives, and their children. Such families living in one household that consist of relatives in addition to the nuclear family are called *extended families*. Normally (in the United States, about 90 percent of us), a person lives in two families during his or her lifetime: a family of orientation (within which one is born) and a family of procreation (within which one is married).

The Family: The Socialization Function

A family is a primary group living in one household that is expected to socialize children. The family forms the child; the family is responsible for making the individual a member of society. Although other individuals and groups also have this responsibility, the family has the earliest and the most important responsibility. Because it is a primary group, relationships are close, and interaction is intense and ongoing. Because the family is the first group within which the individual develops, the child is most vulnerable to influence (he or she has little to compare to what he or she learns there). When social critics bemoan the decline of the family, it is usually the perceived loss of the socialization function that is most problematic. That is because this function is probably the most important one for the continuation of society. "Without the family, how will the child be able to develop conscience, abilities, confidence, close relationships, and values?" "Without the family, how can the child learn responsibility toward others and toward the society as a whole?"

The Family: Economic and Social Functions

In almost every society, the family also acts as an economic unit, although the nature of this function changed considerably in the nineteenth and twentieth centuries from a "unit of production" to a "unit of consumption." In most societies and historically, families worked together on farms, in stores, and in businesses. Manufacturing was done cooperatively in households. Children were economic necessities because they contributed to the family's livelihood, and children inherited the occupations of their parents. This made the family a cooperative unit of economic production. Increasingly, the family has changed to an economic unit of consumption. Children and adults still depend on one another to buy and share goods and services—consumption—but their labor is now separated and done outside the household.

Families also have social functions: protection of the individual members, religious education and practice, recreation, and education. Families took on the primary responsibility for caring for the elderly and for those in the family who were ill. Gradually, these functions, too, have become less important as industrial urbanized society increasingly relies on government, police, physicians, churches, recreation centers, television, the mass media, schools, hospitals, and nursing homes.

The Family: The Social Class Placement Function

The family also places individuals into the social structure of society. In many societies, parents directly pass down occupations to children; families confer privilege (wealth, for example), prestige, and power (or lack of it) on their children. In almost every society, there is a close proximity between parents' and children's relative position in society. Parents socialize children about where they belong and what they should expect in life. In industrial society, placement is more open to individual achievement rather than just family placement, but even here, educational values and opportunities arise from class-based families, and direct contacts in the occupational and political worlds matter. It is difficult to research all the subtle ways in which the family functions for individual placement, but there is little disagreement among social scientists that family makes a significant difference in almost every society, including our own. Modern life may lessen this influence, but it does not erase it.

The Family: The Expressive Function

William Ogburn (1934) has had the most impact on our understanding of how the various functions of the family have changed in modern society. In addition to pointing out how the family began to lose its economic and social functions to nonfamily institutions, Ogburn also alerted us to one way the modern family is playing a much larger role than ever before: It has become increasingly important for individual happiness, personal growth, emotional development, and psychological support. Children also "came to be seen as needing not only discipline and economic support, but also attention, affection, and loving care" (Cherlin, 1997, 44). The American family evolved from an institution that served primarily economic and social needs to one that served personal and psychological ones. Modernization has brought individualism, and individuals have increasingly come to expect individual happiness and meaning through the family. Modernization has gradually shifted the function of the family from strictly the "instrumental functions" (the more practical and public functions necessary for the continuation of society) to what we call the "expressive functions" (the more psychological and private functions necessary for personal happiness).

The family, therefore, serves an expressive function. *It is a place where people seek intimacy, love, and encouragement.* It is increasingly a "private" place where the individual's personal needs are met. Throughout history, most families have probably met this function to at least some small extent, but clearly this function has become increasingly important in modern society. And it is this function that has increasingly become the measuring stick for marital satisfaction.

The Meaning of the Family: A Summary

We are, therefore, left with this definition—tentative, but useful—of the family: *The family is a primary group that lives in a single household whose universal function is to have the primary responsibility for the socialization of children. It also has important economic and social functions, and it is important for placing children into the class system. Increasingly, it has taken on important expressive functions, where all the members are expected to find a place of intimacy, love, and personal happiness.*

MARRIAGE AS AN INSTITUTION

Marriage is an excellent example of an institution. We are born into a society that regards marriage as an important groove to follow. Although people can find personal happiness and meaning without marriage, much of how other people act toward us tells us that we "just have to get married" to live productive lives, and if we do not marry, there is something wrong with us. Peter Berger, describing a couple in the moonlight, reminds us that the man hears an "inner voice" commanding marriage. This inner voice "was instilled in him by society, reinforced by the countless pressures of family lore, moral education, the mass media, and advertising." Society provides the individual "with a formula—to desire is to love is to marry" (1963, 68, 69). Colonial American communities had bachelor taxes, and single women who inherited land were often required to marry soon after or lose that land. Benjamin Franklin expressed the wisdom of his day: A single man "is an incomplete animal. He resembles the odd half of a pair of scissors" (1745).

It is easy for those of us entering the twenty-first century to laugh at Ben Franklin or to reject Peter Berger's 1963 analysis, but the vast majority of people in the world still get married, and the vast majority of Americans in every generation continue to get married. In the United States, nearly 90 percent of whites and 70–75 percent of African Americans eventually marry (Cherlin, 1997, 479). Indeed, people might get divorced far more often today than they did in the past, but most of us end up getting married again . . . and even again. "Marriage is not in danger of disappearing among Americans, and it remains the preferred form of union . . . Most people choose to marry at some time in their lives . . ." (Cherlin, 1997, 480).

From recent data (2006), 28 percent of the women over 15 never married (up from 22 percent in 1970). Thirty-three percent of males over 15 had never married in 2006, up from 28 percent in 1970. The percentage of marriage in the population has been declining since 1980, undoubtedly because of the number of people who have decided to cohabit. The divorce rate is also down: 22.6 of married women in 1980 to 17.5 per 1,000 in 2005. About 8.1 percent of coupled households are made up of unmarried, heterosexual partners (U.S. Today, July 18, 2005). From 1960 to 2000 the proportion of white children living with both parents declined from 90.9 to 75 percent; among black children the proportion was 79 to 46.7 percent. Most of this decline was in the 1970s; from 1996 to 2005 the percentage stabilized and increased slightly. Some sociologists, such as David Popenoe are very critical of our trends: "The United States has the weakest families in the Western world because we have the highest divorce rate and the highest rate of solo parenting" (U.S. Today, July 18, 2005 and U.S. Census Bureau, http://www.census.gov/population/socdemo/ms-la/tabch-3.txt.). Other sociologists, such as Arlene and Jerome Skolnick (2007, 3), see the trends differently:

> The United States has the highest marriage rate in the industrial world. They either have, or want to have, children. Further, surveys reportedly show that family is central to the lives of most Americans. Family ties are their deepest source of satisfaction and meaning, as well as the source of their greatest worries (Mellman, Lazarus, and Rivlin, 1990). In sum, family life in the United States is a complex mixture of both continuity and change.

It seems that the statistics and the trends are difficult to discern. In general, the divorce rate since 1980 has become stable and seems to be slightly down. About 80 percent of the population marries during their lifetime, although the trend is going down. As the population gets older and the norms change, the number of people choosing to live in nonmarried households goes up. It is difficult to determine exactly where we are going as a society, but marriage seems still important to the vast majority of people in the United States, divorce is slightly down, and the number of children with one parent has increased significantly since 1960, but has recently stabilized.

Peter Stein (1976) reminds us how powerful society is in its pressures for us to marry: Encouragement from parents and friends, the desire to leave home, loneliness, guilt, no recognition of workable alternatives, desire for children, examples of peers, romantic view of marriage, sexual attraction to someone, security, prestige, and sexual availability are some of the most important pressures. Stein also points out that although such pressures are still great, in modern society there are increasing pressures for not marrying—especially having to do with independence and personal opportunities. In recent years, the choice to remain single has become especially important for women, many of whom believe that if they are going to succeed in the educational and economic worlds, they must postpone marriage or not get married at all. Consequently, increasing numbers of people are staying single, and those who are marrying tend to do so later in life. Because increasing numbers are choosing to be single longer, refusing marriage is no longer considered foolish, weird, immoral, or selfish as it once was. Marriage is still important, but it is not the institutional imperative it once was.

The Changing Structure of Marriage

Before the age of industrialization (the mid-nineteenth century), the woman was considered to be the property of the man. Sometimes this typical structure is called "owner-property" (Scanzoni and Scanzoni, 1988, 244–248). The wife was owned in the same way land or money was owned. She was dependent; her whole identity was tied to the man she married. Her position within the family was that of wife-mother, and her prestige depended on her husband and on how well she served her husband. The husband was expected to provide for the economic needs of his wife, which increased her dependence and his power. The wife was expected to meet her husband's sexual needs, but the relationship was less characterized by companionship, empathy, and affection than is true in later forms of the institution.

In the middle of the nineteenth century, this relationship gradually changed to what might be referred to as "head-complement" (Scanzoni and Scanzoni, 1988, 24–51). Here, the power differential is not as great; the wife changes from being property to having some rights, and the husband becomes increasingly responsible for his wife's emotional and sexual needs. The structure is based more and more on a complementary division of labor, where the husband remains the head but there is more of a mutual dependence. The marriage becomes more of a joint venture, each actor complementing the other. The wife is more of a partner and suffers less authoritarian control by her husband. Yet the role expectations for each keep the man as head with greater power. As manufacturing is taken out of the home and into the factory, the wife becomes the housewife responsible for the running of the household. In the economic world, the male and female roles are increasingly separated, and the economic function of the family becomes more of consumer rather than producer. Gradually, the family becomes increasingly important for emotional fulfillment and real companionship. Husbands and wives increasingly become lovers and friends.

Since World War II, the marriage relationship has become increasingly equal in the United States. This occurred largely because large numbers of women joined the paid labor force outside the home. By doing this, the woman became less dependent on the man for economic survival and brought to the marital relationship a better bargaining position, a greater equality. Together with widespread use of birth control, a smaller family size, increasing formal education, and an important feminist movement, the family structure was significantly altered. Women questioned the head-complement relationship, demanded more rights, and eventually became recognized by law as people rather than as property (Scanzoni and Scanzoni, 1988, 251–255).

Most marriages today are still not equal because the woman is still considered a "junior partner" (Scanzoni and Scanzoni, 1988, 251–255); she works outside the home but might not follow a continuous and stable career. The trend is definitely in the direction of equality, however, as women continue to pursue careers and achieve educational equality with men.

It is too easy sometimes to miss the very broad changes in society that bring about change in something like the family structure. Among the most significant trends in our society are longer life, fewer children, and a shorter period in the woman's life devoted to having and raising children. In the early part of the twentieth century, the last child to leave home did so when his or her parents were in their fifties, shortly before the end of their lives. Today, adults in their twenties may have two children, and those children gradually become more and more involved in other societal institutions by the time they are three or four years old and are gone from the home by the time their parents enter their early forties. It is difficult for the individual to continue to believe that a housewife-mother role is the only important role in a woman's existence when most of her life is now lived without children in the household. How can we expect the family to be the same in a society that has undergone such changes?

MARITAL SATISFACTION

It is amazing how often humans get married with so much hope and excitement, yet shortly after become dissatisfied and even horrified. Why? Why does marriage sometimes satisfy the individuals involved and sometimes not? Why do some individuals stay in an unsatisfactory relationship, while others separate and get divorced (often to try marriage over again with someone else)? The questions surrounding marital satisfaction are difficult. The topic is complex and even contradictory. Indeed, we know, for example, that people who are least satisfied with marriage are not necessarily those most likely to get divorced. For many of us, our marriage becomes habitual, passively accepted, a "mistake" we just come to live with. Divorce is not the only outcome of unsatisfactory marriage. Passive acceptance of that marriage or continuous frustration, conflict, and aggression may also result.

By emphasizing the expressive side of marriage, the twentieth century has significantly altered the family in society. The family is no longer held together simply by satisfying economic and socialization needs. Instead, the emotional needs of each partner are added; marriage is held together because it now provides opportunities for each partner to have a friend, a listener, and a lover. This added function in marriage produces a new set of stresses on the marriage relationship. And because individual happiness becomes increasingly important to us, if marriage does not meet these expectations, people will fill them elsewhere, either outside the marriage or by divorce and remarriage. In a very basic sense, the problem with modern marriage is that we expect too much from it. Few of us are capable of meeting a spouse's expressive needs for 30, 40, or 50 years. Who among us is capable of being an amateur psychologist, sexual magician, and a good friend to a single person "for as long as we both shall live"? As long as the expectations were instrumental, people were likely to stay together because the relationship itself was critically important to their protection and survival. However, once personal happiness became important, commitment increasingly depended on personal emotional needs, and people came to judge marital satisfaction on whether or not "I am happy, I am fulfilled, I am loved, I achieve my own goals in life."

> . . .the major historical change in family values has been one from a collective view of the family to one of individualization and sentiment. Over the past several decades American families have been experiencing an increasing emphasis on individual priorities and preferences over collective family needs. This individualization of family relations has also led to an exaggerated emphasis on emotional nurture, intimacy, and privacy as the major base of family relationships . . . [however] this has also eroded the resilience of the family and its ability to withstand crises.
>
> (Hareven, 1992, 317)

Whether or not this change is a good one depends on our personal values, but undoubtedly, higher rates of divorce will be one of its outcomes.

Divorce

Divorce has been on the rise in American society since 1860. The divorce rate has leveled off in the 1980s and 1990s, but it does not seem to be going down considerably. About half of today's marriages in the United States will end in divorce. This is one of the highest rates in the world, but other industrialized nations are rapidly catching up to us. Many observers attribute the high rates to industrialization and urbanization—more specifically, to the ethic of individualism accompanying these developments. In addition to this, increased equality in the marriage relationship means that both parties have an equal voice in whether the marriage lasts, and higher expectations for marriage as well as longer life spans for the partners put additional strains on marriage. Over time, as people turn to divorce as a solution to an unsatisfactory marriage, divorce becomes more of an acceptable solution; divorce becomes a legitimate institution.

It is difficult to predict which marriage will end in divorce. Social class, level of education, religion, or even marital satisfaction do not predict very well who decides to get divorced. E. Mavis Hetherington, Tracy C. Law, and Thomas G. O'Connor write this summary on what research reveals about the "precursors of divorce"; it is a useful place to begin understanding the complexities involved:

> Neither marital satisfaction nor sheer frequency of disagreements is a good predictor of divorce. Instead, styles of conflict resolution involving disengagement, stonewalling, contempt, denial, and blaming are likely to be associated with divorce. . . . A second

common marital pattern associated with later divorce is one in which couples have little conflict but have different expectations and perceptions about family life, marriage, and their children, and have few shared interests, activities, or friends.

(1993, 210–211)

Without question, divorce has become an acceptable option in society because individuals feel they have a right to choose whom to marry and how long to stay married. This claimed right is directly tied to the individualism fostered by American culture:

An autonomous courtship system where the participants choose their own mates is conductive to high divorce rates. . . . The more one is culturally taught to seek love as the basis for marriage, the more likely it is that one will break up the marriage entirely and seek another love when the original love relationship deteriorates.

(Reiss and Lee, 1988, 287)

CHILDREN AND SOCIALIZATION IN THE FAMILY

In most societies and in most periods of history, to marry was to have children. Indeed, for most human beings, children are a central part of life. Modern Western industrial society is different. Having children, like most other things, has become an option; it is not (especially with the new birth control technology) something taken for granted. In an age of individualism, people will calculate rewards and costs associated with having and raising children, and many will decide that the cost is too high. One of the results is the trend toward smaller families (two children) in society; another is the rising number of childless marriages.

The family remains a very important agency for the socialization of children. We take on human qualities through interaction in the family. The family teaches us symbols, helps shape our self, constitutes our first role models and our first introduction to the rules of society, and forms our earliest perspectives on the world. The family teaches us who we are and gives us the love and security necessary to make us independent adults. Through it all, most of us become social beings, members of society who are able to cooperate with others, and who act according to a conscience heavily influenced by rules we learn within the family. The family remains central to both the individual and society. It is still, to use the language of sociologists, *the* "primary group."

Divorce does not necessarily mean the undermining of the family or its socialization function. It is increasingly clear that those who get divorced eventually get married again (even though this trend is going down slightly in recent years because more divorced people are turning to cohabitation). The family then changes to one with other adults who become stepparents and often share responsibility for the socialization of the children. The role of stepparents is still an ambiguous one in society, but many individuals have learned to cope and have become effective socializers of children who are not biologically theirs but who live in their household (Furstenberg and Cherlin, 1991, 77–95).

Finally, the negative effects of divorce on children depend considerably on certain circumstances. This is a complex issue, and the research findings are often difficult to interpret. However, research does make it clear that divorce is usually traumatic for children initially, especially for teenagers. Over the long run, the children normally adjust. Some research does suggest that there may be harmful long-term negative effects on children, but it is not clear whether this is simply because of the divorce itself. A clearer finding is that divorce and adjustment without serious social conflict between the parties have the least harmful effects on children. If all the adults involved—biological parents, stepparents, adoptive parents—exhibit a concern for the children's welfare rather than continuing to engage in destructive conflict, the long-term effects will not usually be great, and the socialization of the children will probably be better than if a conflict-ridden marital relationship continues (Furstenberg and Cherlin, 1991, 62–76).

One of the other outcomes of divorce that may considerably affect the children is the fact that the income of the family almost always goes down; for some, this becomes a difficult adjustment in standard of living. In the vast majority of cases, the woman gains custody of the children and, especially if she remains single, she has a much lower income than she is used to; for many children, this adds to the adjustment problems.

INDIVIDUAL CHOICE AND THE CHANGING FAMILY

One of the basic themes in this chapter is that the modern American family is undergoing profound and rapid change. This is not simply because of a conspiracy by some group trying to destroy our society, nor is it simply caused by television, declining morality, or declining schools. And this change is not simply the result of the declining importance of the family, either. The real change is toward a state of deinstitutionalization (toward a society in which *personal choice* in how to live prevails) rather than an end to the family itself. People are deciding what to do with their lives—before and during marriage—rather than being told what to do by society. There is an increasing legitimacy of choice rather than simply a certain groove to follow. This is especially true of the middle class:

> Marriage must now compete with alternatives such as staying in school longer to obtain a higher degree, taking more time to develop a career, living with a partner without marrying, or having children outside of marriage. Among middle-class young adults, this competition is increasingly judged by a single criterion: self-fulfillment. And by this criterion, marriage does not always come out the winner. Most Americans still want to marry, but have less of a need to do so. Most want children, but they also value other uses of their time and money. . . . Many are ambivalent about marriage, at once drawn by its promise of intimacy and wary of its commitments and constraints.
>
> (Cherlin, 1997, 8)

Abortion, homosexuality, divorce, and cohabitation reflect choices that become an integral part of modern industrial life with its focus on the individual. None are completely free choices because there are always forces that limit choice, but our society increasingly makes a wider range of choices more legitimate—and therefore easier for the individual to make. We are witnessing a trend away from tradition and the power of community, less commitment to the family as an end in itself, and less conformity to the expectations of others. The rise of individualism, so much tied to industrialized urban society, is difficult if not impossible to reverse.

For many critics, these trends are bad for the individual and dangerous to society. Without question, these changes mean new psychological stresses and problems, and probably contribute to a decline in community. For many people, these trends cause increasing selfishness and hedonism; for society, they can bring a decline in law and order. However, we also cannot forget that these trends also mean more freedom for the individual, more control over his or her own life, and more choice in how to live. It has also meant more rights for women and children, and greater opportunities to leave a destructive home. The change in the family is therefore inevitable and brings a mixed blessing. The family changes because society changes, and changes in the family, in turn, change society. My generation's image of sex, family, marriage, and children is a unique one; my children will not see these matters as I do, just as I do not see them as those who went before me did. No one summarizes the importance and complexities of the changes that are occurring in the family better than Arlene and Jerome Skolnick:

> The world at the end of the twentieth century is vastly different from what it was at the beginning, or even the middle. Families are struggling to adapt to new realities. . . . But a knowledge of family history reveals that the solution to contemporary problems will not be found in some lost golden age. Families have always struggled with outside circumstances and inner conflict. Our current troubles inside and outside the family are genuine, but we should never forget that many of the most vexing issues confronting us derive from the benefits of modernization few of us would be willing to give up—for example, longer, healthier lives and the ability to choose how many children to have and when to have them. There was no problem of the aged in the past, because most people never aged; they died before they got old. Nor was adolescence a difficult stage of the life cycle when children worked, education was a privilege of the rich, and a person's place in society was determined by heredity rather than choice. And when most people were hungry illiterates, only aristocrats could worry about sexual satisfaction and self-fulfillment.
>
> In short, there is no point giving into the lure of nostalgia. There is no golden age of the family to long for, not even some past pattern of behavior and belief that would guarantee us harmony and stability if only we had the will to turn to it.
>
> (1997, 13–14)

SUMMARY

Generally, sociologists regard the family as a central part of human society. It functions in every society for the socialization of the young. The institutions that make up the family have undergone considerable change in the twentieth century, and it is important to understand what these changes have been and why they have occurred. The family that dominated American society until the mid-twentieth century (the housewife-mother, breadwinner-father, and children) constitutes a very small percentage of families today. Here are some of the ideas highlighted in this chapter on the changing family:

1. It is difficult to define the family because we too often define what we *want* the family to be instead of recognizing that it differs in time and place.
2. In every society, the family is a primary group that has responsibility for the socialization of children. In every society, the family is an economic unit; but in modern industrial society, it has become more of an economic unit of consumption rather than of production. In every

society, the family has several social functions; but in modern industrial society, these functions have increasingly gone to other institutions in society. In every class society, the family is important for the placement of individuals into the class system; but in modern industrial society, this function is less important. In modern industrial society, the family has increasingly taken on an expressive function, becoming a place where psychological and private functions are even more important than many of the more instrumental functions.

3. Marriage remains an important institution in modern society. Much of society pressures us down that path. However, marriage has increasingly become an option for people because they have become more individualistic and more concerned about personal fulfillment.
4. The structure of marriage has changed greatly in modern society. The expressive function has become much more important. The marriage relationship has become more equal in the United States, developing from an owner-property relationship to a head-complement relationship to a junior partner relationship and continuing toward an equal relationship.
5. In part, the strain on modern marriage occurs because we expect marriage to do more than the instrumental functions. We expect it to provide us with personal happiness and intimacy.
6. Divorce is increasingly accepted in modern industrial society with its emphasis on individualism. We tend to claim it as a right if our marriages are unsatisfying.
7. The family is still extremely important for the socialization of children. It forms the core elements of the individual, and it is necessary for cooperation in society and for social order.
8. The real cause of change in the family is the greater emphasis on individualism in society. Increasingly, we choose to marry, we choose whom we marry, we choose when to marry, and we choose if and when to end the marriage.

QUESTIONS TO CONSIDER

1. What is family? Describe what you think it is and contrast your definition with the definition developed in this chapter.
2. This chapter has emphasized the family as undergoing great change in society. Some people would call what is happening the "decline of the family." Is this what is happening, or is it simply change? Give some reasons why this change might be a good thing. Give some reasons why it might not be. What is your overall opinion?
3. What does this chapter view as the reason the family is changing as much as it is? Do you agree? What is left out there?

REFERENCES

Berger, Peter L. 1963. *Invitation to Sociology.* New York: Doubleday.

Cherlin, Andrew. 1997. *Public and Private Families.* New York: McGraw-Hill.

Franklin, Beni. 1745. "Advice to a Young Man on Choosing a Mistress." In *The Papers of Benjamin Franklin.* Ed. Leonard Labore and Whitefield Bell, Jr. New Haven, CT: Yale University Press, 1961.

Furstenberg, Frank F., Jr., and Andrew J. Cherlin. 1991. *Divided Families: What Happens to Children When Parents Part?* Cambridge, MA: Harvard University Press.

Hareven, Tamara K. 1992. "Continuity and Change in Family Life." In *Making America: The Society and Culture of the United States.* Ed. Luther S. Luedtke. Chapel Hill: The University of North Carolina Press, pp. 308–326.

Hetherington, E. Mavis, Tracy C. Law, and Thomas G. O'Connor. 1993. "Divorce: Challenges, Changes, and New Chances." In *Normal Family Processes*. 2nd edn. Ed. Froma Walsh. New York: The Guilford Press.

Mellman, Mark, Edward Lazarus, and Allan Rivlin, 1990. "Family Time, Family Values." In *Rebuilding the Nest*. Ed. David Blankenhorn, Steven Bayne, Jean Bethke Elshtain. Milwaukee Wisc: Family Service America.

Ogburn, William, with Clark Tibbitts. 1934. "The Family and Its Functions." In *Recent Trends in the United States*. Ed. The President's Research Committee on Social Trends. New York: McGraw-Hill.

Reiss, Ira, and Gary R. Lee. 1988. *Family Systems in America*. 4th edn. New York: Holt, Rinehart, and Winston.

Scanzoni, Letha, and John Scanzoni. 1988. *Men, Women, and Change: A Sociology of Marriage and Family*. 3rd edn. New York: McGraw-Hill.

Skolnick, Arlene S., and Jerome Skolnick. 1997. *Family in Transition*. 10th ed. Needham Heights, MA: Allyn & Bacon.

Skolnick, Arlene S., and Jerome H. Skolnick. 2007. *Family in Transition*. 14th edn. Needham Heights, MA: Allyn & Bacon.

Stein, Peter J. 1976. *Single*. Englewood Cliffs, NJ: Prentice-Hall.

U.S. Bureau of the Census. 1990. *Current Population Reports: Consumer Income*. Series P-60, #168, 1989. Washington: U.S. Government Printing Office.

RECOMMENDED READING

Ammerman, Nancy T. 2005. *Pillars of Faith American Congregations and their Partners*. Berkeley, CA: University of California Press.

Bowles, Samuel, Gintis Herbert, and Melissa Osborne-Groves. 2005. *Unequal Chances: Family Background and Economic Success*. New Jersey: Princeton University Press.

Clarke-Stewart, Alison, and Cornelia Brentano. 2006. *Divorce: Causes and Consequences*. New Haven, CT: Yale University Press.

Coontz, Stephanie. 2005. *Marriage, a History: From Obedience to Intimacy or How Love Conquered Marriage*. New York, NY: Viking Press.

DeParle, Jason. 2004. *American Dream: Three Women, Ten Kids, and a Nation's Drive to End Welfare*. New York: Penguin Books.

Edin, Kathryn, and Maria Kefalas. 2005. *Promises I Can Keep: Why Poor Women Put Motherhood Before Marriage*. Berkeley, CA: University of California Press.

Harris, Scott R. 2006. *The Meaning of Marital Equality*. New York: University of New York Press.

Hertz, Rosanna. 2006. *Single by Chance, Mothers by Choice: How Women are Choosing Parenthood without Marriage and Creating the New American Family*. United Kingdom: Oxford University Press.

Hull, Kathleen E. 2006. *Same-Sex Marriage: The Cultural Politics of Love and Law*. Cambridge, UK: Cambridge University Press.

Keister, Lisa A. 2005. *Getting Rich: America's New Rich and How They Got That Way*. New York: Cambridge University Press.

Loe, Meika. 2004. *The Rise of Viagra: How the Little Blue Pill Changed Sex in America*. New York: New York University Press.

Merry, Sally E. 2005. *Human Rights and Gender Violence: Translating International Law into Local Justice*. Chicago, IL: University of Chicago Press.

Pleck, Elizabeth H. 2000. *Celebrating the Family*. Cambridge: Harvard University Press.

Skolnick, Arlene S., and Jerome H. Skolnick. 2000. *Family in Transition*. 11th edn. Needham Heights, MA: Allyn & Bacon.

Stacey, Judith. 1996. *In the Name of the Family: Rethinking Family Values in the Postmodern Age*. Boston: Beacon Press.

Sullivan, Maureen. 2004. *The Family of Woman: Lesbian Mothers, their Children, and Undoing of Gender*. Berkeley, CA: University of California Press.

Sullivan, Oriel. 2006. *Changing Gender Relations, Changing Families: Tracing the Pace of Change Over Time*. New York: Rowman & Littlefield.

Tichenor, Veronica J. 2005. *Earning More and Getting Less: Why Successful Wives Can't Buy Equality*. New Jersey: Rutgers University Press.

Paul Gaugin, French, (1848–1903). The Day of the God (Mahana no Atua), 1894. Oil on canvas, 68.3 × 91.5 cm. The Art Institute of Chicago, Hellen Birch Bartlett Memorial Collection, 1926.198. *Photography © The Art Institute of Chicago.*

14

Religion, Society, and the Individual

"Religion," wrote Peter L. Berger (1967, 25), "is the human enterprise by which a sacred cosmos is established." This sacred cosmos, and the human quest to understand its meaning for the individual and society, is the core of all religious ideas and practices, and it is central to the development of sociology. Sociology, since its launch during the Industrial Revolution, has sought to understand just why religion is essential to all human groups and societies, and how sacred ideas inspire social action and group identity.

The early founders of the science of sociology made important enquiries on the role of religion in the emerging modern European and American societies: Auguste Comte (1798–1857), Ferdinand Toennies (1855–1936), Emile Durkheim (1858–1917), Karl Marx (1818–1883), and Marx Weber (1864–1920). These social scientists saw religion as an important feature of social life and sought to understand its role for both the individual and the society. They also saw the transformation of religious beliefs due to the incredible social changes brought about by the Industrial Revolution in Europe, beginning in the middle eighteenth century, and wrote about how religion was itself impacted by this great social transformation.

THE INDUSTRIAL REVOLUTION: RELIGION AND THE BEGINNING OF SOCIOLOGY

The Industrial Revolution was, in many ways, a necessary condition for the birth of the science of sociology because it completely transformed European society: Without this great transformation, the science of sociology might not have existed. The Industrial Revolution changed how people lived with the growth of large industrial cities. It changed how and where most people worked, from small farms that were close to their homes, to now laboring in factories far removed from village life. It radically altered people's sense of identity and social connection. In essence, the Industrial Revolution led to a complete transformation of social life, beginning with the growth of scientific ideas and knowledge, which was now seen as a panacea

197

for all of human problems. Indeed, scientific explanations were now displacing religious ones as the principal means of understanding the world and its problems. The Industrial Revolution was transforming the very idea of community, and the founders of sociology were keen to write about those changes.

The early observers of this great social transformation brought a uniquely sociological perspective to the treatment of religion and social change. Each of these writers saw religion as a product of social interaction and human groups. As human groups change, so do their ideas about religion; and as religion changes, so do groups. Although they held different views on the role of religion, they agreed that its ideas and practices had important functions for both the individual and the group. Each had a prediction as to what religion will become in the age of industry, science, individualism, and cities.

AUGUSTE COMTE (1798–1857): THE DEATH OF THE SACRED

Arguably the "father" of sociology, the Frenchman Auguste Comte saw religion as an antiquated institution that embodied the most primitive stage of human social and cognitive development. Religion was a way of seeing and understanding the world based on *faith*, and it appealed to theistic (God-based) reasoning to explicate natural phenomena; but it was a paradigm whose reign was quickly being surpassed by technical thinking and the scientific method. Comte believed that religion and religious thought were superstitious relics of the past, and that modern societies had little need for this way of understanding the natural and social world. According to his theory of human progress, religious faith was the most infantile of human social thought, while scientific ideas represented the apogee of human rational thinking.

Comte's views on religion were best expressed in his theory called "Law of the Three Stages." He believed that all human societies as well as human individual development passed through three stages of collective-cognitive development: the theological or fictitious, the metaphysical or abstract, and the "positive" (that is, empirical; scientific). Comte, in his book *Positive Philosophy, Vol. 1*, said that "The progress of the individual mind is not only an illustration, but an indirect evidence of that of the general mind . . . Now, each of us is aware, if he looks back upon his own history, that he was a theologian in his childhood, a metaphysician in his youth and a natural philosopher in his manhood." (Comte, [1896] 1975, 41).

The Theological stage, which for European societies comes to an end with the Medieval period, was one of superstitious reasoning where society employed theistic explanations for the order of things. In the Metaphysical stage, humans looked to themselves (in philosophy, abstract thinking, and logical reasoning) for answers to the problems of society. Finally, the Metaphysical stage gave way to Positive or Scientific societies where science, and the scientific method properly applied, would answer all questions about the order of things. The Industrial Revolution, beginning in the mid-eighteenth century in Europe, gave rise to such scientific societies.

Religion and religious sentiments such as prayers, rituals, and the like were products of a world that neither possessed the cognitive nor material tools to solve its problems or to answer questions of ultimate causes. Auguste Comte's *Positive Philosophy* foresaw the gradual erosion of religious and sacred ideas because as societies become more modern and technologically sophisticated, they have less need to appeal to superstitious or spiritual causes to explain human phenomena. Modernity and scientific ways of thinking would continue to erode the power of the sacred; technology would eradicate or significantly lessen the many problems that long plagued human societies. For instance, medical innovations could now extend the life of modern citizens, while agricultural technologies could produce greater crop yields to end persistent problems of famine and food insecurity. Society's use of philosophy and then science would bring great knowledge, and there would be much less need for religious explanations.

FERDINAND TOENNIES (1855–1936): RELIGION AND COMMUNITY

The German sociologist Ferdinand Toennies (1855–1936) wrote that a great change in European social life was occurring as a result of the Industrial Revolution. In his 1887 book, *Gemeinschaft und Gesellschaft (Community and Society)*, Toennies used the German word "Gemeinschaft," or community, to describe the type of social bonds that existed prior to the growth of industrial cities. In community, or Gemeinschaft, people were closely connected and had a strong sense of collective solidarity or unity with each other. This type of society was often rural and agrarian, and people shared deep personal and social bonds. Toennies laments the decline of this social order as a direct result of the growth in industrial cities. With this transformation, a new type of social order was born, "Gesellschaft," or urban society, a place associated with weak social ties, and where a person's sense of connection would come principally through his or her occupation or job. Gesellschaft societies had a division of labor that was complex, with many occupational categories as opposed to simply agriculture. Toennies described Gesellschaft, or urban settings, as socially disconnected places that were "transitory and superficial" (Toennies, [1887] 1957), but these societies were also ones where individualism was on the rise, and people's identities were no longer exclusively tied to kinship, place of birth, or their village. The Industrial Revolution broke the most basic bonds that held society together. Moreover, because Gesellschaften societies were no longer tied to tradition and were based on scientific thinking, they tended to belittle the place of religion in people's lives. As such, Toennies believed that religion would eventually "cede supremacy to science" in Gesellschaften societies ([1887] 1957, 226). In urban, industrial societies, religion would give way to "public opinion" (Toennies, 1957, 231) as the prevailing morality: people look to each other to determine what is moral and what is not, in opposition to religious codes like the Decalogue (The Ten Commandments).

Urban societies also gave rise to a "new individual," one that was more self-reliant and less connected to social groups, traditions, and religious organizations and practices. This self-reliance, or new individualism, is another reason why religion was losing its power in people's lives in Gesellschaft. In the industrial city, people were forced to depend on themselves to address their own needs, whereas in the village, or Gemeinschaft, people could rely on each other by virtue of their membership in the group. Self-reliance and excessive individualism erode the need for sacred sentiments and collective rituals, and reduces peoples' reliance upon religion to deal with personal problems.

In many ways, Toennies' views on religious secularization in modernity are very similar to Auguste Comte's. Both writers believed that modern societies would eventually discard the idea of the sacred in favor of scientific rationality. However, while Auguste Comte saw this as an example of social progress, Ferdinand Toennies was skeptical. He believed that humans had an innate need for deep social connections, the kind of attachments found in village life (Gemeinschaft), and specifically the kind of solidarity religious groups propagate. Toennies felt that modernity and urban societies, with their over-reliance on scientific and economic rationalities, and their emphasis on excessive individualism, would produce people with a strong sense of disconnection from each other. For this reason, Toennies laments that industrial societies were superficial and too individualistic.

KARL MARX (1818–1883): RELIGION AS THE OPIATE OF THE MASSES

Karl Marx, one of the architects of socialism and communism, saw religion as a tool of social control over people in society. He believed that religion was used by powerful elites to control the actions and thinking of the masses, namely industrial workers. Religion is the product of our social life, but for Marx, it is a tool of those who control wealth and power in society. Religious sentiment is meant to subdue and manage the opinions and actions of exploited workers in industrial societies.

Karl Marx was deeply critical of the use of religion. Religion exists not because humans and societies need it, but because the powerful people need it to retain the inequality that exists in capitalist society. After all, didn't Christianity preach that "the first will be last, and the last will be first" (Matt, 19, 30)? And if the reward of "the last" is in a kingdom to come, then why should the poor, huddled masses of the industrial world, seek to challenge and alleviate conditions of economic exploitation and entrenched poverty? Karl Marx's theory saw religion as a social creation by the powerful for their own interests.

> Man makes religion, religion does not make man. In other words, religion is the self-consciousness and self-feeling of man who has either not yet found himself or has already lost himself again . . . Religion is the sigh of the oppressed creature, the heart of a heartless world, just as it is the spirit of a spiritless situation. It is the opium of the people.
> (Marx, [1844] 1964, 41–42)

From Karl Marx's vantage point, religion was a tool of the privileged elites (the bourgeoisie) that kept industrial workers (the proletariats) passive and alienated. Their hope in a "kingdom to come" makes the most distressing and oppressive social situation bearable, and this optimism, or "opium of the people," reduces the possibility of grassroots social movements to attain new rights and privileges. All religious thinking produces a type of "false consciousness," or distorted worldview, in the minds of the working classes in industrial society. And the "false consciousness" that religion promulgates prevents workers from seeing the injustice and unfairness of their social conditions, hence making revolutionary change less likely to occur. In order for workers to transform their condition of industrial oppression, they must first cast off religious fallacy as the previous quotation suggests. Religion is linked with everything else in society. It is allied with political institutions, education, military, police, the judicial system, media, and law, as instruments of social control in every society that is characterized by inequality.

Marx's colleague and closest confidant Friedrich Engels took a more analytical approach in theorizing the meaning and function of religion in industrial society. He was open to the possibility that religion can be a transformative force for oppressed people, and indeed, religion has come to play a key role in many social movements in the twentieth century, such as the American Civil Rights Movement and the movement for India's independence from British colonial rule. Yet, in the end, both Engels and Marx were weary of the otherworldly emphasis of religion, and its tendency to ignore problems in the here and now, especially the misery of the working classes. Both believe religions tend to draw their adherents' attention away from the immediate problems of this world.

EMILE DURKHEIM (1858–1917): MEANING AND FUNCTION OF RELIGION

It was the French sociologist Emile Durkheim who provided sociology with its most salient definition of religion as well as the role of religion in society.

Religion and the Creation of the Sacred

In his book *The Elementary Forms of the Religious Life* (1915, 62), Durkheim noted that "a religion is a unified system of beliefs and practices relative to sacred things, that is to say, things set apart and forbidden—beliefs and practices which unite into one single moral community called a Church, all those who adhere to them." For Durkheim, all religious expressions—ideas, rituals, objects, actions— are part of the sacred world as contrasted to the profane world. The profane world deals with the ordinary or mundane, the everyday and the physical. Religion is an attempt to encourage the idea that the universe is more than the physical; it is mysterious, holy, and sanctified and deserves reverence. Religion attempts to influence us to believe that there is something in the universe more than the profane: certain sacred truths, certain sacred morals, certain sacred objects, and certain sacred rituals.

Religion's Creation and Function Is Social

Durkheim does not claim that the sacred world actually exists—it may or may not— but in order to ensure the continuation of society, people must believe it exists. The sacred is ultimately important to the continuation of the collective.

Emile Durkheim thought that religious ideas and practices were "eminently social . . . religious representations are collective representations which express collective realities" (22). Religion is socially created by people, and it comes to represent their distinct assemblages. Religion is a socially created system of ideas and practices that represents the very group that adheres to its precepts and doctrines, and nowhere is the eminently social character of religion as strongly embodied as in the totemic idol or God.

It was through his study of the religious practices of the Australian Aborigine that Durkheim came to his most important position that religion is more natural and social than supernatural, and that the worship of the totem was actually the worship of society because it symbolized the group and was endowed with sacred meaning. In a word, the iconic totem was *God*, and ultimately, the worship of God in the form of the totem was really the worship of society: "Religious forces are therefore human forces, moral forces" (Durkheim, [1915] 1995, 421). Emile Durkheim sees religion as playing crucial roles in society, both pre-industrial and modern ones. The universality of religion arises because it binds people together, and gives them a sense of collective solidarity or unity, what he calls the "collective conscience" (Durkheim, 1972, 222). Religion bonds people in the community; it brings separate individuals into a collectivity.

Religion Creates and Upholds the Morality of Society

Durkheim believed religion plays an important role in the morality of society. Morality is clothed in the sacred; it is the social conscience that individuals are supposed to internalize so that the community can continue. "Moral education could only be essentially religious, as was morality itself. Only religious ideas could serve as the basis for an education that, before everything, had as its chief aim to teach man the manner in which he ought to behave towards religious beings" (Durkheim, 1972, 240). The "Golden Rule," the Ten Commandments, the Five Pillars of Islam, and other such moral protocols, along with sacred texts, such as the Hebrew and Christian Bibles and the Islamic Koran, promote morality to the collective conscience and influence the internalization of social norms and religious precepts. All societies are moral collectives of people who accept a set of moral principles that are sacred and taught to them through religion, government, schools, and family.

Religion Is Important for the Individual

Peter Berger (1967) highlights Durkheim's view that religion brings a sense of meaning and purpose, which protect against the condition of "anomic terror," or the feeling that the world is one of "disorder, senselessness, and madness" (Berger, 1967). Durkheim thought that in addition to being a social creation and function, religion is "also a means of enabling men [and women] to face the world with greater confidence" (Durkheim, 1972, 227). By encouraging unity and common morality, it also guides the individual in direction that anchors life. Indeed, in his book *Suicide*, where he describes reasons for the suicide rates in society, he explicates the two most important types of suicide in industrial society: *egoistic suicide*, where individuals are not integrated into society, and *anomic suicide*, where rules are so conflicting and changing that the individual does not know what to really believe.

The Future of Society

Like the previous founding sociologists, Durkheim treats religion as a product of human interaction and society. In some sense, he believes that the worship toward a God or totem actually is the worship of the community itself. The bonds and morality that arise from religion seem essential for society. Industrialization in Europe made him wonder what society will become in an age of individualism, cities, factories, economic progress, and rapid change. Believing that religion was necessary for society, much of his intellectual life was full of conflict, wondering how society could exist without the sacred world that religion taught. In his earliest book *The Division of Labor in Society* (his PhD dissertation), he examines the possibility that unity in society will become increasingly structural, that it will be the interdependence of people (hence, the division of labor) rather than their common culture and morality, or people's sameness, that would create unity in the modern world. However, as many writers suggest, the rest of his life he does not go back to this theme, probably indicating that he could not convince himself that the division of labor would be successful as a basis for unity. The weakening of the collective conscience may become a serious problem, and in turn, the continuation of society would be threatened.

MAX WEBER (1864–1920): RELIGION, THE RATIONALIZATION OF LIFE, AND SOCIAL CHANGE

Max Weber was very interested in the role of religion in society and conducted sociological studies of Buddhism, Christianity, Judaism, and Islam. In fact, among the early founders of sociology, Max Weber offers the most comprehensive analyses of religion in the modern world. Like each of the previous sociologists, he was also interested in social change, and he was a keen observer of how religious thought contributed both to capitalism and to the development of the Industrial Revolution.

The Protestant Ethic and the Spirit of Capitalism: Religious Thought Influences Economic Action

One of Weber's most important works was his book *The Protestant Ethic and the Spirit of Capitalism*. Weber's thesis was that religious asceticism (self-discipline) was an important impetus behind the development of the spirit of capitalism in Western Europe. A certain view of religion contributed to an economic system.

Weber ([1904] 1958, 35) begins his analysis by posing a quandary: "Why were the successful capitalists of modern business enterprises in European countries 'overwhelmingly Protestants'?" Why did Protestantism seem to encourage capitalistic values in the population, values that encouraged "absolute unscrupulousness in the pursuit of selfish interest by the making of money?" (Weber, [1904] 1958, 57). It was a certain Protestantism—propagated by John Calvin (1509–1564), a French Protestant—that taught that salvation was *not* a matter of free-will, faith, or good works, but rather being chosen—determined by God—at the point one has a soul.

The Calvinists believed those who would be chosen would assume a kind of Christian asceticism that prized highly self-control, hard work, and fruits of rational conduct in business and social enterprises. To Calvinists, the most severe sin was the sin of idleness, and poverty became the certain sign of being numbered among those predestined for hell's fire. Consequently, Calvinists disciplined their bodies and minds for austere, pious labor, not toil for conspicuous consumption (for this would be a lack of self-control and irrational business practices), but rather hard work for the purpose of acquiring wealth as a sign of being among God's elect. The outcome was as follows: saving, investing, and acquiring property and land, while living pious lives. Weber argued this is what created a spirit necessary for capitalist venture. This is what influenced exact accounting and bookkeeping, rational organization, and the continued pursuit of profit in the expansion of commerce in Calvinist communities.

Max Weber developed the idea of the importance of the "Protestant ethic" in American and certain European societies. And, interestingly, once the Protestant ethic helped create capitalism, the religious aspect—predestination by God—was no longer necessary to believe. It was the origin of capitalism that Weber emphasized, and, as most of us are aware, much of our culture still emphasizes hard work, discipline, accumulation of wealth, and rational business practices. Of course, our current emphasis on spending and consumerism has origins not related to Puritanism.

Rationalization of Life and the Future of Religion

Weber's most basic idea has to do with what he called the "rationalization of life." By rationalization, Weber is describing the increasing propensity of people to apply scientific and logical thinking to every situation in order to achieve goals. He believes that this is an important trend in society: the turning away from traditions, feelings, and spiritual values, and toward bureaucratic management and organization, the use of technology to accomplish goals, and the evaluation of every action on the basis of efficiency and effectiveness. Rationalization dominates every domain, from law and politics, to economic production, educational administration, and even religion. Rationalization relates to religion in three ways:

1. Rationalization, because it undermines tradition, feeling, and spiritual values, also undermines religion. Science causes us to seek knowledge through rational processes; the past is no longer the basis of what we believe and do; problem solving trumps ethics, customs, and feelings. That which was once a mystery to human beings becomes rational. Like Comte, Toennies, and Durkheim, Weber predicts that an expanding modernity will bring the decline of religious ideas and practices.
2. Weber saw the increasing use of *the rational* in religion itself. People will eventually evaluate what is taught to them rather than accept sacred views. Tradition will no longer be important to their lives, and instead of intimate churches, more and more huge bureaucratic and impersonal organizations will become common. Communicating, praying, learning, ministering, and proselytizing will move from traditional ways to highly rational ways, and what was once emotional will become impersonal.
3. Weber does not regard rationalization as either good or bad. It is a mixed blessing. For example, he argued, although it may be that science and rational thought will ultimately

give us more understanding of the universe, something important will be lost in our lives. The magic will be gone, and the sacred will be lost. Weber wondered if rationalization would make life much less exciting when the unexplainable was dissected by science, and scientific answers began to undermine wonder.

Charismatic Authority and the Role of Religion in Social Change

To Weber, the rationalization of life is a trend that constantly changes the society. However, change also occurs through revolution, and religious leaders play critical roles throughout history. Charismatic leaders are actually created out of dissatisfaction in society, and organize and attract followers into social movements that, in turn, cause conflict with society as it exists, and ultimately bring about social change. Weber's description of charismatic authority emphasizes that the leader is created to be a special person—apart from ordinary humans—chosen not by force, nor law, nor tradition, but God, fate, history, or some other *sacred quality*. Charismatic leaders— Moses, Jesus, Mohammed, Luther, for example—have helped create new religions. Charismatic leaders—Napoleon, Joan of Arc, Hitler, Gandhi, and Dr. Martin Luther King, for example—have altered society itself, but their claims and their followers' perceptions were that they are above the natural profane world, chosen by something more, something sacred, often a supernatural being. To Weber, religion plays an important role in much of society's development through leaders who are believed to be religiously chosen.

Weber: A Summary

Throughout his work, Weber teaches the importance of ideas as sources of what humans do. We are not the same as other animals. We are not only actors who are impulsive, habitual, or emotional, but also actors who are motivated by thought, ideas, goals, and values that we come to believe. Religion represented to Weber the importance of humans as cultural/ideational beings, and so he would spend much of his academic work on religion. He explains to us what happens to religion as the world is becoming more rational, and he shows us that religious ideas and charismatic leaders—thought to be chosen by higher authority—are central to social change. In much of his work—most importantly in *The Protestant Ethic and the Spirit of Capitalism*—he explains the influence of religious thought on human actions, and thus society.

THE HERITAGE OF SOCIOLOGY FROM THE EARLY SOCIOLOGISTS: CONCLUSION

The classical sociologists regarded religion as a part of a society's culture; it is a set of ideas, morals, and values. Religion tends to be in conflict with science, modern thinking, and institutions. It creates a sacred order. It is an important reason for the actions of people. It influences society's direction; it controls people in society; it answers basic questions for many; it gives meaning to life. It brings members of the community together; it also encourages change through charismatic leaders and movements. Modern life tends to undermine religion, and the classical sociologists have serious questions about the future of society without the central role religion has traditionally occupied. Some—such as Comte and Marx—believed that the decline of religion would mean progress, even a more perfect world. Others—such as Toennies, Durkheim, and Weber—had real concerns about the inevitability of declining religiosity in modern society.

THE STUDY OF RELIGION IN THE LATE-MODERN WORLD

The classical theorists we have examined up to now became the anchor for what sociologists have been studying about religion throughout the twentieth century and into the twenty-first. Their ideas on the function of religion and its role in society form the basis for continued scientific debates and further empirical study. The overarching question is the same: What is the influence of religion over peoples' lives and societies in late-modernity?

Secularization: Is Religion Becoming Less Important Today?

Most of the founders of sociology supported the "secularization thesis," the belief that industrial urban society with its rational-scientific character would eventually erode the influence of religion and the sacred in people's lives. Recently, however, there is vigorous scholarly debate concerning the secularization thesis. Modern life, according to many critics, does not inevitably cause secularization; modern life and religion are much more compatible than we thought.

Defenders of the Secularization Thesis.   Those who continue to accept the secularization thesis developed by the classical sociologists still believe that industrialization and urbanization will replace community, law will replace tradition and morality, and relativity will replace certainty. Thus, religion is becoming less important. Church attendance, belief in the sacred, and the declining centrality of religion in people's life, is slowly becoming part of modern life.

In his classic essay on the secularization thesis entitled "The Concept of Secularization in Empirical Research," Larry Shiner (1967) argued that several types of secularization are taking place in the modern world, namely (1) a decline in religious beliefs and practices, (2) the turning away from supernatural or religious explanations toward natural or scientific ones, (3) the disentanglement of society from faith, where religion and spiritual practices becomes the domain of individuals and are kept in their private sphere, and (4) the de-sacralization of the culture, leading to the erosion in Durkheim's traditional binary of *sacred and profane*, where religious beliefs are seen as the products of human culture just as other ideas.

The strongest evidence for the secularization thesis is Western Europe, where rates of religious practice and church attendance are among the lowest in the world, and where, according to the British sociologist Grace Davie, most people might *believe* in God but not actually *belong* to an organized religious body or attend religious services, a type of secularization she calls "believing without belonging"

(Davie, 1994). Accordingly, many sociologists—especially in Europe—predict the United States will inevitably become like Europe. The theory has become almost a law of social change for some: modernization brings secularization.

Critics of the Secularization Thesis. Sociologists who are critical of the secularization thesis believe that the world continues to be religious, and find support for their position in the religious practices of Americans (and the non-Western world more generally) and in the rise in global religious fundamentalism. Indeed, recent research data from the *Pew Forum on Religion & Public Life* on the importance of religion and the intensity of religious practice in people's lives, what sociologists call *religiosity*, show that the United States continues to be a very spiritual nation, with 96 percent of Americans reporting a belief in God or a "supreme being," 40 percent reporting that the Bible is the word of God, and with over half of Americans reporting monthly attendance at religious services and 25 percent attending weekly (Masci and Smith, 2006). Statistics on America's religiosity seem to suggest that the secularization thesis, on the declining significance of religion in modern scientific societies, is far from inevitable, and that religion still remains an increasingly potent force in late-modern life.

Peter Berger, in his classic book on religion, *The Sacred Canopy: Elements of a Sociological Theory of Religion* (1967, 107–108), distinguishes between two types of secularization: secularization on the level of "culture and society" and secularization of "individual consciousness." The former type refers to the separation of church and state in the arena of politics and law, and the declining importance of religious content from things like art, philosophy, science, popular literature, music, and the like. Secularization of individual consciousness, on the other hand, is where people do not use religion to interpret or guide the situations of their lives nor of the world. Although Berger predicted in 1967 that secularization of both types would characterize life in the United States, in 1997 he proclaimed, in a stunning reversal of his previous support, that the secularization thesis is *dead*:

> I think what I and most other sociologists of religion wrote in the 1960s about secularization was a mistake. Our underlying argument was that secularization and modernity go hand in hand. With more modernization comes more secularization. It wasn't a crazy theory. There was some evidence for it. But I think it's basically wrong. Most of the world today is certainly not secular. It's very religious.
>
> (Berger, 1997, 974)

Another prominent scholar, Rodney Stark (1999), goes a step further in proclaiming that there has never been sufficient empirical data to support the secularization thesis and that it should be abandoned as a failed sociological theory. Indeed, Stark argues that much of the American landscape is still very devout, and religious arguments are inherent in almost all of the impassioned cultural debates today. The opposition to extending the rights of marriage to gay and lesbian couples is largely framed in religious terms as anathema to a Biblical definition of matrimony. Many people who reject a woman's right to abortion typically cite arguments on the sanctity of life to justify their activism. Likewise, politicians and laypersons who support prohibitions on the use of new stem-cell lines in biomedical research rely on religious arguments to support their claims. And who can forget the actions of the Kansas Board of Education, who on November 8, 2005, voted in a six to four decision to allow "Intelligent Design" to be taught alongside Darwinian Evolutionary Theory in its publicly funded schools? What these and many other "culture war" issues suggest is that modernity has not resulted in a situation where faith-based beliefs and practices are socially marginalized or kept private and out of public spheres. Rather, many sociologists believe the debates and issues facing society are wrapped within religious arguments.

The Role of Fundamentalism

One important reason that religion continues to be important is that many organized religions have changed; they have altered their ways in order to keep their congregations in tact. This is especially true for "mainline religions"—Judaism, Catholicism, and many large Protestant denominations. There is a trend to keep religion alive by appealing to those who wish to continue to be religious, yet moving away from tradition and adjusting to modernity.

Others, however, retain their traditions and are more critical of modernity. These groups tend to have religious views and practices that align with fundamentalism. Evangelical Protestants, Orthodox Jews, Muslims, and many recent immigrants embrace their traditional religious identities and customs. So, for example, private religious schools become more ubiquitous, denominations continue to impose limits on the participation of women in traditional male roles, regular attendance in religious ceremonies and activities is common, and the sacred view of the universe is central to their lives.

Fundamentalist religions support a strict and literal interpretation of sacred text, even when those interpretations conflict with prevailing scientific consensus, such as the case with evolution and the Kansas School Board, or when the text runs contrary to the ideals of social movements that seek new rights for historically excluded groups, as with the case of same-sex marriage. But fundamentalism is more than just a straightforward reading and literal interpretation of sacred texts. In the United States, fundamentalism has also come to mean the rejection of religious pluralism, the rejection of religious groups who try to accept modern values and ideas, and the rejection of humanist groups who do not emphasize the supernatural. In addition, fundamentalist groups continue to support conservative political figures and causes (see Jacobs, 2006).

Fundamentalism also raises concerns about the separation of church and state, and on the role of religion in a democratic society. When fundamentalist religious ideas are fused with political practice, the natural outcome is a movement toward a theocratic government. A theocracy is a type of government that is ruled by divine authority, where leaders and citizens look to sacred texts to establish laws and rules of conduct. In a theocracy, there is no separation of "church and state" because the church" *is* the state. Modern examples of theocratic nation-states are Iran, Saudi Arabia, and Afghanistan (under Taliban rule). Each of these states relies upon sacred religious texts or traditions to conduct their political affairs and to draft laws that conform to strict religious codes. Theocratic governments try to control all parts of a person's life, and are opposed to religious pluralism, individualism, and many democratic principles.

Fundamentalism is an important reaction to modernity. Instead of altering religious beliefs and practices in order to adjust to social change, fundamentalists attempt to hold onto tradition the best they can. Most will accept much of the technology of the modern world (television, internet, computers, machinery, even the newest weapons of war, for example), but they try very hard to keep tradition, values, ideas, and rules as sacred and unchanging. Fundamentalism is one way religion has continued to flourish in the United States. Along with denominations that choose to integrate religion into modern life, the American religious landscape has taken a different path than Western Europe's.

The real issue for critics of fundamentalism is the conflict between fundamentalism and democracy. The important question is, are sacred ideas and practices, private religious schools, excessive community controls over the individual's actions, thoughts, and communications, and the rejection of modern discoveries compatible with democratic principles?

Organized Religion and Individual Spirituality

One of the most interesting trends in late-modern societies is the emergence of a new type of religious practice that is very distinct from those of the past, and is best described using the *religiosity* versus *spirituality* binary. When sociologists speak of religiosity, they are typically describing things such as church membership or affiliation, rates of attendance, and belief of a deity and/or the supernatural. The higher a person's religiosity, for instance, the more likely he or she is thought to have membership in a formal religious organization, to attend weekly or monthly worship, and to report belief in God or some supernatural being. In recent years, however, the term *spirituality* has come to describe a trend that departs from these organized traditional beliefs and practices.

Many sociological studies report that spirituality is about *personal* beliefs and practices in the quest to experience fulfillment and well-being: The emphasis is usually on feelings and emotions, meaning, and personal faith (see Hodge and McGrew, 2006). Spiritual practices might include everything from new age disciplines such as yoga and transcendental meditation, to various divination practices (séance, astrology, fortune telling, tarot cards, etc.). Moreover, several studies report that spirituality is becoming an increasingly reported type of religious identification, sometimes including a supernatural being (see Glendinning and Bruce, 2006; Voas and Bruce, 2006). In addition to turning inwards for their spiritual fulfillment, people who identify as *spiritual* tend to disavow the guidance of traditional organizations and authorities such as churches, synagogues, and mosques, which they see, in skeptical terms, as hierarchal and patronizing moral organizations (see Aupers and Houtman, 2006).

Finally, spirituality tends to be a highly individualistic form of religious practice when compared to the collective and congregational nature of traditional religious customs. The emphasis is on freedom of choice (see Heelas et al., 2004). Under this approach, people are responsible for their own spirituality, which is gained through a process of "shopping around" in a very open and diverse marketplace of sacred ideas and practices. What is unique about this approach is the imposition of rational choices and decision-making processes to determine which spiritual practice "fits" best and which one produces the finest personal outcome or feeling. It is unlike religiosity, which is usually connected with affiliation in a highly organized traditional community. It is not a stretch to suggest that spirituality is well suited for late-modern societies that are themselves highly individualistic and inwardly directed, and this is exactly what Ferdinand Toennies foresaw in his writings.

Those who are critical of spirituality without organized religion often argue that encouraging individuals to seek spirituality without clear direction within a highly religious community may always be a choice for individuals; but it is very unlikely that that a modern society such as the United States will be able to continue to retain its level of religiosity without attractive and successful organized religions.

SUMMARY: THE SOCIOLOGY OF RELIGION

The founders of sociology were fascinated by religion, and all of them saw that modern society was transforming the place of religion in people's lives. They believed that religion was an important creation in all societies in the past, and wondered what would become of religion in the future. Marx and Comte welcomed the end of religion; Toennies, Durkheim, and Weber perceived religion to be a necessary part of society, providing meaning, order, community, morality, explanation of the universe, and an important source of change.

Durkheim, probably more than any of the others, saw religion as a special attempt to create a sacred order in the universe, a necessary recognition that life is more than profane existence, a way that people were able to interact peacefully, work together, feel part of community, and create a shared morality. Weber's interest was to use religion as an example of how important people's ideas and values were important to the nature of society and social change. Weber, more than the others, saw the tremendous changes in twentieth-century society—changes he called rational—and did the most to understand the relationship between modern life and secularization. Toennies' dichotomy of Gemeinschaft (community) and Gesellschaft (society) highlighted the point that religion in the modern world would become more and more individualistic rather than communal. Marx simply saw religion as a way of controlling the masses; Comte saw it as a way of looking at the world in a simple and childish way.

In many ways, the questions of the early sociologists are the same questions most of us still wonder about. Does modern society mean a decline of religion or simply a change in religion? Is a pluralistic-democratic society a way that people are able to enrich their religious life, or is it a way of undermining religious life? What is the relationship between religion and science—must they be in conflict or together can they make life more understandable and meaningful? Is fundamentalism the way for religion to survive in the modern world, or is altering religion the way? Is religion bringing people together in society or is it tearing us apart? What will life be like if religion becomes less and less important to society and to individuals? Is the rise of spirituality without organized religion evidence of change or is it an example of secularization?

Religion is a fascinating subject. It is difficult to study, but it is very important for understanding society and individuals. It is a topic almost all sociologists think about; it is also a topic everyone should think about if he or she wants to understand human society.

QUESTIONS TO CONSIDER

1. Auguste Comte believed that modern societies would eventual cast off their dependence on religious ideas and institutions, which he saw as relics from the theological stage of human social development. Do you believe that modern societies can do without religious sentiments and institutions? Please explain why.
2. Karl Marx said that religion was the opiate of the masses. What does this statement mean really? Can you think of examples today where religion functions as an "opiate" for the collective consciousness?
3. What are your opinions on the secularization thesis? Do you believe that modern societies are indeed secular? If so, what evidence can you provide to support this claim? On the other hand, if you believe that modern societies are still very religious, then what evidence might support your conviction?
4. Are there ways in which the secularization of society is a good thing? Are there ways in which the secularization of society is a bad thing? Explain.
5. Emile Durkheim saw the imposition of moral codes as one of the most basic and important functions of religion. Do you agree? In the absence of, or the significant decline in, religious practices, where would society get its shared morality?
6. How religious are you, and what factors account for your religiosity? If you are religious, does your religion inform your views on wider social issues like gay marriage, abortion, military conflicts, and social problems like poverty and crime? If yes, why, and if no, then why not?
7. Which founder of sociology (Comte, Marx, Weber, Durkheim, Toennies) is closest to your own views on religion and the scared, and why?
8. Can you identify fundamentalist influences on American politics and culture today? What are these issues, and how are fundamentalists using religious ideas to make their claims?
9. Would you describe yourself as *spiritual* or *religious*? Please explain.

REFERENCES

Aupers, Stef, and Dick Houtman. May 2006. "Beyond the Spiritual Supermarket: The Social and Public Significance of New Age Spirituality." In *Journal of Contemporary Religion*, 21(2): 201–222.

Berger, Peter L. 1967. *The Sacred Canopy: Elements of a Sociological Theory of Religion.* New York: Anchor Books.

Berger, Peter L. 1997. "Epistemological Modesty: An Interview with Peter Berger." In *Christian Century*, 114: 972–975.

Comte, Auguste. 1896. "Positive Philosophy Vol. 1." In *Auguste Comte: The Foundations of Sociology.* 1975 edn. Ed. Kenneth Thompson. New York, NY: Halsted/Wiley.

Davie, Grace. 1994. *Religion in Britain Since 1945: Believing without Belonging.* London, England: Blackwell Press.

Durkheim, Emile. 1915 [1995 A New Translation by Karen E. Fields]. *The Elementary Forms of the Religious Life*. New York: Free Press.

Durkheim, Emile. 1972. *Selected Writings*. Edited, translated, and with an introduction by Anthony Giddens. Cambridge: University Press.

Glendinning, Tony, and Steve Bruce. September 2006. "New Ways of Believing or Belonging: Is Religion Giving Way to Spirituality." In *British Journal of Sociology*, 57(3): 399–414.

Heelas, Paul, Linda Woodhead, Steel Benjamin, Karin Tusting, and Baron Szerszynski. 2004. *The Spiritual Revolution: Why Religion is Giving Way to Spirituality*. Oxford, UK: Blackwell Publishers.

Hodge, David R., and Charlene C. McGrew. Fall 2006. "Spirituality, Religion, and the Interrelationship: A Nationally Representative Study." In *Journal of Social Work Education*, 42(3): 637–654.

Jacobs, Anton K. 2006. "The New Right, Fundamentalism, and Nationalism in Postmodern America: The Marriage of Heat and Passion." In *Social Compass*, 53(3): 357–366.

Marx, Karl. 1844. "Contribution to the Critique of Hegel's Philosophy of Right." In *On Religion*. 1964 edn. Ed. Karl Marx and Friedrich Engels. New York: Schocken Books.

Masci, David, and Gregory A. Smith. 2006. "God is Alive and Well in America." In *Pew Forum on Religion & Public Life*. Accessed August 15, 2007: http://pewresearch.org/pubs/15/god-is-alive-and-well-in-america.

Stark, Rodney. Fall 1999. "Secularization, R.I.P." In *Sociology of Religion*, 60(3): 249–273.

Toennies, Ferdinand. 1887. *Community & Society: Gemeinschaft und Gesellschaft*. 1957 edn. New York: Harper & Row Publishers.

Voas, David, and Bruce, Steve. April 2006. "Is Religion Giving Way to Spirituality?" In *Sociology Review*, 15(4): 14–16.

Weber, Max. 1958. *The Protestant Ethic and the Spirit of Capitalism: The Relationship Between the Economic and Social Life in Modern Culture*. New York: Charles Scribner's Sons.

RECOMMENDED READING

Ammerman, Nancy T. 2005. *Pillars of Faith American Congregations and Their Partners*. Berkeley, CA: University of California Press.

Emerson, Michael O., and Rodney M. Woo. 2006. *People of the Dream: Multiracial Congregations in the United States*. New Jersey: Princeton University Press.

Engels, Friedrich. 1844. "On the History of Early Christianity." In *On Religion*. 1964 edn. Ed. Karl Marx and Friedrich Engels. New York: Schocken Books.

Freund, Julien. 1969. *The Sociology of Max Weber*. New York: Pantheon Books.

Goldberg, Michelle. 2006. *Kingdom Coming: The Rise of Christian Nationalism*. New York: W.W. Norton.

Lifton, Robert Jay. 2000. *Destroying the World to Save It: Aum Shinrikyo, Apocalyptic Violence, and the New Global Terrorism*. New York: Owl Books.

Shiner, Larry. 1967. "The Concept of Secularization in Empirical Research." In *Journal for the Scientific Study of Religion*, 6: 207–220.

Weber, Max. 1963. *The Sociology of Religion*. Boston, MA: Beacon Press.

Wilson, Bryan R. 1982. *Religion in Sociological Perspective*. New York: Oxford University Press.

Cliff Dwellers by George Bellows. *Los Angeles County Museum of Art.* Los Angeles County Fund.

+ 15 +

The Meaning and Uses
of Sociology

This book is meant to be one introduction to the discipline and perspective of sociology. It is an attempt by two authors to describe what the meaning of sociology is to them.

Throughout this book, there has been one dominant theme: Sociology is a perspective that focuses on the social nature of the human being. Other perspectives in social science examine the human being, but not with this central focus. The biologist, the chemist, and the psychologist may say that there is more to human beings than their social nature, and they are, of course, correct. No claim can be made that sociology has the whole or final answer. Instead, like all perspectives, sociology is an exaggeration, it starts with a set of assumptions that seem reasonable and consistent with known evidence, and it goes from there, trying to get as much mileage as possible through theorizing and testing.

The concepts described in this book create the basic parameters, or outline, of sociology. Instead of simply defining sociology in one simple sentence (for example, "the scientific study of society"), it is better to see sociology as the study of these concepts: socialization, social action, interaction, social patterns, social organization, social structure, culture, institutions, social order, power, conflict, family, religion, and change—to name the most central.

Throughout this book, there has been an attempt to describe some of the ideas that are central to sociology—ideas that should prove important for students understanding the human being. Let us review these ideas.

Human Beings Are Social and Socialized. We are born dependent on others. We survive because of them; we learn how to survive from them; we are socialized by them. Socialization is no small matter. Through socialization, we take on the ways of society and become members of society. We learn to control ourselves through the rules and perspective of society, thus making society possible. Through socialization, we develop symbols, self, and mind, qualities that make us both human and, to some extent, free. Finally, either because of socialization or because of our nature, humans come to live their whole lives around others, subject to the rules that dominate all social life.

215

Humans Are Social Actors: We Interact, and We Create Social Patterns.   Because we act around others, they become important influences on what we do. We consider them as we act; we are social actors in almost every situation. Interaction — mutual social action — socializes us, influences our actions and ideas, and, over time, influences the development of social patterns. Social patterns, once created, take on a life of their own, influencing actors in interaction. It is such patterns that form the basis of social organization.

Humans Live Their Lives Embedded in Social Organization.   We are in the center of many organizations, most of which we had no part in creating. Dyads, groups, formal organizations, communities, and society are, to some extent, the walls of our prison. Each represents rules we are expected to follow.

Social Structure Is an Important Social Pattern in All Social Organization.   It positions each actor, tells each actor what is expected (role), gives the actor an identity and perspective, distributes power, privilege, and prestige. What we do, what we are, and what we believe are linked to our positions in many social structures.

Society Is a System of Inequality.   This system of inequality includes class, gender, and racial/ethnic group positions. These social structures are far-reaching, are very hard to change, and place us in positions that are very important for our entire lives.

All Social Organization Has Culture.   Culture, too, is a social pattern. It is what people share as they interact: their ideas, values, goals, and norms. Our actions are influenced by what our social organizations teach us. What may seem to us like free choice often turns out to be products of the culture we have learned.

Institutions Are Social Patterns That Exist in Society.   We are all born into a society that has developed certain ways of doing things. Although these ways appear to be natural or right, they are always alternatives. Institutions are what we inherit from our ancestors. Societies generally have political, economic, military, kinship, educational, health care, and recreational institutions. Institutions are necessary for the continuation of society; institutions control individual choice.

Social Order Is Necessary for All Social Organizations.   Order is achieved through controlling the human being. Control is achieved through social structure, culture, institutions, socialization, feelings of loyalty, and social controls. Social controls include the designation of certain people to be outside the acceptable: the condemnation of some as deviant. The human being is part of a world that demands a certain degree of order and control. Although we all do not conform, and although no one conforms completely, society has many ways to encourage conformity. Without order and control, organization would be impossible and the human being would also be impossible.

Social Power Is Part of All Human Relationships.   As people act in relation to one another, they exert resources in order to achieve their will. Some win; some lose. Some influence; some are influenced. In general, sociologists see society as a system of unequal power, usually with an elite in control.

Human Beings Develop Symbols, Self, and Mind in Interaction with Others. Symbols, self, and mind are qualities that change our relationship with our environment, including other people. Instead of simply responding to stimuli, instead of simply being conditioned by others, we become active, thinking, self-directing, problem-solving, free beings. These qualities are central to what we are; they are also qualities we develop only through our interaction.

Social Organization Is Always in the Process of Change. It is easy to get lost in the permanence of organization; in fact, change is as much a part of organization as permanence and stability. There is no one reason organization changes. Change is complex and many faceted.

The Family Exists in Every Society. It is diverse across societies. Its structure and its functions have changed dramatically in the twentieth century as modern society has emphasized individual choice. The family remains important in modern society, but it is no longer a fixed entity. More and more people are making choices about whether or not to marry, whether or not to have children, what kind of gender roles to follow, and what should be done if a marriage is not satisfying.

Organized Religion is a Central Part of Almost Every Society. Religion is an attempt in society to separate a sacred universe from a profane universe. Traditionally, it holds society together, it helps bring the individual to feel part of society, and it reaffirms the morality of society. Religion thrives in traditional society; in modern society religious reactions to secularization include adjustments by organized religion, fundamentalism, and individual spirituality.

These are the core ideas contained in this book. Sociology is exciting because of these ideas. If taken seriously, many of these ideas challenge the taken-for-granted truths that many people hold. If taken seriously, these ideas can show us aspects of the human being we have never really considered.

Of course, sociology is also a discipline that has accumulated lots of facts. There are textbooks filled with these facts. There are scientific journals filled with studies of the human being never mentioned in this short introduction. The purpose here is to introduce only the core; there is much more if you are interested in pursuing it.

THE USES OF SOCIOLOGY

Why study sociology? Consider the following.

First, some students are attracted to sociology as either a major or minor field of study. It is interesting, challenging, and applicable to the kinds of questions that concern them. Sometimes, sociology becomes a bridge to an appealing occupation. It prepares the individual for many diverse occupations by teaching social research skills, by making one sensitive to organizational and interactional patterns, and by providing a body of knowledge that can be applied to almost any occupation that involves working with people.

Knowing sociology contributes to understanding; it contributes to being an educated person. To those who regard truth as an important value, who believe that there is nothing more exciting than understanding self, others, society, and humanity, sociology is important to study and know.

Sociology can be applied to one's own life. It helps the individual understand why people around him or her act the way they do. It aids an understanding of one's own identity, thinking, and action. It can also be applied to understanding all the organizations of which we are a part and can be useful for achieving our goals in these organizations.

Sociology is liberating; it is a step toward having more control over one's life. We are social beings; from the beginning of our lives, we have been socialized by family, friends, teachers, and others. Much of what we know we have not scrutinized very carefully. At the least, the sociological perspective exposes the culture and the nature of society to the individual, making it possible to understand oneself better and to realize that to make choices is to be able to step back and look objectively at the control exerted by our various social organizations.

Not all students will be affected by studying sociology, and those who are affected may very well not understand in ways that the authors intended. The authors of this book, however, believe that sociology is more than simply our job. The study of sociology continues to alter our understanding of the world and the values we use to make judgments about what is happening around us. Specifically, we continue to understand and apply the following profound insights:

1. To be different is not to be wrong. Social organization, other people in interaction may think us funny or immoral or dumb, but our strangeness is part of their social definition only.
2. We are prisoners in social organization. Much of what we do is determined by the structures, cultures, and institutions within which we are located. Yet there is something liberating even about this knowledge — it is one step in making choices, it is one step in living something approaching a free existence. Peter Berger makes this point in *Invitation to Sociology* (1963): Sociology can provide one with an understanding of the rules of the game, the roles we are assigned — and this knowledge is the first step to consciously playing the roles, dealing with those more powerful than we are, and determining our own action in the face of others' rules.
3. Berger underlines another idea we have found in sociology: Things are not what they seem to be. We are cultural animals; our views of the world are a result of socialization, so that what most of us regard as just "common sense" has been transmitted to us by our groups. Sociology has made us realize that superficial explanations do not constitute understanding — we have a passion for understanding life that sociology has helped us develop.
4. Sociology has made us more realistic about what is possible in society. On one hand, we know that social change is inevitable. One cannot wish change away; and one must come to deal with it both in the larger society and in one's own personal existence. And we have also become less impatient about what we think America can become. We still have ideals that we feel are worth working for, but we have also come to terms with what can be expected realistically, given the power of social structure, culture, institutions, socialization, social controls, and people's loyalties.

If we think not about ourselves as individuals but about the society at large, there are justifications for a perspective like sociology, a science of society. It is vitally important to study human beings objectively and to draw conclusions not only about what we *think* the world *should be* like, but on what it actually *is* like. There should be financial support for sociological research so that we can more fully understand action and also avoid the kinds of problems ignorance leads to. It is better to know than to be ignorant, and it is better to know about human beings and society objectively so that we do not have to accept the word of those who "claim to know" what they are talking about (usually, they turn out to be people who agree with us). Finally, sociology has something to offer policy makers not in telling them what to do, but in helping them understand what will happen if, for example, schools remain segregated; or family life becomes increasingly diverse; or the government does or does not regulate television, addictive drugs, or health care. Sociologists have made important contributions to America's consciousness in race relations, poverty, crime, gender roles, social power, religion, and family life. This consciousness may not be a comfortable one, but it is absolutely necessary if we are not to live with myths we may have accepted without serious investigation.

Sociology is promising—it offers the student much. If you are still interested, come back to it. Think of this book as a beginning, a core, a brief encounter, an invitation.

QUESTIONS TO CONSIDER

1. What is sociology? What are its most important ideas? In what ways, if any, is it different from what you imagined it to be before you read this book?
2. Every perspective makes certain assumptions. What are the assumptions of sociology? Do you agree with them?
3. Do sociologists hold certain values? That is, after claiming that sociology is supposed to be "value-free" in its investigation, the author may reveal a set of values (commitments) that underlie the whole perspective. Can you identify any?

REFERENCE

Berger, Peter. 1963. *Invitation to Sociology*. Garden City, NY: Doubleday.

RECOMMENDED READING

The following works are aimed in part to investigate the meaning and uses of sociology as a discipline or perspective.

Charon, Joel M. 2000. *Ten Questions: A Sociological Perspective*. 4th edn. Belmont, CA: Wadsworth.
Clausen, John A. 1986. *The Life Course: A Sociological Perspective*. Upper Saddle River, NJ: Prentice Hall.
Inkeles, Alex. 1964. *What Is Sociology? An Introduction to the Discipline and Profession*. Upper Saddle River, NJ: Prentice Hall.
Johnson, Allan G. 1997. *The Forest and the Trees: Sociology as Life, Practice, and Promise*. Philadelphia: Temple University Press.
Mills, C. Wright. 1959. *The Sociological Imagination*. New York: Oxford University Press.
Stephens, W. Richard. 1995. *Careers in Sociology*. Boston: Allyn & Bacon.
Turner, Stephen, and Jonathan H. Turner. 1990. *The Impossible Science: An Institutional Analysis of American Sociology*. Newberry Park, CA: Sage.

Weber, Max. 1905. *The Protestant Ethic and the Spirit of Capitalism.* 1958 edn. Trans. and ed. Talcott Parsons. New York: Scribner's.

Weber, Max. 1919. "Science as a Vocation." In *Max Weber: Essays in Sociology.* 1969 edn. Trans. and ed. H. H. Gerth and C. Wright Mills. New York: Oxford University Press.

Wilson, Everett K., and Hanan Selvin. 1980. *Why Study Sociology? A Note to Undergraduates.* Belmont, CA: Wadsworth.

Wolfe, Alan. 1989. *Whose Keeper? Social Science and Moral Obligation.* Berkeley, CA: University of California Press.

Index